JASO OCCASIONAL PAPERS No. 9

Series Editor: Jonathan Webber
General Editors: David Gellner and Robert Parkin

GOVERNING THE NUER

DOCUMENTS IN NUER HISTORY
AND ETHNOGRAPHY, 1922–1931

BY

PERCY CORIAT

Edited with Introductions and Notes by

DOUGLAS H. JOHNSON

JASO

Oxford 1993

JASO OCCASIONAL PAPERS

1. VERONIKA GÖRÖG-KARADY (ed.)
   Genres, Forms, Meanings: Essays in African Oral Literature

2. RUI FEIJÓ, HERMINIO MARTINS and JOÃO DE PINA-CABRAL (eds.)
   Death in Portugal: Studies in Portuguese Anthropology and Modern History

3. B. A. L. CRANSTONE and STEVEN SEIDENBERG (eds.)
   The General's Gift: A Celebration of the Pitt Rivers Museum Centenary, 1884–1984

4. R. H. BARNES, DANIEL DE COPPET and R. J. PARKIN (eds.)
   Contexts and Levels: Anthropological Essays on Hierarchy

5. JOY HENDRY and JONATHAN WEBBER (eds.)
   Interpreting Japanese Society: Anthropological Approaches

6. PETER CAREY
   Maritime Southeast Asian Studies in the United Kingdom: A Survey of their Post-War Development and Current Resources

7. WENDY JAMES and DOUGLAS H. JOHNSON (eds.)
   Vernacular Christianity: Essays in the Social Anthropology of Religion Presented to Godfrey Lienhardt

8. HUGH D. R. BAKER and STEPHAN FEUCHTWANG (eds.)
   An Old State in New Settings: Studies in the Social Anthropology of China in Memory of Maurice Freedman

9. PERCY CORIAT
   Governing the Nuer: Documents in Nuer History and Ethnography, 1922–1931
   Edited by Douglas H. Johnson

Africa World Books Pty Ltd.

P.O. Box 130 Wanneroo, WA 6065, Australia

ISBN: 978-0-9943631-5-2

Copyright © JASO 1993. All rights reserved.

Printed under license from JASO.

Africa World Books reprint 2018.

Typeset in 11-point Garamond at Oxford University Computing Service.

JASO, the Journal of the Anthropological Society of Oxford, is a journal devoted to social anthropology. Launched in 1970 as a hard copy journal it is now an online journal, JASO-Online, a joint collaborative project between JASO, the Society and the School of Anthropology and Museum Ethnography of the University of Oxford. JASO-Online is available as a free download at http://www.isca.ox.ac.uk/publications/jaso/introduction/

Governing the Nuer

Percy Coriat, 1928 (Coriat collection)

PREFACE

I FIRST came across Percy Coriat's neglected writings on the Nuer in 1972 when beginning research on the history of the Nuer prophets. They appeared to me then, even in the early stages of my research, to be of a quality quite different from other contemporary administrative reports. I came to appreciate his work all the more after doing fieldwork among the Gaawar and Lou Nuer in 1975–6, when I met many persons who had known Coriat well. My research on Nuer history then brought me in touch with persons in Britain who knew either Coriat or his work, and I was particularly pleased to meet his widow, Mrs Kay Coriat, in 1977. She allowed me full access to her husband's few remaining papers and photograph collection before donating these papers, and some of her own, to Rhodes House, Oxford.

This volume presents all of Coriat's known major writings on the Nuer, with the exception of his 1939 article on Guek (Coriat 1939). A preliminary list of his reports was published in *JASO* in 1981 (Johnson 1981*b*). I later discovered a number of his other papers in the Sudan, some in Khartoum, but most were in Malakal and Bor before I transferred them to the Southern Records Office in Juba. It is possible that more documents may be found, but the prospect is not hopeful. His reports on the Lou were transferred from Abwong to Akobo in 1937 but were destroyed when the Akobo office burned down in 1939. Some of his writings on the Gaawar may still be in Fangak. None had been transported to New Fangak when I visited the office there in my capacity as Assistant Director for Archives in the Regional Ministry of Culture and Information in 1981. I was told that some of the oldest district reports had been left in a storeroom in old Fangak when the administrative headquarters was moved in 1976. I subsequently learned that many of those papers were damaged or destroyed when old Fangak was attacked and looted by 'Anyanya II' guerrillas late in 1981. I have not been able to visit the offices in Bentiu, but record-keeping in the early days of Western Nuer District was haphazard at best. However hopeful we may be that a more complete corpus of writings might one day be compiled, that hope should not delay the publication of the substantial body which has already been gathered together.

This volume is not a complete collection of all of Coriat's papers; it is not an attempt to document an entire life. Most of Coriat's official correspondence consists of shorter letters addressing specific administrative questions. His personal letters sometimes do contain information not found in his official reports. I have thought it best to make reference to these shorter letters in the notes and introduction, to illuminate and enhance his substantial reports. I have indicated to the reader where the shorter correspondence can be found as an aid to further research. The papers which have been included in this collection have been chosen because of the contribution they make as sources of information on Nuer history and on the administrative history of the Southern Sudan. They demonstrate Coriat's value to us as a reporter at the same time that they serve to document his own work among the Nuer.

Quite apart from the specific value these reports may have to anthropologists as early descriptions of the Nuer, they have a more general interest for historians and others concerned with the study of the colonial period in Africa. There is still a need for the detailed examination of the local work of district officers in colonial administration. Personal memoirs and reminiscences of colonial officials are frequently anecdotal, retelling the series of old dining-out stories which have become ingrained in the memory through repetition, and leaving out the practical details of administration. Academic studies of the Sudan Political Service have tended to offer character sketches or generalized evaluations, analysing the members of the SPS in the context of their own kind, and according to their own values (see, for instance, Collins 1983, Collins and Deng 1984, Kirk-Greene 1982, Daly 1986). With one exception (Deng and Daly 1989) they have ignored, for the most part, that fundamental question of the administrator's relations with the people he ruled. This volume, by focusing on Coriat *and* the Nuer, tries to redress the balance.

Many persons have helped me in compiling information about the Nuer and the government during the period covered by these reports, and others have contributed directly to my knowledge of Coriat's life. In the Sudan I must make special acknowledgement of my friends the late Kulang Majok (former Native Authority policeman among the Gaawar), Ruot Diu (Dual Diu's half-brother), John Wicjaal Buom Diu, Philip Diu Deng (whose grandfather, Akuei Biel, was appointed chief of the Luac Dinka by Coriat), the late Stephen Ciec Lam, and the commissioners of Upper Nile Province when I was first there, their Excellencies Peter Gatkuoth Gual and Philip Obang. In Britain I would like to acknowledge the help of Professor Richard Gray and Dr Paul Howell, CMG, OBE (for reading and commenting on the manuscript), Dr Gabriel Giet Jal, Mr Stephen Abraham Yar (who has been most helpful in providing information for notes to the Western Nuer documents), Mr Adrian Struvé, Mr Christopher Tracey, the late John Winder, the late K. D. D. Henderson, CMG, the late Lt.-Col. J. H. R. Orlebar, OBE, Major L. E. Humphreys, MC (retired to Canada), Mr B. J. Chatterton, Mr Edward Aglen, Mr E. G. Coryton, Mrs Patricia Vicars-Miles, Mrs Jean Eastwood, the late Mrs Kay Coriat, Mrs Honor Baines, Mr Gordon Leith (Assistant Librarian, RAF Museum, London), Flight Sergeant Brian Birkin (Squadron Historian, no. 47 Squadron, RAF), the Sudan Archive at the University of Durham, and Rhodes House Library, Oxford.

Permission to publish Coriat's official reports has been very kindly granted by Dr Muhammad Ibrahim Abu Salim (Secretary-General, National Records Office, Khartoum), and the late Mark Loro (Deputy Director for Archives, Southern Records Office, Juba). Mrs Honor Baines has given permission to reproduce some of her father's private papers and photographs from his albums; and Mrs Jean Eastwood has kindly allowed me to reproduce photographs taken by her late husband, Brigadier Gerald Arthur Eastwood, DSO, OBE. I am also grateful to Miss Terese Svoboda for permission to quote her translation of the song given in n. 26 to document 3.3.

Jonathan Webber steered the book through the press, sometimes by fax from Poland and elsewhere. He also helped me tread the difficult path between strict accuracy to Coriat's texts and sensitively editing them in a way that would help readers to understand them. Connie Wilsack performed a similar role with regard to the editing of maps and tables. Nick Clarke redrew the maps, designed the plate section, and harnessed his own creative abilities to those of the Mac to capture the spirit of the period in his cover design. But thanks are due most of all to Stephen Ashworth, who laboured to produce a handsome book despite having to learn a new typesetting system while the book was in production.

Publication has been made possible by a subvention from the British Academy, which is gratefully acknowledged here. The Coriat family has also generously contributed towards the cover illustration and the reproduction of the photographs in this volume.

Finally, I would like to acknowledge the help of my wife, Wendy James, who asked the type of questions anthropologists would like answered about Coriat's contribution to the ethnography of the Nuer.

D.H.J.

Oxford
April 1992

CONTENTS

Abbreviations   xi
Glossary   xiii
Note on Documents   xv
List of Plates and Maps   xviii

Editor's Introduction
Percy Coriat's Life and the Importance of his Work   xix

DOCUMENTS IN NUER HISTORY AND ETHNOGRAPHY, 1922–1931
BY PERCY CORIAT
Introductions and notes throughout by Douglas H. Johnson

Section 1: Central Nuer
Introduction   5
1.1 'Easy but Uncertain'   6
1.2 'The Gaweir Nuers' (1923)   12
1.3 'Transfer of Barr Gaweir to Zeraf Valley District' (1926)   36
1.4 Bloodwealth Payments (1926)   53
1.5 'Southern (Abwong) District: Handing-over Notes' (1929)   56

Section 2: Fixing the Boundary
Introduction   85
2.1 'Settlement of Ol Dinka–Gaweir Nuer Boundary Dispute' (1925)   86
2.2 'Nuer–Dinka re Settlement Intertribal Boundary' (1931)   91

Section 3: The Nuer Settlement
Introduction   99
3.1 Gwek Diary (1927)   101
3.2 'General Report: Patrol S8 (Lau Nuer) 1928'   108
3.3 'Nuer Settlement–Gun Lau (Guncol) Area' (1929)   123
3.4 Notes on Political Prisoners in Malakal (1931)   149

Section 4: Western Nuer
Introduction   155
4.1 'Western Nuer District' (1931)   157
4.2 'Administration–Western Nuer' (1931)   184

Section 5: The Administrator and Anthropology
Introduction 191
5.1 'Notes on a Paper on the Nuer Read by Mr. E. Evans-Pritchard at a Meeting of the British Association for the Advancement of Science, September 1931' 193

List of Works Cited in the Introductions and Notes 201
Subject Index 207

ABBREVIATIONS

ADC	Assistant District Commissioner
AMC	Archivio Storico della Congregazione dei Missionari Comboniani, Rome
AMO	Assistant Medical Officer
BD	Bor District (notation used on district files now in the SRO)
Civsec	Civil Secretary's files (in the NRO)
CMS	The Church Missionary Society
Coriat MSS	Coriat papers (Rhodes House, Oxford, MSS Afr. s.1684)
Dakhlia	Dakhlia (Arab., Department of the Interior) files (in the NRO)
DC	District Commissioner
EA	Egyptian army
EHJP	Ecology and History of Jonglei Province (tapes and transcripts of interviews undertaken in Jonglei Province, 1981–2, now deposited in the SRO)
END	Eastern Nuer District files (in Nasir and the SRO)
GGR	Governor-general's annual report: Reports on the Finance, Administration, and Condition of the Sudan
Intel	Intelligence Department files (in the NRO)
JAH	*Journal of African History*
£E.	Egyptian pound, the currency of the Sudan until 1956, roughly equivalent at this time to £1. 0s. 6d
LND	Lou Nuer District files (in the SRO)
MA	(Arab.), *mulazim awal*, rank of first lieutenant in the Egyptian army and Sudan Defence Force
m/ms	Milleme: one-thousandth of an Egyptian pound; one-tenth of a piastre
MO	Medical Officer
MP	Mounted Police
MPMIR	Mongalla Province Monthly Intelligence Report
MT	(Arab.), *mulazim tani*, rank of second lieutenant in the Egyptian army and Sudan Defence Force
NRO	National Records Office, Khartoum
OC	Officer commanding
pt.	Piastre: one-hundredth of an Egyptian pound
SAD	Sudan Archive, Oriental Library, University of Durham

SCR	Strictly Confidential Report (notation on files in the confidential section of district and province offices)
SDF	Sudan Defence Force (separated from the Egyptian army in 1925)
SGS	Sudan Government Steamer
SIR	*Sudan Intelligence Report*
SMIR	*Sudan Monthly Intelligence Report*
SMR	*Sudan Monthly Record*
SNR	*Sudan Notes and Records*
SRO	Southern Records Office, Juba
TD	Torit District files (in the SRO)
UNP	Upper Nile Province (notation used on province files in the NRO and SRO)
UNPMD	Upper Nile Province Monthly Diary
Willis MSS	C. A. Willis papers (in the SAD)
ZD, ZVD	Zeraf District and Zeraf Valley District files (in the SRO and New Fangak)

GLOSSARY

Note: Words are given as they appear in the original manuscripts, with standard transcriptions provided in parentheses.

ardeb (Arab., *ardabb*), measure of capacity, about 200 litres
bimbashi (Turk.), the rank of major in the Egyptian Army and Sudan Defence Force, the lowest rank allowed a British officer
buluk amin (Turk.), the rank of company quartermaster sergeant in the Egyptian army and Sudan Defence Force
durra (Arab.), sorghum
felucca (Arab.), a type of sailboat used on the Nile
fulah (Arab., *fula*), pool of water
hish (Arab.), to weed; used in the sense of clearing and repairing roads
jallaba (Arab.), merchant
jallabia (Arab.), long cotton garment worn in the Sudan, associated in the south with Northern Sudanese merchants
kaid el 'amm (Arab.), commander-in-chief of the Sudan Defence Force
kantar (Arab.), measure of weight, about 100 lb.
khor (Arab.), watercourse, dry throughout part of the year
kujur (colloq. Arab.), used indiscriminately by Muslim Sudanese to describe pagan spiritual figures, roughly equivalent in derogatory meaning to the English 'witchdoctor'
mahr (Arab.), bridewealth
mamur (Arab., *ma'mur*), junior Egyptian or Sudanese administrative official, subordinate to the British DC
marah, see *murah*
markaz / marakiz (Arab.), district headquarters
merisa (Arab., *marissa*), beer brewed from sorghum
meshra (Arab., *mashra'*), landing place on a river
mudiria (Arab.), province headquarters
murah (colloq. Arab.), cattle camp
namlia (Arab.), mosquito-proof house
nas (Arab.), 'people'; used by DCs, even in the Southern Sudan, when referring to 'their people'
onbashi (Turk.), rank of corporal in EA, SDF, and police
rotl / rtl (Arab.), measurement of weight, roughly one pound

serraf (Arab.), government store-keeper
shawish (Arab.), rank of sergeant in the EA, SDF, and police
shen / shieng (Nuer, *cieng*), a territorial or social unit of indeterminate size; applied to the family homestead, segment of a lineage, clan or tribal territory
sudd (Arab., *sadd*), blocks of matted vegetation obstructing river channels
temargi / temargia (Arab.), local medical orderlies
toich (Western Nilotic, *toc* or *toic*), riverain pastures, used during dry season
wakeel (Arab., *wakil*), assistant, agent
zariba (Arab.), thorn hedge, or a fortified camp in the Southern Sudan

NOTE ON DOCUMENTS

Most of the documents reproduced in this volume are taken from carbon copies, which are very often the only copies extant in the files. This has posed some problems in transcription, for, quite apart from the lack of clarity in some places, it is not always possible to know which errors in the text were corrected in the final report. This is particularly true of tables; some entries seem erroneous but there was no way of knowing how to correct them. Most reports were typed by Coriat himself; only documents 2.2 and 3.4 bore the initials of a clerk, and 5.1 was apparently typed in Khartoum for general circulation. I have not felt that any great purpose would be served by an exact transcription of errors in the text. I have therefore corrected obvious typographical mistakes (such as transposed characters) and have inserted missing letters where needed. However, a minimalist approach has been used in the editing of the documents so as to reproduce as far as possible the character and appearance of the originals, and I have therefore retained certain idiosyncracies in grammar and spelling, particularly of non-English words. No significant changes have been made to punctuation and capitalization, other than in section and sub-section headings and to make consistency within individual texts; or to paragraphing, except in the case of document 3.2, where the original paragraph divisions were not always clear.

Where the original documents had titles, these titles have been retained and are reproduced on the Contents page within quotation marks. Documents 1.4, 3.1 and 3.4 were untitled and have therefore been given descriptive titles.

Each section of the book has an introduction by the editor, and each document is preceded by a short introduction by the editor, set in italics. All editorial insertions within the text of the documents are contained within square brackets and have been confined to material which either identifies names or clarifies points in the text. Botanical names for plants mentioned in the documents are taken from Broun and Massey 1929. Some Nuer words are given more modern spellings the first time they appear in each document. Coriat's spelling of Nuer words is not consistent, but the spelling in the later documents conforms more closely with the standard phonetic system proposed in the 1928 Rejaf conference on linguistics. In general, Coriat uses 'sh' where 'c' is now normally used, and a 'w' instead of 'u'. Where only minor alterations are involved I have not felt it necessary to provide a variant. It did not seem necessary to use the full range of phonetic symbols for Nilotic vowels; in general, I have tried to follow a broad transcription for proper nouns similar to that used in Evans-Pritchard's monographs. The names of the two main Nuer tribes that Coriat dealt with, the Lou and Gaawar, appear consistently in the documents as 'Lau' and 'Gaweir', and no alteration has been made to this. The commonest form of certain geographical names, such as Bahr el-Jebel and Bahr el-Zeraf, is also retained, even when such spellings may not be the most accurate modern transcription. I have employed a simplified transcription for Arabic names, titles, and ranks, as the retention of diacritical marks is not crucial in this context.

Wherever possible, individuals mentioned in the texts have been identified in the notes. In many Nuer and Dinka cases, as well as with some Sudanese and British officials, I have been unable to find additional identifying material in either the oral or archival sources available to me.

The documents reproduced here were found in the following locations:

Doc. 1.1 'Easy but Uncertain', Coriat MSS; also appeared in *Heritage; A Journal of Southern Sudanese Cultures* (Regional Council for Arts and Letters, Juba), Vol. I, no. 1, 1982, pp. 43–6.

Doc. 1.2 'The Gaweir Nuers', published as an addendum to H. C. Jackson's 'The Nuers of the Upper Nile Province' (*SNR*, 1923) when the latter was reprinted as a pamphlet in 1924 by the Intelligence Department in Khartoum.

Doc. 1.3 'Transfer of Barr Gaweir to Zeraf Valley District', SRO UNP 66.B.10.

Doc. 1.4 Bloodwealth Payments (Coriat to governor, Upper Nile Province, 30.06.26), SRO BD 66.B.3.

Doc. 1.5 'Southern (Abwong) District: Handing-over Notes', Coriat MSS.

Doc. 2.1 'Settlement of Ol Dinka–Gaweir Nuer Boundary Dispute', SRO UNP 66.B.11.

Doc. 2.2 'Nuer–Dinka re Settlement-Intertribal Boundary', SRO BD 66.B.3.

Doc. 3.1 Gwek Diary, Coriat MSS.

Doc. 3.2 'General Report: Patrol S8. (Lau Nuer) 1928', NRO Civsec 5/2/11.

Doc. 3.3 'Nuer Settlement—Gun Lau (Guncol) Area', NRO Civsec 1/3/8; also Coriat MSS.

Doc. 3.4 Notes on Political Prisoners in Malakal (Coriat to governor, Upper Nile Province, 27.11.31), NRO Dakhlia I 1/2/6.

Doc. 4.1 'Western Nuer District', NRO Civsec 57/2/8; also Willis MSS, SAD 212/14/224-51.

Doc. 4.2 'Administration—Western Nuer', Coriat MSS.

Doc. 5.1 'Notes on Paper on the Nuer Read by Mr. E. Evans-Pritchard at a Meeting of the British Association for the Advancement of Science, September 1931', NRO Dakhlia I 112/12/87.

Two other significant notes by Coriat, which are not reprinted here because they contain information already included in the above, are:

'Barr or Southern Gaweir—Précis of Note by Coriat 19.1.1923', NRO Dakhlia I 112/13/87.

'Note by P. Coriat Esq.', 02.08.28, NRO Civsec 5/3/12 [on the 'Gaweir March'].

LIST OF PLATES AND MAPS

PLATES

The plates are to be found after page lvi

Frontispiece Percy Coriat, 1928 (Coriat collection)
1. Manyel Deng, 1928 (Eastwood)
2. Guer Wiu and Deng Mayan, *c.*1926 (Coriat)
3. Wan Tyeir and son, 1928 (Romilly)
4. Lat Makuai, *c.*1926 (Coriat)
5. Akuei Biel, *c.*1926 (Coriat)
6. Garang Wui, *c.*1926 (Coriat)
7. Deng Kir, *c.*1926 (Coriat)
8. Them Jang, *c.*1926 (Coriat)
9. Coriat and Mayan Lam, parading Dinka chiefs' police for a bathe at Thul, S8 patrol, 1928 (Eastwood)
10. Beating two chiefs' police for lying, 1928 (Eastwood)
11. Prisoners, S8 patrol, 1928 (Coriat)
12. Coriat interrogating a prisoner, S8 patrol, 1928 (Coriat collection)
13. Nuer 'hishing' the road, 1928 (Romilly)
14. Dual Diu (in shirt on right), outside Coriat's tent, Fajilil, 1928 (Eastwood)
15. Major Wyld in Dual Diu's cattle camp, Gaweir March, 1928 (Coriat)
16. Coriat climbing the Mound, 1928 (Coriat collection)
17. Guek, with ruins of the Mound in background, 1929 (Eastwood)
18. Mayan Lam, Wyld, Coriat and Tunnicliffe with Guek's trophies, 1929 (Eastwood)
19. 'Peace treaties': Tunnicliffe, Alban, Coriat, Kerr, 1929 (Coriat collection)

MAPS

Map 1. Nuerland within Upper Nile Province, 1954	xxii
Map 2. Upper Nile Province, 1926	xxxv
Map 3. Western Nuer, 1930	160

Editor's Introduction

PERCY CORIAT'S LIFE AND THE IMPORTANCE OF HIS WORK

The Nuer have fascinated anthropologists and Africanists ever since the publication of the first volume of Evans-Pritchard's Nuer trilogy in 1940. This fascination has been as much due to the innate qualities of *The Nuer* as to the Nuer themselves. The quality of Evans-Pritchard's ethnography has inspired generations of anthropologists and there has now grown up a small industry of secondary commentaries on *The Nuer*, and to a lesser extent on the Nuer, an industry which has sought to use Nuer ethnography as a vehicle for propounding new theories in social anthropology. Evans-Pritchard has remained the main source of information, but other sources produced by administrators, missionaries and even early explorers have been brought in to confirm or refute his analysis. Very little attempt has been made to assess the quality of these other sources, nor has there been much attempt to supplement published with manuscript material.

In all this activity the writings of Percy Coriat have been largely ignored, and because ignored they have been underrated. He published only two pieces in his lifetime: 'The Gaweir Nuers' (reprinted here as document 1.2) and 'Gwek the Witch-doctor and the Pyramid of Dengkur', *Sudan Notes and Records*, 1939. Yet Coriat is our first authoritative European source on the Nuer. He was one of the first British administrators to become fully conversant in the language in the 1920s; his nine years' administrative experience brought him into contact with a broader territorial range of Nuer than any of his successors; and he left behind a scattered but substantial body of writings which have never been systematically used by scholars and which are presented to the wider public for the first time in this volume.

Before the 1920s all that was written and published on the Nuer was based on information extracted through other languages, usually Arabic and Dinka. All the main nineteenth-century European explorers, such as the Poncet brothers, John Petherick and Ernst Marno, communicated to the Nuer through Arabic. Marno did learn some Nuer from a Lou slave-girl, but she seems to have been the only Nuer he tried to converse with in her own language (Poncet 1937, Petherick 1869, Marno 1874). The early British administrators, such as H. H. Wilson (1902–5), K. C. P. Struvé (1905–10), and C. H. Stigand (1916–18),[1] also used Arabic or Dinka. Stigand had a wider experience in African linguistics than most of his colleagues and produced the first Nuer–English vocabulary (Stigand 1923), but it was compiled with the aid of a Dinka government interpreter. H. C. Jackson (1921–2)[2] used the same interpreter (Bilal Said, or Tut Deng)[3] as his main source of information for his lengthy but somewhat miscellaneous notes (*SNR*, 1923). Captain V. H. Fergusson[4] who, because of his dramatic murder in 1927, is probably the best remembered of all Nuer administrators, also communicated solely through Dinka and Atuot interpreters, using a mixture of Dinka and Arabic. Many of the men listed above published brief articles or reports on the Nuer, and these have been cited more widely than Coriat's own. Few scholars have taken into consideration the manner in which they collected their information. Even Evans-Pritchard, in his lengthy critique of sources on the Southern Sudan (1971), excluded administrative writings from his survey, though his own work indicates that he was well aware of both their value and limitations.

It was only in 1921–2 that two British administrators learned to speak Nuer. The first was John Lee, who served at Nasir among the Eastern Jikany from 1921 to 1929. Unfortunately he committed very little to paper, and not much of his official correspondence survives today. He is still remembered with respect by the Eastern Jikany because of his efforts to establish peaceful contacts with them after the 1920 punitive campaign, and his role in the early history of Nuer administration should not be underestimated merely because it is unrecorded on paper. From the point of view of scholarship, however, he is not an early

---

1. Bimbashi H. H. Wilson, inspector Upper Nile Province 1902–4, senior inspector 1905; K. C. P. Struvé, OBE, junior inspector Upper Nile Province 1906–9, senior inspector 1909–10, governor 1919–26; Major C. H. Stigand, inspector Nasir 1915–16, governor Upper Nile Province 1916–19. Details of the service of British officials in the Sudan are taken from Bell and Dee n.d., Daly 1984, the *Sudan Government Gazette*, and other official sources.

2. H. C. Jackson, deputy governor Upper Nile Province 1920–2.

3. Bilal Said (Tut Deng): Jackson (1923: 59) claimed Tut Deng was a Dinka adopted into the Nuer. He came from the Eastern Jikany area and was initiated into the Maiker age-set before being captured by a Mahdist raiding expedition in *c.*1888. He was interpreter to the governor of Upper Nile Province as early as 1906 (*SIR* 148 (Nov. 1906), 3), then became a merchant trading on the Sobat (*SIR* 207 (Oct. 1911), 5), returned to government service as interpreter in Nasir, and ended his service as chief government interpreter in Malakal in *c.*1920–3.

4. Captain V. H. Fergusson, OBE, seconded from EA in 1919, DC Eastern District Bahr el-Ghazal 1921–7.

major historical or ethnographic source.

Coriat soon followed Lee, spending the rainy season among the Gaawar at Ayod in 1922, and obtaining a working knowledge of the language. As the documents in this collection show, his understanding of both the language and the people grew over the next eight years. We are fortunate that though Coriat, like so many district commissioners, disliked paperwork, he did not make a fetish of an aversion to 'bumf'. He did his office work well and produced a series of highly detailed and informative reports on major issues and events in Nuer administration. It is these reports which make the core of this book. What makes these unique reports even more special is that all of Coriat's immediate successors among the Lou, Gaawar and Western Nuer—Pletts, Sherratt, Wedderburn-Maxwell, Alban and Romilly[5]—continued the older, mainly non-literate tradition of administrative reporting (see Thesiger 1987: 261). We have very few official records immediately following on Coriat's reports.

Coriat's writings are those of the archetypical district commissioner, being concerned with the local details of the district rather than with amateur ethnography or administrative theory. Unlike H. C. Jackson before him, he was not inspired by Frazer's *The Golden Bough* and did not try to fit his own writing on the Nuer into the outline of topics presented in that massive work. Intellectualism of any sort amused him, and he was equally indifferent to professional administrative theory as to scholarship. He was energetic in setting up the structure of 'native administration' in his districts, but he wasted no time analysing it. Again, this distinguishes his reports from those of many of his successors. Administrative writing on the Nuer in the two decades after Coriat left Upper Nile Province was very much dominated by theories of native political structures and administrative devolution. This theoretical concern was in many ways encouraged and facilitated by Evans-Pritchard's writings, which began to be published in *SNR* in 1933. It is perhaps significant that those who wrote most about the theory of devolution as applied to the Nuer political structure—Armstrong, Corfield, Lewis and Winder[6]—all eventually rose high in the provincial administrative hierarchy, most becoming governors. Coriat remained a district officer throughout his career in the Sudan Political Service.

---

5. G. S. Pletts, ADC Zeraf 1923–7; W. G. N. Sherratt, ADC Zeraf 1930–4, DC Zeraf 1935–6; H. G. Wedderburn-Maxwell, ADC Frontier District 1926–7, ADC Zeraf 1927–31, DC Zeraf 1931–2, DC Western Nuer 1937–46; Captain A. H. Alban, DFC, ADC Abwong 1929–35, ADC Akobo 1935–7, DC Pibor District 1937–41, HBM consul Gore, Western Abyssinia 1942–50; Captain H. A. Romilly, SDF 1924–8, joined Sudan Political Service 1929, ADC Western Nuer 1930–1, DC Western Nuer 1931–6, DC Eastern Nuer 1937–46.

6. C. L. Armstrong, DSO, MC, DC Nasir 1930–1, governor Upper Nile Province 1939–40; F. D. Corfield, MBE, ADC Nasir 1931–2, DC Nasir 1932–6, governor Upper Nile Province 1948–50 (author of the Corfield report on Mau Mau); B. A. Lewis, ADC Zeraf 1935–8, DC Pibor District 1942–4, deputy governor Equatoria Province 1952–3; J. Winder, ADC Pibor District 1936–7, DC Zeraf 1938–42, deputy governor Upper Nile Province 1948–51, governor 1953–5.

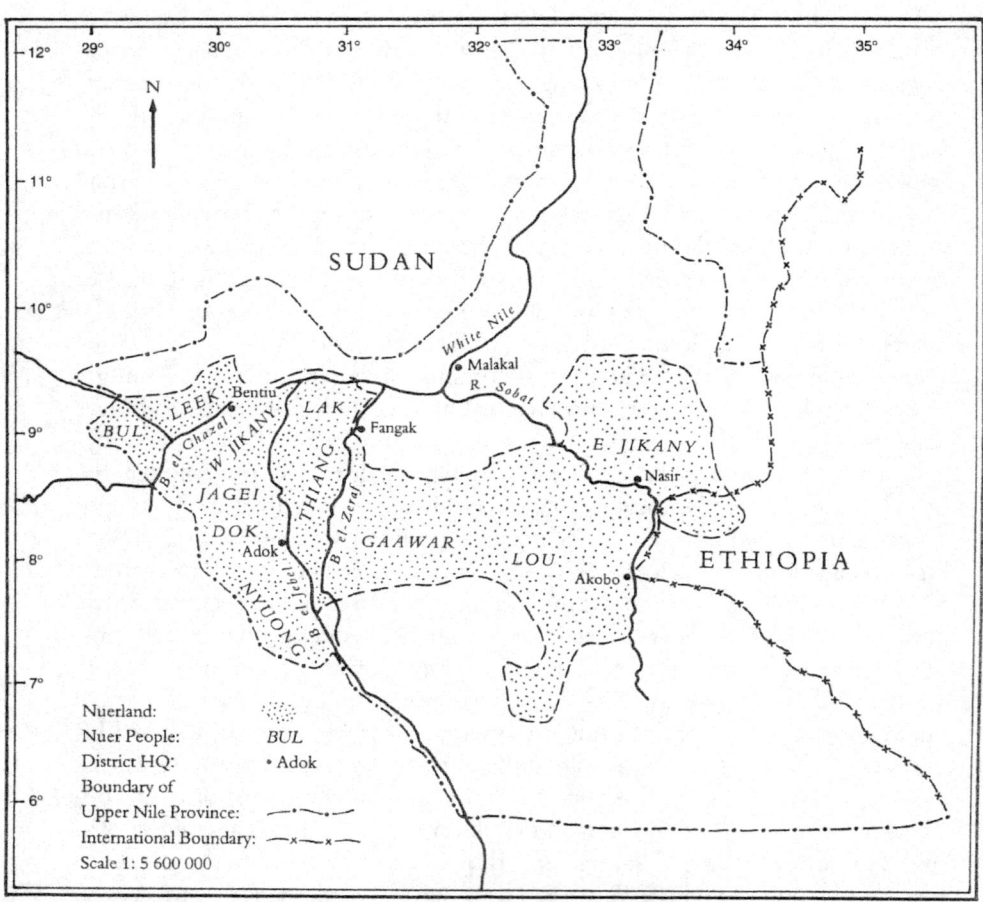

MAP 1 Nuerland within Upper Nile Province, 1954

Coriat thus stands at a pivotal point in our knowledge about the Nuer. He came to know the Nuer before they were fully integrated into the administrative structure of the Anglo-Egyptian Sudan, and before they became grist for several theoretical mills. He was a source of information for Evans-Pritchard and a friendly critic of his earliest writings. At the same time Coriat was an influential participant in a number of events during a crucial period in Nuer history; he was not an independent and neutral observer of Nuer society. His reports can be understood only in the context of the time they were written, his personal relations with the Nuer, and his career in the administrative service. I will thus first summarize his career before analysing the impact of his work and the signficance of his writings.

Coriat's Career in the Sudan

Much has been written about the educational qualifications, intellectual achievements and social respectability of the members of the Sudan Political Service (Collins 1972, Collins and Deng 1984, Kirk-Greene 1982, Mangan 1982). Coriat was considered by his contemporaries to be in many ways a model DC, a man whose style was to be emulated. Sir James Robertson, a former civil secretary of the Sudan and governor-general of Nigeria, later wrote, 'In the Sudan Service, where I knew him, Corry had a splendid reputation.... We, who served in other Sudan provinces, heard fabulous accounts of his work in the difficult Nuer country.... I met him first in Kordofan, and was most relieved in 1936, when due for transfer, to hear that I was to hand over my district of Western Kordofan to him. I could not have asked for a better successor' (Robertson n.d.: 3–4). Western Kordofan was one of the most prestigious districts in the Sudan; it was the training ground of a number of civil secretaries, and Coriat was the only contract officer ever to serve there. Despite this, he does not fit the collective stereotype of the service which was so carefully created by its members and by the handful of scholars who have studied it since.

Coriat's family background was cosmopolitan. There was a distant connection to Thomas Coryate, the seventeenth-century traveller of 'Coryats Crudites', who introduced the fork to English tables. Coriat himself was born in London on 29 August 1898; his father served for some time as British consul in Morocco, and the family lived in London, Morocco and Spain. Coriat received a standard pre-war education first at Warrington Private School in London, and then at the Perse School in Cambridge. Perse, a school with a sound academic reputation, did not normally produce men for either the Sudan or the Colonial service. Coriat was its only son to find his way to the Sudan, and that by an unusual channel.

Coriat was sixteen and still at school when the First World War broke out.

Though under age for military service he was extraordinarily tall (6 ft 4 in) and was able to enlist as a trooper in the Bucks Hussars Yeomanry in October 1914. All of his war service was spent in the Near East, first on garrison duty in Egypt, then at Suvla Bay at Gallipoli, in the Sanussi campaign of 1915–16, and finally in Palestine in 1916–17. He lost an eye at Suvla Bay but was still considered fit cannon-fodder. In 1916 he was promoted to corporal and then to lance-sergeant. At Nablus Hill, in Palestine, he was again wounded in 1917 and won the French Croix de Guerre. Before being discharged from the army in April 1918 he was awarded the Distinguished Conduct Medal (DCM), a rare and coveted decoration awarded only to other ranks, not to officers. His military service with the ranks was thus in many ways more distinguished and valorous than some of his later Sudan colleagues who emerged with commissions, and his experience in the mounted infantry was to stand him in good stead during his service among the Nuer.

Back in England Coriat was at something of a loose end, farming in Berkshire for a time until the family suddenly lost most of its money. He was then forced to look for employment and joined the Sudan Cotton, Fuel and Industrial Development Company as an agricultural assistant. The company, with John Wells as its technical director, planned a vast scheme for turning the *sudd* of the Upper Nile into blocks of fuel (Collins 1983: 296–7). It became known colloquially as the 'John Wellington Wells Company', partly because of the name of its director and partly because, like Gilbert and Sullivan's sorcerer, it went up in smoke. Coriat was stranded at his site on Lake No, refusing to abandon the local workers until they were paid. There is an improbable story of how he and his co-worker, Captain Vicars-Miles,[7] eventually escaped by canoe and camel to Khartoum, only to find the company's office closed and the safe empty. There is also a more likely tale that he and Vicars-Miles were washed away by a flood and were found floating in Lake No on the wreckage of their camp. What is certain is that Coriat became very ill and was brought by steamer to Malakal to recover. The governor, K. C. P. Struvé, was apparently annoyed at the prospect of having to oversee the embalming of Coriat's body for shipment back to England in the event of his death (Ben Assher 1928: 222), but Coriat recovered and was recruited locally into the Sudan Political Service, staying on in Upper Nile Province.

Coriat's employment in the province was due entirely to Struvé. There was an affinity between the two men which lasted until Struvé's death. Both were tall and both came into Sudan administration through unusual channels. Struvé had the more orthodox background, having obtained a modest geology degree at Oxford in 1899. From there he went to Egypt, employed first as Inspector for Rotations in the First Circle of Irrigation and then in an agricultural land company which, like the John Wellington Wells company of later fame, went bust, leaving Struvé stranded in Egypt. After interviews with Lord Cromer and

7. Captain A. L. W. Vicars-Miles, MC, Sudan Political Service 1922–45.

General Wingate[8] he joined the Sudan civil service. Like Coriat, Struvé had suffered and recovered from severe illnesses early in his career, and because of this was considered robust enough for an appointment in Upper Nile Province.[9]

This similarity in their lives would have been enough to establish a rapport between them, but there were other reasons for their friendship. Struvé had been one of the first civilians to join the Sudan service after the Reconquest (1898), and he was the first civilian to be sent to Upper Nile Province before the First World War. He was the province's first civilian governor after the war, but in 1920 most of his staff were still professional soldiers. Coriat, who had had a distinguished war career, was neither an officer nor a part of that class of administrator whose military approach to administration Struvé so deprecated and was trying to replace. In a difficult province Coriat, with his robust sense of humour, was a good companion. Struvé, who became a father at the advanced age of fifty—a year before he retired from the Sudan—came to treat Coriat virtually as a son. Coriat was one of only two Sudan colleagues with whom Struvé remained in touch after leaving the country in 1926.

The Sudan government placed a strong emphasis on 'character' in selecting recruits for administrative service, and character was produced by the right social background and training in the officer corps or at university. Coriat was neither an officer nor a graduate, but his social background, while unusual, was acceptable. As his former house-master from Perse was at pains to emphasise in a formal letter of recommendation, Coriat was 'a gentleman in the best sense of the word'. He was not an Oxbridge 'blue'—that varsity proof of hardiness which was considered essential for the hard life in the Sudan—but he had demonstrated his robustness in other ways. He had survived Gallipoli, Palestine, the loss of an eye, and flood and fever on Lake No. His war decorations proved his valour; his yeomanry experience proved he could ride and shoot; and he was on the spot. Despite occasional hinted reservations about his 'Latin' paternity, he was a satisfactory recruit. Thus it was that he was sent almost immediately to Ayod as a temporary contract probationer.

Ayod is a beautiful spot. Situated on a sandy knoll within the Duk ridge, it is amply covered with large shady trees. Its wells produce clear, fresh water. The Gaawar Nuer found it a welcome refuge from floods at the end of the nineteenth century, and it was chosen as the site for a government police post in 1918. Being far from the rivers it was difficult of access and only two inspectors had previously paid it intermittent visits. A track had been cut through the bush from the Sobat to Ayod in 1921, and it was Struvé's intention to bring the Gaawar under closer administrative control by placing Coriat there throughout the rains of 1922. This was an unprecedented experiment in rural

---

8. Lord Cromer, British agent and consul-general in Egypt 1883–1907; Sir Reginald Wingate, governor-general of the Sudan 1899–1916.

9. I am indebted to Mr Adrian Struvé for this account of his father's early career. Collins (1983: 127) mistakenly describes Struvé as a short man.

administration, since all other government posts in the province at the time were established on the rivers.

The accommodation of the post was less than adequate. Arab slavers had established their *zariba* there in the 1860s and the outline of their trench was (and is) still visible. Within this rectangle a previous inspector had constructed a mud, mosquito-proof house, which Coriat found to be full of holes and with only half of its floor cemented (the cement slab can still be seen and is occasionally incorporated into huts built on the site). Coriat's stint during the rains (which he describes in doc. 1.1 below) was difficult, cut off as he was from any other government post or mail from home for three months.

This enforced isolation imposed hardships, but it also forced him to seek company with the Nuer in a way that no other previous DC had done. He learned the Nuer language (though speaking it, as some now are still able to recall, in the clipped tones of a regimental sergeant-major); he was given the honorific name Kulang-Girkuac (usually shortened to Girkuai); and formed many strong personal friendships among the Nuer men with whom he had to work. This is evident in his personal comments in his handing-over notes of 1926 (doc. 1.3). Nyang Macar, a veteran of Deng Laka's rise to power in the nineteenth century (see doc. 1.1), was one of his earliest friends. So was the chief Guer Wiu[10] and—what was more important politically—so was Dual Diu, the prophet Deng Laka's son and successor.

Dual Diu had never before been on completely easy terms with government representatives. His father had been courted by government and had even received a visit from the governor in 1906. After his death in 1907 the government dealt only with Deng Laka's elder sons, Wol and Macar Diu. Macar was prodded into rebellion in 1913 and both he and Wol died on a cattle raid against the Twic Dinka in 1914.[11] Dual had by that time inherited the divinity Diu, which had also inspired his father, and led the Gaawar on a series of retaliatory raids against the Dinka. From 1914 to 1918 there was intermittent warfare between the government and Dual, but the government did not have the resources to press a conclusion.

In 1918 Dual made his formal submission to an inspector from neighbouring Mongalla Province and publicly welcomed the building of the government post at Ayod, near his own home at Buk. But the inspectors who visited Ayod had little real contact with Dual. Coriat's predecessor, Borradaile,[12] decided that Dual was 'conceited' and showed him little public respect. Coriat, however, came to regard Dual as a 'great friend', and it was on the strength of this friendship

---

10. See below, doc. 1.2, note f to table entitled 'Gaweir Shens'.

11. For accounts of government dealings with Deng Laka and his sons Wol and Macar Diu, see Matthews 1907, Struvé 1909, Wauhope 1910 and 1913, Owen 1910, O'Sullivan 1910, and Kulang Majok, text 2.5, in Johnson, in preparation.

12. C. Borradaile, Sudan Political Service 1920–2, who wrote about his experiences in Ayod in Ben Assher 1928.

that Dual was drawn progressively into the administrative orbit, shedding his reluctance to meet directly with government officials, and eventually agreeing to leave his home and visit Malakal not once, but twice, in 1923 and 1924.[13] Coriat exchanged visits with Dual, first in the company of his interpreter, Manyel Deng,[14] and then on his own. Coriat and Dual are still remembered during this period as *maath ti ca kayndien reet*, 'friends who cannot be separated'.[15] This was to make Dual's subsequent treatment by the government all the more bitter, as it was felt that Coriat had in some way betrayed him.

Coriat's sense of humour and affability stood him in good stead in his contacts with the Gaawar. He found the list of criminals he was bequeathed intensely amusing, and 'long did he laugh, and loud, in his appreciation of the Ayod casebook' (Ben Assher 1928: 223). He is still remembered as a man who could be approached by anyone, and that if he liked a man he would walk along, hand in hand, conversing, just as any Nuer did. His sociability is commemorated in his 'ox-name'. Nuer honorific names usually describe the colour pattern of an ox presented as a 'name-ox', but Coriat's name describes a special type of leopard-skin (*kuac*) with bells sewn on it and worn at dances. He appears, then, to have been a stylish dancer. The impression he created at dances is recalled in the following song, recorded by Fr. Crazzolara in 1931, and still well known in Western Nuer:[16]

Kulang Gierkwai cako peen ne nyaal	Kulang Girkuai we met over a girl
Kwiy ne gate	He does not know his son
Ci Kulaang ben	Kulang has come
Ci Gieerkwai ben	Girkuai has come
Ci maanke dhwoony dhwoonydien	And the women are dancing rythmically
Ci wuuti tang gaar late	And the men are jumping in order
Ci wuuti yiaadmaan kan	And men have taken the skins of women

13. *SMIR* 348 (July 1923), 5; 363 (Oct. 1924), 4.

14. See below, doc. 1.1 n. 6.

15. SRO EHJP8, Kulang Majok, 24 May 1982, transcribed and translated by Stephen Tut Puol. Other parts of Kulang Majok's testimony concerning Gaawar–government relations are to appear as texts 2.5 and 4.8 in Johnson, in preparation, where it is compared with and frequently corroborated by contemporary records.

16. John Winder (personal communication) recorded Coriat's ox-name as 'Kolong-Kerkwac', explaining that 'a "ker" was a beast with a stripe down its back and "kwac" was, of course, a leopard marking'. Crazzolara transcribes it as 'Gierkwai' (the diphthong replacing the final 'c'), and in all the interviews I have recorded the name has been pronounced either 'Girkuac' or 'Girkuai'. Stephen Abraham Yar (Nyuong Nuer) has given me the explanation of the name used here, though he has also suggested that it might refer to a *kuac* (spotted) ox with a special *gier*, or bell. The song, of which these are only the opening lines, is found in Crazzolara, 'Nuer Customs', AMC A/112/4. The translation is by Stephen Yar, who explained that it describes the effect Coriat had on a dance, where the girls danced their best to attract his attention, and the men redoubled their efforts to regain the attention of the girls. Though Crazzolara implies that the song is a Gaawar composition, it is still sung in Western Nuer, usually as a lullaby to calm crying children.

After his first year in Ayod he exchanged full bridewealth in cattle for Nyanliedh Ruac, a woman from a respectable family. When Coriat finally left the Lou and Gaawar in 1929, he placed Nyanliedh in the care of his old friend, Guer Wiu, with cattle for her maintenance. Though she had no children by Coriat, she later had some by her chosen consort and, because of the original exchange of bridewealth, they are considered Coriat's family (see Coriat's own explanation of this custom in doc. 1.2, under 'Marriage Rights'). A proportion of the bridewealth of each of the daughters has been reserved for him, and as recently as 1975 Gaawar in Ayod acknowledged that a small herd had accumulated for his use, should he ever return to claim it.

Coriat's friendships were highlighted, in a way, by his very toughness. It is still recalled that once, while mounted, he picked a man up by the hair of his head, trotted some distance, and then dropped him. Coriat and his horse are remembered as a fiercesome pair, especially during the Nuer Settlement of 1929, when Coriat 'tamed the Nuer'. There is even a story that his eye was plucked out by a thorn branch as he pursued the Nuer on horseback through a forest.

The way in which Coriat could take a liking to a person for his own qualities, whatever the circumstances, and the way in which he could also pursue his duties with a sternness which bordered on cruelty are contrasted in two stories told by Kulang Majok, a Bar Gaawar who served Coriat as a Native Authority Policeman ('Chiefs' Police'), and who was close enough to Coriat to help collect his bridewealth cattle. The first concerns Kulang's recruitment into the Chiefs' Police, the second a manhunt for the murderer of an Arab merchant in 1924.

Kulang had just been initiated into the 'Pilual' age-set shortly before Coriat first arrived at Ayod. One of Kulang's sisters had recently divorced her husband, even before he had completed the marriage payments. The ex-husband came around to Kulang's father's homestead with a policeman to reclaim the cattle he had paid, but Kulang speared and wounded the policeman rather than let him take the animals. Coriat later came searching for Kulang and arrived at the homestead preceded by his interpreter, Manyel Deng, and the Gaawar chief, Guer Wiu. When they arrived Kulang and his brothers fled. But then Kulang thought to himself,

> 'I better come back or Girkuai will kill father'. So I returned.... I went to the barn and brought out a big ram, like that. I went and took the tail of a giraffe recently killed which was hanging up in the barn. I went to meet him. He asked Guer, 'Who is that person?' Guer told him, 'He is Kulang, the son of a man called Majok Juc'. [Coriat] asked me, 'Are you the person who speared the policeman?' I said, 'Yes'. He said, 'We go home.' When we arrived home he got off the back of his horse. The police took the horse and tied it to a post. The police walked with horses [i.e. they rode] because it was the rainy season. He took his chair and put it there on the ground. My father came and sat on the ground with his head bowed. He thought we were all going to be killed. When I brought the ram and the tail [Coriat] said, 'You, are you the one who speared the police?' I said

yes. He said, 'Why didn't you run away?' I said, 'No. There is no place I can run to'. He told me to take the ram back to the barn because it had a *kujur* [Arab., spirit]. He then said, 'You will even be given a chief's cloth'. I said no. He said, 'No, I must give it to you. If you fear the government because you are young, you will walk together with Guer Wiu.'[17]

Kulang Majok returned with Coriat to Ayod the next day. Instead of being arrested he had been offered the appointment of government chief, which the conferring of the cloth implied. Having stabbed a policeman, he now found himself enrolled in Guer Wiu's police.

Not all Nuer who came up against the law got off so lightly. The second story, about Pathot Cakuen (mentioned in doc. 1.3), illustrates the harsher side of Nuer administration at this time. Early in 1924 Pathot, a Gaawar from Rupciengdol, and another man murdered an Arab merchant. Kulang Majok was out hunting elephants when Coriat arrived at Rupciengdol and sent for him. On arrival Kulang found that Coriat had rounded up all of *cieng* Dol's cattle and promised their return only if the section produced Pathot and his father Cakuen Jok. Coriat then offered Kulang a reward of a captured cow if he personally brought Cakuen in. Kulang refused.

> I told him, 'No! He is my maternal uncle. If he sees it is me [taking a cow from his section], and if you kill him, he will curse me. He will say, "My sister's son, you kill me!"' [Coriat] said, 'You *must* go!' I told him, 'I will not go!' He went to Guer Wiu, Guer who was his big chief. He said, 'Guer!' Guer said, 'Yes'. 'I told Kulang to go find Cakuen. He said he cannot go because Cakuen is his maternal uncle.' Guer told him, 'He is right. He cannot go'. [Coriat] said, 'Ah! Is he right?' Guer said, 'Yes'.[18]

There is a special relationship which exists between a mother's brother and a sister's son, a relationship of affection and security which is often absent between a Nuer man and his paternal kin, with whom he is frequently in competition (Evans-Pritchard 1951: 157–8, 162–7). It prevented Kulang from doing his duty as a policeman, at least as Coriat understood that duty. Yet Coriat accepted Guer Wiu's judgment and avoided placing Kulang in an impossible position. However, others within *cieng* Dol, Cakuen's agnatic kin, were less reticent. A man named Wei Joak caught Cakuen and beat him brutally with an iron bar. Cakuen was then taken to Rupciengdol while Coriat was absent in another village. Kulang found his uncle in the morning.

> I found him sitting on the ground with his head bowed. . . . I cried, my tears were running down my cheeks. He said, 'My sister's son do not cry, the Turuk will kill you. As for me, *cieng* Dol has killed me'. At about this time Girkuai arrived along with two *ma'murs* and the rest of the horsemen. As soon as he arrived he was told that Cakuen was caught. He came on his horse and slowly he circled round, and circled round, and circled round Cakuen. He said, 'Cakuen!' Cakuen said,

17. SRO EHJP8.
18. Ibid.

'Yes'. He said, 'Why did you bring up your son so badly? Your son, who killed an Arab, he is like someone who kills a woman. Is not an Arab like a woman? Would you say that he has killed a man?'

He then dismounted and his horse was taken away while he sat down. When he finished drinking his tea he sent for Cakuen. He asked Cakuen, 'Where is your son?' Cakuen said, 'My son has run away'. 'You don't know where he is?' He said, 'I don't know his place'. [Coriat] then said, 'All right'.

Cakuen was then taken away. He was just sitting listlessly, doing nothing, because he was an old man. The sun reached the late afternoon. We then heard that Cakuen's son who killed the Arab had been found and he was shot. [Coriat] then said, 'Right. It is finished. Tomorrow we will go to Guer's cattle camp'. . . .

The next morning when people left, the old man was tied [with a rope around his neck] to a horse's back. A Turuk on horseback was pulling him. When the people had gone a short distance, he died. The Turuk dismounted and untied the rope that was holding him. He died at once. They went and informed the villagers that 'the old man named Cakuen is there under the thorn tree. He is dead. You go and bury him there'. The villagers, those from his own section, went and buried him. . . . [Pathot] was also caught when he was found in Guer's territory. The DC said that he would take him by canoe to Tithbel for treatment. He also went and died there. Cakuen and his son, they both died together, they both died.[19]

Kulang Majok was a witness to all or part of these events. Coriat gives a more restrained account of this incident in his 1926 handing-over note (doc. 1.3), saying merely that Cakuen died in prison (by which, perhaps, he meant 'in custody'). It is clear even from his report that the pursuit and death of both Pathot and his father created considerable tension within *cieng* Dol.

The year 1924 continued to be one of tension in the province, mainly because of nationalist agitation in Khartoum and other towns of the Sudan. Coriat was on leave in England during August when the White Flag League began its demonstrations in Atbara, Khartoum and Omdurman. All leave was cancelled as absent administrators were recalled to their stations. The provinces remained quiet throughout that month and Coriat had an uneventful journey to Malakal. He was in his district on the Bahr el-Zeraf in late September when there was a demonstration of loyalty to the king of Egypt among the Sudanese troops in Malakal. Coriat returned to the province headquarters in time to take part in a police sweep through the native quarter. Nothing more happened until November, when Sir Lee Stack, governor-general of the Sudan and Sirdar (commander-in-chief) of the Egyptian army, was assassinated in Cairo. This was followed by mutinies in Khartoum and Talodi, in the Nuba Mountains neighbouring Upper Nile Province. Struvé sent Coriat with nearly fifty policemen to Talodi to arrest the Egyptian officers of the mutinous battalion, and the story of how he did so has become part of the folklore of the Sudan Political

---

19. Ibid. Kulang Majok indicated with a gesture that the rope was tied around Cakuen's neck. This was the usual way prisoners were tied at that time (see Plate 11).

Service. The officers are said to have set off overland for Malakal:

> On arrival at the only waterhole en route they found it occupied by a piratical figure with a revolver and a black patch over one eye, who informed them that they were under arrest. Having no idea of whether their government had repudiated them they thought it best to comply and were marched down to Tonga under escort of Coriat and a couple of Upper Nile policemen.[20]

Other, less dramatic changes also occurred in 1924. In that year Coriat completed a brick house at Ayod but was transferred to Abwong when the Lou Nuer were included in his district. He was also taken on in the permanent and pensionable service, losing the contract officer's bonus and taking a drop of pay from £600 a year to £480.

Coriat had begun visiting the Lou as early as 1923. His transfer to Abwong, however, did not bring him into as close contact with the Lou as his stay in Ayod had done with the Gaawar. Abwong, founded in 1904, had several brick buildings. As it was on the river Sobat it was in easy communication with Malakal, but it was set in Dinka country, far from the heart of the Lou. The geographical and political centre of the Lou Nuer at that time was Weideang ('Dengkurs' on government maps), a good fifty miles from Abwong. Coriat was not able to engage in the type of reciprocal visits with Lou chiefs which had been common with the Gaawar. He was much more dependent on those Nuer who were willing to journey to see him at Abwong. The greater personal distance this imposed between Coriat and the Lou is demonstrated in his assessment of chiefs in his 1929 handing-over notes (doc. 1.5). Out of forty-three chiefs and prominent men listed, eight are dismissed as 'useless', 'untrustworthy', or in some other way unreliable. By contrast only one of the twenty-three Bar Gaawar chiefs listed in his 1926 Bar Gaawar handing-over notes (doc. 1.3) is described as 'useless', while others have personal virtues mentioned to mitigate their administrative failings. It is clear that Coriat had more friendships among the Gaawar than among the Lou, and this may have had some bearing in the way events later developed in 1927–8.

Four Lou whom Coriat did come to know, like, and rely on were Dhiew Dieng, Guet Thie, Lam Tutthiang, and his son Mayan Lam, the government interpreter at Abwong. Dhiew tried to mediate between Guek and Coriat in 1927, but having failed, absented himself entirely from the conflict, thus earning himself a reputation for double-dealing on both sides.[21] Guet Thie and Lam Tutthiang were long-standing opponents of the prophet Ngundeng and

---

20. Henderson 1987: 102. The Malakal demonstration took place on 22–27 Sept. 1924, and the Talodi mutiny on 27 Nov. (*SMIR* 362 (Sept. 1924), 7; 364 (Nov. 1924), 5). Coriat was not so single-handed in his arrest of the Egyptian officers as Henderson suggests. He was accompanied by forty-seven Mounted Police led by a Shilluk police captain who, like Coriat, had won a DCM in the war (K. C. P. Struvé, 'Annual Report. Upper Nile Province, 1925', *Reports of Governors of Provinces for the Year 1925* (Khartoum: McCorquedale, 1926), p. 411).

21. See below, doc. 1.5, doc. 3.1 n. 32, doc. 3.2.

his son Guek and were later to provide Coriat with anti-Guek information.²²
Mayan Lam (see Plates 9 and 18) was required by his position to be more unambiguously in the government camp than the chiefs, but his long-term residence in Abwong virtually removed him from everyday Lou political life.

One man with whom Coriat never got on was Guek Ngundeng. He was one of the younger sons of the prophet Ngundeng, but he did not become possessed by his father's divinity, Deng, until some ten years after Ngundeng died. Guek was a young man of no great position during the Lou patrol of 1917. Following the combined events of the Lou defeat and the coming of the great flood of 1918, Guek fled to the home of his maternal relatives in the Jikany area, and it was there that he first became possessed by Deng. He returned to his own home shortly after the flood subsided and in the early 1920s began repairing his father's Mound (which Coriat calls a 'pyramid') at Weideang.

When it became known that Guek was possessed by Deng, people from as far away as Nasir began to come to him to have their disputes settled, with the aid of his divinity. This brought him into competition with the government, who claimed the ultimate right to hear legal cases. H. C. Jackson, then senior inspector (deputy governor) of Upper Nile Province, went to visit Guek in 1921 and established some form of diplomatic relations between the government and the prophet, with Guek's brother Bol acting as intermediary (Jackson 1954: 162–8; Coriat 1939: 228).

In 1923 Coriat received alarming reports while in Ayod that Guek was planning to raid the Dinka of neighbouring Mongalla Province. Coriat thereupon made an unannounced visit to Guek, some three days' march away, only to be told by Bol Ngundeng that Guek was unable to see him. Coriat nevertheless camped near the Mound. Early in the morning after his arrival, Coriat was awoken by loud shouts coming from the direction of the Mound. As the sun rose he could see Guek 'standing erect on the top and still shouting raucously'. Guek remained on top of the Mound all that day and disappeared during the night. A few days later he visited Coriat's camp, and 'by the evening we were almost affable'. Some form of a workable arrangement was established, Coriat dealing directly with Guek on the level of 'sub-chief' in the hierarchy of chiefs he was then trying to create. In two subsequent visits Coriat again found that Guek would ascend the Mound at night and spend the day on top of it, but in 1925 Guek returned Coriat's visits and came to Abwong (Coriat 1939: 227, 229).

Guek's behaviour was in stark contrast to that of Dual Diu's. Dual seems to have had a shrewder appreciation of government officals than Guek, and there is no record of him ever appearing before Coriat in a state of possession. The easy, friendly visits between the two men had no parallel with Guek. Guek's appearance also went against him. While Dual was close to seven feet tall

---

22. For Guet Thie, see below doc. 1.5 n. 17; for Lam Tutthiang see below, doc. 3.3 n. 27; for Mayan Lam see below, doc. 1.5 n. 65.

and powerfully built, Guek was squat with stumpy limbs (Jackson 1954: 164; Coriat 1939: 226). He also tended to drool in Coriat's presence, which did not improve the impression he made. It is no wonder that Coriat thought of Dual and Guek in completely different terms. Dual was scarcely a *kujur* at all, while Guek became 'the witchdoctor'. Throughout Coriat's reports Dual appears a reasonable and capable head chief of the Bar division of the Gaawar. As for Guek, 'the more I became acquainted the less did I consider him fitted as a Chieftain...' (doc. 3.2).[23] Guek took very little active part in the new administrative system Coriat was creating for Nuer leaders, but from 1923 to 1926 the two men were on reasonably good terms, and Coriat had no cause for complaint or alarm. It was only after 1926, with a change in province personnel, that things began to go wrong.

The Lou only gradually became Coriat's main concern. Even after his transfer to Abwong, the Gaawar and their southern Dinka neighbours occupied a good deal of his attention. As early as 1909 a province boundary had been fixed to coincide with a 'tribal' boundary between the Gaawar and Lou Nuer on the Upper Nile Province side, and the Ghol and Nyareweng Dinka on the Mongalla Province side. This increased rather than diminished inter-tribal tensions, as the opposing province administrations tended to side with their own people (Johnson 1982a). Coriat gave his own, informal assessment of the border in 1925:

> That southern boundary between our two districts [is] a tricky one and it requires both D.C.'s to pull together.... The trouble there is that my Nuers on my side are deadly enemies of the Dinkas on the other side and require constant watching to stop them knocking blazes and the fear of both places into the Dinkas. The Dinkas on the other hand being a mean crowd are deadly jealous and scared of the Nuers and go prancing in to the D.C. at Duk with hair-raising tales of Nuer attacks, forays, alarms and gory massacres. If the D.C. there is inclined to believe them without referring to this side a certain amount of unnecessary wind and confusion is raised. On the other hand if he and I work together he takes no notice of the artful Dinka unless there is good reason to do so. Even if nothing happens and any credit is put on the Dinka yarns without hearing our side of the case, the Nuers get to know there is wind up and think 'Government believes we are going to slosh the Dinka and we'll get it in the neck. Let's have a run for our money' and thereupon proceed to do so.[24]

During the period Coriat was assigned to the Gaawar three different DCs were appointed to the neighbouring district in rapid succession. Not all had learned the complexities of their district before they were transferred, and not

---

23. Collins (1983: 123–4) misrepresents Coriat's views on the prophets when he states that Coriat tried to convey to Willis the prophets' peaceful role in Nuer society. Coriat always thought of Dual as a warrior leader and blamed Guek for the attack and annihilation of an army patrol in 1916.

24. Coriat to Kathleen, 12.10.25, Coriat MSS.

all got on with Coriat. But in 1925 Major J. W. G. Wyld, DSO, MC[25] was appointed to Bor, and in 1926 both he and the northern half of his district (Duk Fayuil) were transferred to Upper Nile Province (see Map 2).

Coriat and Wyld hit it off immediately. Wyld was the son of H. C. Wyld, the Merton Professor of English Language and Literature at Oxford who once declared that 'no gentleman goes on a bus'. Though clearly a gentleman, the younger Wyld was not himself a university man. He had, instead, 'a fine record and some rather bad luck' (as Coriat put it), being a regular officer who served in Mesopotamia, France, north Russia and Iraq before marrying a White Russian refugee and leaving the army to farm in South Africa. There he was swindled and had to return to England, where he joined the Sudan Political Service and was sent to Bor, bringing his wife with him (the only European woman below the rank of governor's wife to be allowed south). Struvé thought Wyld 'rather brilliant' but a bit of a fire-eater who needed reining in. Coriat thought him 'a most excellent fellow'.[26] In a still snobbish service, with its subtle distinctions of social background and character, Wyld and Coriat shared a non-varsity background and similar war experiences. They toured the border together in the dry season and trained the mounted police in Kodok during the rains. It was to be a lifelong friendship. Like Coriat's friendship with Dual Diu, it undoubtedly facilitated administration. It was not, however, without its difficulties, as the events of the Gaawar march in 1928 were to show.

The year 1926 was one of many changes for Coriat and the province. In the dry season he handed the Bar Gaawar over to Fangak, headquarters of the Zeraf Valley inspectorate. During the rains, while on leave in England, he married Kathleen (Kay) King, his fiancée of some years, who had to stay behind in England when he returned to the Sudan. It was also the year that Struvé retired as governor. Coriat had hoped that Angus Gillan,[27] the deputy governor of neighbouring Nuba Mountains Province, would replace him, but instead the province got C. A. Willis, the former director of intelligence in Khartoum.

Willis was a controversial appointment. He was undoubtedly an energetic man, but his handling of many sensitive issues connected with his department had made him highly unpopular with his colleagues (Daly 1980: 34–6; Hasan 1979: 468–9). Struvé in particular was appalled by the idea that Willis was to succeed him, seeing the choice as a repudiation of his own cautious and gradual approach to administration. Coriat at first welcomed the new governor and his infusion of new energy into the province. He was 'a thruster', he had 'pluck and imagination', and he could get Khartoum to listen to him (or so Coriat hoped). But this favourable first impression did not last long. Coriat and Willis

25. Major J. W. G. Wyld, DSO, MC, ADC Bor-Duk District 1925–31. See Plates 15 and 18.

26. K. C. P. Struvé, 'Handing-over Notes July–Aug., 1926', SAD 212/9; and Coriat to Kathleen, 12.10.25, Coriat MSS.

27. Sir Angus Gillan, KBE, CMG, deputy and acting governor Nuba Mountains Province 1921–8, governor Kordofan Province 1928–32, assistant civil secretary 1932–4, civil secretary 1934–9.

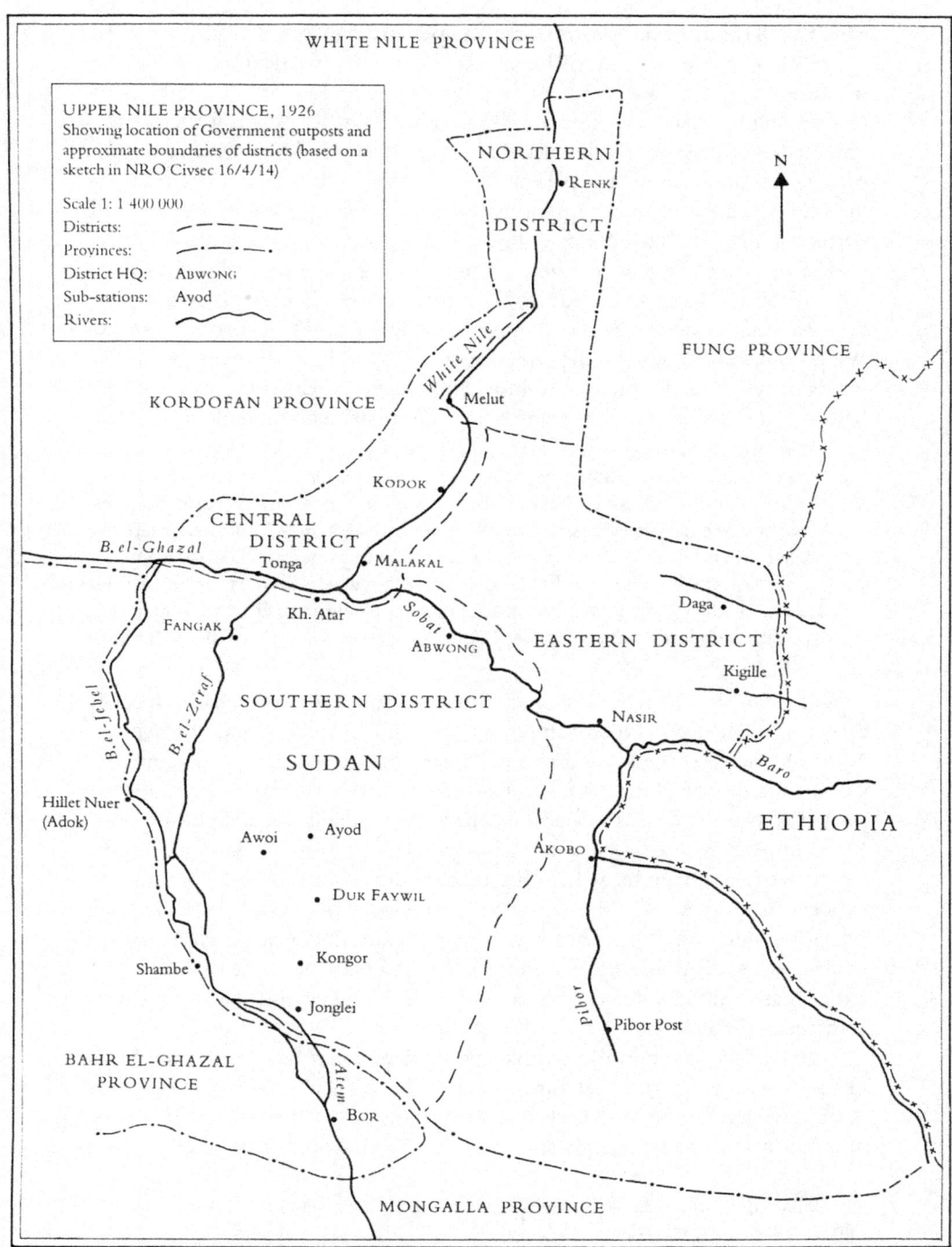

Map 2 Upper Nile Province, 1926

were to fall out for both professional and personal reasons.

Willis had the reputation of being one of the best classical Arabic scholars in the service, and as director of intelligence seemed to have prided himself in knowing the 'native mind'. But Upper Nile Province was not the north; a knowledge of classical Arabic was of no use there. He knew next to nothing of the province's Nilotic peoples and, as one of his subordinates later recalled, 'he blundered about in the unfamiliar world of the Upper Nile', never really coming to grips with the complexities of his new situation. It is perhaps for this reason that he often gave the impression of being resentful and jealous of his subordinates' greater knowledge of the province. He frequently treated them tactlessly, acknowledging his own mistakes gracelessly. There were times when Willis seemed to resent his dependence on Coriat in Nuer administration.

Coriat was already one of the most experienced DCs in the province and had demonstrated a versatility which Struvé warmly recommended:

> Fiery youthful energy, tempered by an admirable sense of discipline and deference to his chief's views. Has an amazing driving force, which carries everthing along with it, till his tribesmen have become a sort of special tribe (?Coriatids), like Nicholson's devotees.[28] Is absolutely tireless at work and should be ordered on leave when his keenness carries him away. I have rather inclined to use him as a sort of knight-errant, and to divert him to anywhere there is serious trouble, always with complete satisfaction to myself. Is a delightful cheery companion, a perfect blend of Latin and Saxon. I hope my glowing opinion of him will find an echo in you.[29]

Willis did have to rely on Coriat almost as much as Struvé had, especially after 1929 when the Nuer Settlement was put into effect and the Western Nuer District was transferred to the Upper Nile. It was just at this time that Coriat, for personal and financial reasons, was trying to transfer to another province. Upper Nile, as a southern province, was still considered unsuitable for European women. Without an independent income Coriat found it too expensive to maintain his wife in England on the lower salary of a pensionable officer. As early as 1927 he tried to transfer to a province where he could bring his wife, but Willis, faced with reorganizing Nuer administration with insufficient staff, refused to let him go. 'Having become more or less a Nuer expert has its disadvantages', Coriat wrote Kay, 'as they don't seem to want to transfer me at all.'[30]

To have any future in the permanent service Coriat had to pass an Arabic exam, both written and oral parts being set in classical rather than colloquial Arabic, which Coriat had little chance to practise. When he failed his first attempt in 1927 he felt his prospects were limited. Coriat then asked to revert

---

28. John Nicholson (1821–57), Indian administrator, after whom a Kashmiri sect, the 'Nikkulseynites', was named.

29. K. C. P. Struvé, 'Handing-over Notes July–Aug, 1926'.

30. Coriat to Kathleen, 02.07.27, Coriat MSS.

to a temporary contract. As a 'contract officer' Coriat was no longer eligible for promotion above DC, but he received a bonus to compensate for not having a pension, and his salary went up to £720 a year. This helped his financial position somewhat, but he was still separated from his wife. It was only with the permission of the governor-general that Kay was allowed to come out late in 1928 to stay with the Wylds in Bor, as no suitable accommodation was then available in Malakal. When Coriat was transferred to Western Nuer District in 1929 the problem of Kay's accommodation came up once more. There was no district headquarters in Western Nuer, only the Sudan Government Steamer *Kerreri*[31] with its leaking, rotting woodwork. Again Coriat put in an application for transfer, again Willis refused it. The *Kerreri* was patched up, and Kay joined her husband on board as he steamed up and down the rivers, visiting the Nuer on the banks. It was only in 1931, with the Nuer settled under a new generation of Nuer-speaking DCs, that Coriat successfully transferred to a more comfortable post, this time Juba, the capital of Mongalla Province. But Willis delayed even this transfer, preferring to keep Coriat among the Nuer until he himself had retired earlier that same year.[32]

These disappointments might have been more bearable had Willis been more tactful. Unfortunately he took an instant dislike to Kay Coriat which he never attempted to hide. It is a remarkable feature of Willis's exile in Malakal that, as the small town began to fill with young DCs' wives, he penned a running commentary of his disapproval to his sister at home.[33] Kay was a country parson's daughter who had lived for a while in Chelsea and established a reputation of her own as a painter and theatre-set designer. Willis doubted that she would survive the rigours of the province, but in this he underestimated her. She was as determined as her husband and was frequently on trek with him in Upper Nile, Mongalla, and later in Kordofan. Her endurance and vigour were admired by other DCs, not all of whom were blessed with such companions. Willis's attitude towards Kay helped to poison his relations with Coriat. Shortly after Willis left the Sudan in 1931 Coriat wrote to Kay, 'I wonder what Chunky doodle is doing. I heard a rumour that he was trying to get the job of Times special correspondent at Cairo. Daily Mail lies would be more his line.'[34] Willis showed an unfortunate capacity to alienate his colleagues and subordinates, and his governorship of Upper Nile was no exception. This was to have a detrimental impact on the direction of Nuer administration.

Two projects which Willis began to implement soon after he came to the province were the organization of Chiefs' Police (to help enforce the decisions of the Chiefs' Courts) and the building of a motor road south through Lou Nuer

---

31. SGS *Kerreri*, a stern-wheel steamer built at Khartoum North in 1903 (Hill 1970: 142).
32. Coriat to governor, UNP, 11.05.29; Coriat to Kathleen, 11.06.31, Coriat MSS.
33. See Willis MSS, SAD 209/12–13.
34. Coriat to Kathleen, 02.07.31, Coriat MSS.

country and Bor district. Both were projects Coriat enthusiastically endorsed and began to implement. The dry season of 1927 was spent recruiting young men into the Chiefs' Police and organizing road gangs for the next dry season's work on road construction. The Chiefs' Police proved popular work among both the Dinka and the Nuer of Coriat's district; road work was less so. Lou dissatisfaction with the road project was articulated by Guek Ngundeng, who up till then had taken little active involvement in local administration.

It was Willis's explanation later that Guek's opposition to the road was based on a realization that the government's plans for progress among the Lou would inevitably reduce his scope for trickery and extortion.[35] Modern Lou, including some of Guek's contemporaries, see the conflict in a different light. Guek, as a spokesman of the Lou, was obliged to represent their objections to being required to provide uncompensated labour on the road. Having done so, he was identified by the government as a ringleader of subversion, and when government preparations for war were reported to Guek, he too had to prepare to fight.[36]

There were, of course, other factors which contributed to Guek's opposition, such as the long-standing rivalry between the families of Guek and Guet Thie (who was supported by, and supported, Coriat). But the Lou version does get some confirmation from the contemporary record, including Coriat's reports in this volume (see Section 3). It is clear from document 3.2 that Guek, while not one of Coriat's favourites, had given little trouble and had not interfered with the creation of the Chiefs' Courts in 1926. It is also clear from documents 3.1 and 3.2 that, while there were some reports of Guek's disaffection in mid-1927 before Coriat went on leave, most rumours circulated after Coriat left the province. Some of these rumours came from doubtful sources, but it was on the strength of such reports that the province government sought, and received, permission to prepare for a military campaign against Guek as early as August. It was only as late as November, shortly before Coriat was due back, that the governor-general insisted that no aggressive action be taken until Coriat had had a chance to assess the situation.

Coriat was met by a pile of telegrams in Khartoum reporting a variety of rumours, including one that Guek was plotting to murder him. On arrival at Abwong he seems to have found some difficulty sifting rumour from fact. He became convinced that the official government interpreter, Mayan Lam (who was no friend of Guek's), was witholding information from him.[37] He also found his new deputy at Abwong, Captain A. H. A. Alban, busy clearing a landing-ground for the RAF. This had been witnessed by a deputation from Guek who had come before Coriat's arrival and whom Alban had received

---

35. Governor, Upper Nile Province, to civil secretary, 06.08.27, NRO Civsec 57/2/8.

36. See Johnson, forthcoming, and Lou text 4.2, in Johnson, in preparation.

37. See Madhir Lam Tutthiang, text 4.2, in Johnson, in preparation.

coolly. A second deputation arriving after Coriat's return, this time including Guek's brother Bol, were received even more coldly. There was, after all, the rumour that Guek planned to entice Coriat to the Mound, where he would be killed. Coriat detained Bol and then toured his district. It is perhaps not surprising that by this time there was evidence that the Lou were preparing for war. Following Coriat's report of what he had observed the government committed itself to a pre-emptive air strike.[38]

The origin of Guek's rebellion can be found, in part, in two contrasting attitudes towards the Nuer prophets: Coriat's and Willis's. Coriat took a pragmatic view towards *kuj*urs. He liked Dual and he disliked Guek for purely personal reasons. *Kuj*urs in general might be treated with caution, but he was willing to work with them, especially if they demonstrated that they could command authority and respect. Even after Guek's rebellion and death, he would advise his successor, 'don't down all Kujurs'. Willis took the more orthodox government line against inspired religious figures in the Sudan, an attitude based on experience with militant Islam in the north and transferred to the south (Johnson 1981a). He equated the Nuer prophets with the charm-selling 'hedge fikis' of Kordofan.[39] It was an inaccurate comparison. Because he expected rebellion he prepared for it, and by preparing for it, guaranteed that it would break out. Willis seemed temperamentally unable to trust Coriat's judgement of his own district and later placed part of the blame for Guek's rising on Coriat for underestimating the seriousness of Guek's potential threat.[40] Coriat was unable to contest his superior's accusation. It was axiomatic that the true test of a DC's work came when he was out of his district. He had done his work well if there was no real trouble in his absence. Guek and the government became set on a collision course while Coriat was on leave. 'Kujurs when they crop up will require to be watched very closely,' he later advised Captain Alban, 'and I think I failed in this, otherwise the 1928 Patrol would not have happened.' Yet he could not disregard all his previous experience. Still a qualification: watch 'kujurs' closely, but 'don't down all Kujurs' (doc. 1.5). Willis's suspicion that Coriat had been too lenient with Guek made it more difficult for Coriat to insist on a more sympathetic approach to Dual Diu later.

It is significant in the assessment of the strength of Guek's rebellion that even after his tour Coriat believed a full-scale campaign could be avoided. At the meeting with the governor and the commander-in-chief at Abwong on 7 December, 'I told them I thought I could avoid a Patrol by being given a Squadron of Mounted Police, but Willis said they couldn't be spared from other District duties, so the General had to decide on the Army being brought in.'[41]

38. See Johnson 1979, Jackson 1927, and Lou text 4.2, in Johnson, in preparation.
39. Governor, Upper Nile Province, to civil secretary, 06.08.27, NRO Civsec 57/2/8.
40. Willis to civil secretary, 27.03.28, NRO Civsec 5/2/11.
41. Coriat to Kathleen, n.d. [*c*. March 1928], Coriat MSS.

It was Willis who was forcing the pace, Coriat who was holding back. Perhaps he was trying to justify his earlier leniency towards Guek, but he was not a foolhardy man and had already been warned of a plot to murder him. For all the rebellion in the air, very few Lou actually tried to fight the government. Coriat's subsequent reports, presented in Section 3, provide very little evidence of widespread hostility to the government or active support for a rising among the Lou. Though troops traversed the country in the dry season of 1928, there were no major confrontations until February 1929, when Guek and a very small number of close followers were cornered at the Mound. Military operations continued for over a year because Guek remained at liberty, not because the Lou were carrying on the struggle. By March 1928 most of the Lou had submitted to government troops, and Coriat noted:

> I believe they are really sorry and realize that the Witchdoctor is not more powerful than the Government. In that way as I have always known, they are like children. Unless there is a rod in the background and it is occasionally shown, they are ready to break discipline, however [much] they like one personally and however much they may see the good of Government.[42]

In the end it was not the Lou who posed the greatest threat, but the Gaawar. Following the RAF's bombing of Guek's village the Lou scattered and many sought refuge with their Gaawar relatives. Coriat's friend, Dual Diu, was then facing a challenge from a new prophet among the Bar Gaawar, Kerbiel Wal,[43] who was reported to be trying to organize a raid on the Dinka. With the completion of the S8 Patrol in Lou in early February, Coriat accompanied the mounted troops to Gaawar country where he met H. G. Wedderburn-Maxwell, the new DC of Zeraf District, and Major Wyld, who had come from Duk Fayuil with a number of Dinka 'friendlies'. An attempt had been made to capture Kerbiel Wal, but he eluded his would-be captors. The Gaawar march was, as Coriat commented, 'quite a peaceable show'[44] except for one incident which was scarcely mentioned in the contemporary reports, but which was to weigh heavily on Coriat's conscience for some time afterwards.

On 27 February 1928 Coriat went to meet Dual Diu at his cattle camp at Fajilil (see Plate 14). Most of the rest of the troops, along with Major Wyld and his Dinka auxiliaries, arrived the following day. Coriat and Dual had a friendly meeting, assuring each other of their good intentions, and Dual's camp was left in peace. This did not satisfy Wyld, who argued fiercely with Coriat that the Gaawar must be disarmed. Had Coriat and Wyld not been such close friends, Coriat might have resisted this imposition. In the end he 'allowed himself to be

---

42. Ibid.
43. Kerbiel Wal: born Gaabuogh Wal of *cieng* Gaakuar of Bar Gaawar, came to prominence in 1927 when he announced he was possessed by a divinity with the ox-name *kerbiel*. He was arrested and exiled to Wau in 1931 and pronounced an epileptic ('Upper Nile Province. Personality Sheet no. 20', SRO ZD 66.K.1). He died in exile.
44. Coriat to Kathleen, n.d. [*c*. March 1928], Coriat MSS.

overpersuaded', and the next morning at dawn the troops surrounded Dual's camp and closed in. A few Lou refugees were picked up, a few rifles were found in the grass, and these were confiscated (see Plate 15).[45]

Dual was furious, not only at the confiscation of his people's rifles and Coriat's apparent bad faith, but at the behaviour of Wyld's Dinka auxiliaries, who mutilated some Gaawar cattle. When Dual complained to both Coriat and Wyld no action was taken, Wyld insisting that his Dinka were incapable of such an act. It was not Wyld but Coriat who got the blame. As one of Dual Diu's half-brothers later recalled:

> One ox, its tail was cut and the other one, its hump was cut by the Dinka. He [Dual] said, 'Children, we have to go to the Turuk'. He came to a Turuk named Girkuai, in his own language Kurieth [Coriat], and told him, 'Now an oxen's tail and hump has been cut by the Dinka. Why? Now, solve our differences... If you do not solve it we will have to fight the Dinka...' Girkuai ignored it. He did not take it under consideration. Then we were bitter about Girkuai's attitude towards us.[46]

None of the British officials involved in the march—Coriat, Wyld, Wedderburn-Maxwell or Romilly (officer in charge of troops)—mentioned Dual's complaint until many months later. Coriat stressed Dual's 'loyalty under trying circumstances' and justified the confiscation of his rifles as only a 'precautionary measure'. Willis was able to report to Khartoum that Dual had remained loyal and the march had helped to discredit the *kujur* who had challenged his authority.[47] But the opposite was the case. Dual, who had remained loyal, had been discredited by the government's treatment of him. In retaliation for both government and Dinka actions he invaded Ghol and Nyareweng Dinka country in August (during the rains), and even attacked the government police post at Duk Fadiat. Throughout the rest of 1928 and 1929 the Gaawar put up a stiffer fight against the government than had the Lou. Guek was killed in February 1929 (see Plate 17). It was not until the end of January 1930 that Dual was captured on the Sobat in Jikany territory. He was to spend the next twenty-three years in exile.

Coriat was fully occupied in the campaign against Guek and took no part in the patrols against Dual. Dual's rising clearly bothered him. 'I'm awfully sorry about Dwal Diu', he wrote at the end of 1928, 'as he was a great friend of mine when I ran that District but I'm afraid he has gone beyond the limits

---

45. See Wedderburn-Maxwell 1928; Wyld 1928; Dual Diu 1930; Gaawar texts 4.8 in Johnson, in preparation; Romilly diaries (1928), SAD G/S 833; B. A. Lewis to B. V. Marwood, 10.06.36, SRO UNP 66.B.11; also doc. 3.4 below. Collins (1983: 136) claims that Romilly and Wedderburn-Maxwell, as well as Coriat, opposed Wyld's insistence on ransacking Dual's camp. There is no evidence of any objections at the time other than Coriat's.

46. See Gaawar texts 4.8, in Johnson, in preparation.

47. 'Note by P. Coriat Esq.', 02.08.28, NRO Civsec 5/3/12. Governor, Upper Nile Province, to civil secretary, 27.03.28, NRO UNP 1/6/31.

of forgiveness from a Government point of view.'[48] When Dual was finally captured and gave the mutilation of his cattle as the reason for attacking the Dinka, Coriat expressed himself in stronger terms:

> I am aware that Dwal was incensed over injuries said to have been caused by Dinkas to one of his Dance bulls during the visit of the Troops on the Gaweir march to his camp near Fasheir. In my opinion Dwal had material cause for grievance at the action taken on the Gaweir march but there can be little doubt he was responsible for the attack on Duk Fayuil.[49]

The dilemma of alien administration of the Nuer is exemplified by this incident. For nearly thirty years the government had insisted to the Nuer that it was the ultimate authority in law and in justice, and that with the coming of government the right of 'self-help' in disputes no longer applied. But there were times when, out of ignorance, or stupidity, or on principle, the government took action which denied the Nuer justice and left them no real alternative to self-help. Yet if they took restitutive action they placed themselves in the wrong with the government which had wronged them. This was clearly as unacceptable to the administrator, who believed the government represented and maintained justice, as it was to the Nuer. It is in this light that we must read Coriat's final document on Dual (doc. 3.4) below. It was written after Willis and Wyld—both of whom were convinced that Dual was a thorough menace—had left the province. While Coriat does not excuse Dual's raid on the Dinka or his taking up arms against the government, he gives a clear indication of the government's (and his own) culpability in provoking Dual's action.

By the end of 1931 Coriat had very little time left in Upper Nile Province. After the death of Guek in 1929 he was transferred to Western Nuer District and was promoted to full district commissioner in 1930. This was a posting which came to him only because the previous DC, Captain Fergusson, had been murdered at the end of 1927.

Fergusson's district was then part of Bahr el-Ghazal Province and was scheduled for transfer to Upper Nile in 1928 as part of the rationalization of Nuer administration. Fergusson had his own methods of administration: he left Nuer courts largely unsupervised and did not impose a cattle tax, but he did enforce cotton cultivation to bring in the necessary money to pay tax in cash. Coriat and Fergusson approved of each other, but however progressive Fergusson's administration was in some respects, he generated antagonisms which eventually led to his own death early in December 1927. 'I had a letter from him', Coriat wrote,

> written two days before his death, in which he was full of his plans and ideas and congratulating himself on his District being peaceable in spite of attempts by various bad hats to cause trouble. He said he was sorry to hear about my troubles (which by that time had started) and hoped all would be well soon. It

---

48. Coriat to Kathleen, 23.12.28, Coriat MSS.
49. Coriat to governor, Upper Nile Province, 10.02.30, SRO UNP 5.A.3/43.

seems that his intelligence from the natives must have been scanty as evidence seems to show that it was an organised effort but it is awfully difficult to tell.[50]

The transfer of the district was delayed until after Bahr el-Ghazal Province completed its own punitive patrol. One of Coriat's first tasks on taking over the new district in May 1929 was to bring the murderers to book and uncover the causes of the conspiracy. One murderer had already surrendered in April. Coriat, who had a far better grasp of the Nuer language than Fergusson, was able to establish, partly through interrogation and partly through the use of a network of secret agents, that Fergusson had not been killed at the instigation of a 'witchdoctor' but through the ambitions of one of his supposedly loyal chiefs. The trial of the second murderer, Gatkek Jiek, caught in June 1930, brought the case to a close.[51]

The murder of a British DC, however, had to be punished, and both murderers were returned to their homes to be publicly hanged. Kay Coriat was with her husband when the second murderer was executed. A large portable gallows was brought by steamer and then by lorry to his inland village. 'The prisoner won our reluctant admiration with his complete look of indifference as he marched on in front or beside us', she later recalled:

> After several days we found the village and camped down. About 500 (?) natives assembled and we had a handful of police. The portable was hoisted, certain measurements taken, a talk to the dependants and we felt rather miserable.... The night was quite moonless and the smoke fires glowed as we turned in under our mosquito nets. I am ashamed to own that I took my husband's revolver and slipped it under my pillow, and lay wide awake. Some one walked near our beds, but my 62 lbs bull terrier seemed wide awake too, and when I heard his deep growl and deeper bark, I felt we were well guarded and I might as well sleep and forget the eeriness of it. Long before dawn we were awake and could hear the continuous sound of flat bare feet moving over to the portable. The dawn had not broken as my husband went over. A long silence, a most dismal howl from Bully, and then an awe inspiring cry rang out. A cry from the avenged to be again revenged. My husband returned and did not speak much and breakfast seemed out of the question so we tried to appear busy over nothing until it was time to move off. Packed up I glanced to where the portable had been and before hastily turning away I saw a slight black body suspended to a tree.[52]

Coriat had one other duty to perform on behalf of Fergusson's memory. In England on leave, he and his wife visited Fergusson's bereaved mother. Mrs Fergusson had hired a ghost-writer to turn her son's journal and letters into

---

50. Coriat to Kathleen, n.d. [c. March 1928], Coriat MSS.

51. See NRO Civsec 5/3/13, 5/4/14–15.

52. Kay Coriat, 'Headlines', Rhodes House, MSS Afr. s 1684 (1). See also her account in Kenrick 1987: 19. The execution of Gatkek Jiek had a disturbing effect on all those involved. 'Hang Gatkek 8 a.m. Extremely unpleasant. He behaves wonderfully', Romilly recorded tersely (Romilly diaries, 28 December 1930, SAD G/S 833). Kay Coriat was even more vivid when, many years later, she recalled that 'Corry was just green' when he returned from the execution.

a book, a book which was a eulogy to 'Fergie's' valour, intuition, competence and sacrifice; a book in which, incidentally, Mrs Fergusson herself figured as the object of her son's greatest love (Fergusson 1930: 171). She also turned her house into a shrine to her son's memory, renaming it 'Kerreri', after her son's steamer, and naming each of its rooms after one of his Sudan colleagues (the initials of the WC were transposed, it is said, to make it the 'C. A. Willis Room'). Before dinner Mrs Fergusson led her two guests into her son's own room, kept just as he had left it, to have a drink in front of his portrait. 'Corry was just livid,' his wife recalled many years later, remembering her own embarrassment, 'it wasn't his style at all.' But he masked his astonishment and is paid the compliment in Mrs Fergusson's book of having a 'fine, generous mind' (ibid.: 285).

Back in the Sudan, conditions of service were quite different in Western Nuer than they had been in either Ayod or Abwong. There were no large administrative centres in Western Nuer District, only a series of landing places which the DC visited on his floating headquarters. From these *meshra*s the DC would trek inland to visit various chiefs and court centres. Coriat shared this trekking with an ADC, but administrative supervision of the Western Nuer chiefs continued to be somewhat loose, as it had been in Fergusson's time. Coriat made a virtue of necessity and argued for the increased autonomy of the chiefs (see docs. 4.1 and 4.2 below), a policy which was discontinued after he left.

As with the Gaawar and the Lou, Coriat came to rely closely on a few chiefs. Buom Diu, the Dok Nuer prophet of the divinity Teny, became one of his favourites, despite being a *kujur*. Buom was an autocrat and imposed a discipline of which Coriat thoroughly approved. They frequently trekked together. In February 1930 they were travelling in Jagei country when they received news of an inter-sectional fight brewing over a murder back in Dok country. Coriat and Buom returned in time to prevent the fight. Coriat lectured the Dok chiefs for not keeping their people in line. 'Chief Buom went a step further by divesting every Headman and Sub-Chief of their shirts and shorts and the group marched out of Adok dressed like ordinary Tribesmen!'[53] Coriat's successors did not share his enthusiasm for Buom, who was later deposed for becoming 'an unconstitutional autocrat'.[54] Perhaps what Coriat admired in Buom was not so much his efficiency as his personality. Buom's son, John Wicjaal, later recalled, 'What I know is that my father was a hard man. Coriat was a hard man. They got on well together.'

All was not austerity during the three years Coriat served in Western Nuer. His wife remembered the nights he would spend sitting on the deck of the steamer swapping stories—usually ribald—with the chiefs gathered there, and how the boat would literally rock with laughter late into the night. We get a

53. P. Coriat to governor, Upper Nile Province, 12.02.30, NRO Civsec 1/4/9.

54. *SMR* 85 (Jan.–Feb. 1936), 6.

glimpse of just what sort of jokes were told on these occasions, and at whose expense, from Coriat's account of one session just before his final departure from the district:

> I had a very amusing chat with Nuel [Juel][55] & Co. last night.... They wanted to know why I was born like them with a tall figure and why I walked like they did. They said all the English were stumpy and walked like an ostrich trotting! One of them put his hand on his hip and imitated Dub [Romilly]. Shrieks of laughter. I took it all in good part and told them most of the English were really tall. It does seem a pity that here, they have only seen Chunky, Pink eye, Dub, Kidd etc. Pawson too is small. We might have had people of Beavan's size easily and it's rather bad luck that the short a—'s are here. Nuel said the women liked my figure![56]

Coriat usually had company during his tours on the *Kerreri* and treks into the interior. Kay was with him much of the time until a determined amoeba hospitalized her in Khartoum. Throughout much of 1929 Captain J. Masterman was Coriat's ADC, and in November 1930 Captain H. A. Romilly, recently transferred from the army to the civil administration, took up that appointment. Romilly had commanded the infantry company from Akobo during the S8 patrol and the Gaawar march. Throughout the early part of 1930 he served with Captain Alban at Abwong and learned Nuer. Coriat was very pleased to get Romilly, especially as he had never much liked Masterman (whom he privately called 'Pink eye') as a subordinate. Coriat also had frequent guests on his steamer, Evans-Pritchard being one. But his favourites were the Italian Catholic missionaries at Yoinyang (Fr. J. P. Crazzolara among them), who 'would sit down with you and have a good stiff drink and didn't bother about putting Mother Hubbards on the natives'. English Protestant missionaries, on the other hand, tended to want to hold prayer meetings on board ship.

Coriat's last year among the Nuer was mainly spent saying goodbye. In February Coriat took Willis and his wife through the district prior to Willis's departure from the Sudan. Then in June and July he accompanied A. G. Pawson, the new governor, on a tour introducing him to his new subjects. Coriat himself then went on leave from the end of July to November, returning to Malakal before Christmas for one final district commissioners' meeting. After Christmas he paid a last visit to Abwong in the company of Romilly. In January 1932 they returned to Malakal to pick up Kay, and then made a leisurely procession by steamer to Juba, stopping at various landing places in Western Nuer District on the way. They finally arrived in Juba on 13 January, where Coriat was to take up a new posting. After the flat plains and swamps of the Upper Nile, Juba

55. See below, doc. 4.1 n. 39.

56. Coriat to Kathleen, 02.07.31, Coriat MSS. 'Dub': Capt. H. A. Romilly; 'Chunky': C. A. Willis; 'Pink eye': Capt. J. Masterman, ADC Western Nuer 1929, assistant commander of police Yirrol 1930; Kidd: Captain H. F. Kidd, MBE, ADC Yirrol 1922–6, ADC Eastern District Bahr el-Ghazal 1927–8, DC Western Nuer District 1928–9; Pawson: A. G. Pawson, CMG, governor Upper Nile Province 1931–4; Beavan: J. Beavan, ADC Renk 1928–31.

presented a completely different prospect. 'Pretty country hills etc.', Romilly noted in his diary, '& Coriats pleased'.[57] The hardships of nearly ten years among the Nuer were finally over.

Coriat's service after the Nuer was varied. He served in Juba between 1932 and 1934 until he was struck by black-water fever (induced by a well-intentioned overdose of quinine administered by archdeacon Shaw). He was then sent to Malakal to recover his health before going to El Obeid in 1935 and serving in Western Kordofan from 1936 until the war. In En Nahud town he became a legend for his direct methods in town planning: he simply burned down buildings erected without planning approval (Henderson 1987: 102–3). With Italy's entrance into the Second World War in 1941 he transferred to the army as a bimbashi (major) in the Sudan Defence Force and served in Eritrea, Cyrenaica and Tripolitania, ending the war as lieutenant-colonel in command of the 1/7 Nuba battalion in the SDF. He was then appointed to the British Military Administration of Tripolitania in 1946 and continued in a variety of capacities in the administration of Libya until 1953. His last important position was commander of the Muscat and Oman Field Force, protecting the new oil wells from desert brigands, in 1953–4 (Coriat n.d.). He was then on the Foreign Office list from 1954 to 1959 and died of cancer in July 1960.

Coriat was able to inspire respect and even affection throughout his career in the Sudan, despite the harshness he often displayed. The expressions of admiration from both Sudanese and British colleagues were genuine. When he left the Zeraf District he reported that 'the Chiefs also were I think sorry to lose me and one simply had to spit in my hand as a farewell compliment, though he knew I disliked the practice!' (spitting is a form of blessing; the more energetic the spitting, the stronger the blessing). When he left Malakal in 1931 the deputy governor, E. G. Coryton, wrote in a personal note, 'there is no need really for me to repeat what is common knowledge, but there is not the slightest doubt that you & Wyld laid the foundation stones of the Southern districts in this Province & found out the difficulties & the remedies necessary. Others coming after have copied or builded [sic] on your foundations. . . . I think you have done magnificently.' Another colleague, Major L. E. Humphreys, MC, recalled some forty years after leaving the Sudan: 'Speaking with Coriat or, even walking with him in the street, you could sense the staunchness and strength of his character and strength of his personality, and he mostly had a short or tight smile on his lips. Dark brown eyes. Bright. Alive. Again I mention his long "frontiersman's" stride, not exactly a prowl but he sure planted each foot strongly on the ground. I would have gone anywhere with him, i.e. into any danger, for you'ld know he'd be at your elbow, or, as in the Indian mutiny days, back to back.' A colleague from his Kordofan days, K. D. D. Henderson wrote, 'we all liked and admired him very much. And that goes for the Sudanese too.' To another Kordofan companion, E. A. Aglen, who later served among the Nuer, 'Corry'

---

57. Romilly diaries (1932), SAD G/S 833.

was always 'one of my heroes'. Perhaps the most remarkable compliment came from a northern Sudanese education officer in Kordofan in the late 1940s who recollected that Coriat was tough, *walakin gelbu dahab* (but his heart was gold) (Henderson 1987: 103). John Winder, recalling his own experiences in Coriat's former district, remembers that when he was faced with 'an old and tiresome cattle case' among the Baliet Dinka on the Sobat, 'I started off by getting my mounted police to round up all the cattle in the neighbourhood and then suggested we all got down to the business. . . . The Dinka did not seem to object to my preliminary actions but admiringly muttered "chap Kerkwac" [Girkuai].' Even today among the Gaawar, his harshest critics are those who were born after he left the province; those elders who knew and worked with him are inclined to be more charitable.[58]

Coriat's Work and Writings

The value of Coriat's writings on the Nuer can be assessed by evaluating his quality as an administrator first, before comparing him with other ethnographers. One must understand his place in the development of Nuer administration, the problems which confronted him, and the administrative constraints on his writing. It is only then that one can discuss the contribution his papers make to understanding administrative history, the history of the Nuer, and Nuer ethnography.

Coriat was a new type of administrator among the Nuer, spending more time with his subjects than had the itinerant inspectors of the past. His attitude towards the Nuer contrasts markedly with the attitudes of most of his predecessors. The immediate comparison is with H. C. Jackson, who was the first official to attempt a lengthy and systematic ethnography. Jackson felt no affection for the Nuer. 'Lazy to a degree, indifferent to the outer world and any suggestion of progress,' he wrote, 'they are a heart-breaking race with which to have to deal. . . . Indeed it is difficult to see how, in the near future any real moral, material or spiritual progress or development can be expected of them.' He wished 'to depict them now as they really are, in all their barbarism and degradation, before the mists of time have enfolded their past in a romance that was never theirs, and assigned to them an attractiveness that they have never possessed' (Jackson 1923: 60). Coriat's surviving writings, including his private correspondence, are free of such remote and hostile judgements. He may have compared the Nuer to children (a common imperial sentiment of

---

58. Coriat to Kathleen, 02.03.27 and E. G. Coryton to 'Coriato', 29.12.31, Coriat MSS; personal communications from Major L. E. Humphreys, K. D. D. Henderson, E. A. Aglen, John Winder and Paul Howell.

superiority); he may have disliked individual Nuer with whom he had to deal; but he spoke Nuer; he had Nuer friends; he had Nuer relatives. As far as the Nuer were concerned he looked and acted more like one of them than any previous British official.

Coriat had both the opportunity and the ability to learn more about the Nuer than anyone before him, but his reports are part of the official record of government. They deal with administrative matters, are written for administrators, and focus on topics of immediate use to administration. Though Coriat knew Nuer, there is little of value for the linguist in his writings. Though it was also important for him to know something about Nuer spiritual and social life, these were not suitable topics for explicit and detailed analysis in the official correspondence of the 1920s. Religious figures, social and political organization, are all discussed and judged according to their relevance to administrative problems. We will find in Coriat's papers more local detail than is often found in ethnographic writings, but less subtlety of analysis. The detail, however, is rich. There are explicit discussions of local politics, rivalries between leaders, problems of environment and economics, matters of law, and relations with other peoples (particularly the Dinka). There is also much which can be inferred about religion and social life. Taken all together, Coriat's writings can add considerably to an appreciation of the theoretical arguments in Evans-Pritchard's ethnography. It is futile to discuss the theory of Nuer politics, for instance, without reference to some examples. Coriat gives us many examples to discuss.

One must not lose sight of the fact, however, that Coriat was reporting about his own time; he was not attempting to define enduring principles of Nuer life. The main historical value of Coriat's reports lies in what he reveals about Nuer–government relations in the 1920s. Even after two decades of contact government activities and policies had not yet begun to dominate Nuer life. The Nuer, both collectively and individually, were trying to work out a *modus vivendi* with an alien power which remained distant, but which made increasing demands and would not go away. That *modus vivendi* could only be made through personal negotiation with individual government representatives. In over twenty years of British attempts to administer the Nuer, Coriat was the first person with whom satisfactory negotiations could take place. The government insisted on the right to collect taxes, to appoint (or at least confirm) leaders, and to settle disputes. These were the three major issues which preoccupied both Coriat and the Nuer for nearly a decade.

Taxation (or the collection of tribute) implied the recognition of subordination to the government, but it was further justified as payment for the services government supplied. In the 1920s about the only service the government did supply (and that erratically) was the maintenance of public order through the settlement of disputes. The Nuer, however, did not see the payment of tribute as a return for a service. Tribute was the necessary price to keep government troops at bay; it was quite literally 'protection money'. Since tribute was collected in items the Nuer needed for their own physical survival—grain and cattle—they had to make a fine calculation in sacrificing present needs for future security. Government health measures, veterinary services and reserve stores against famine were still underdeveloped (if not absent) at this time. In giving up their food to the government, the Nuer got very little in return.

This presented a problem to any thoughtful administrator. Tribute imposed an economic hardship on the Nuer, and the burden was correspondingly increased when tribute was paid in grain (as in the early 1920s), which paradoxically the Nuer were more willing to give up. Not all administrators realized this, many assuming that the Nuer could achieve regular grain surpluses. Certainly Jackson, who never visited the Nuer in the cultivation season, attributed seasonal hunger entirely to Nuer laziness (Jackson 1923: 60). There is nothing easy or assured about crop production in the Upper Nile plains (see Jonglei Investigation Team 1954, Johnson 1988), where abundant crops are produced in only about one year in seven. Coriat had some appreciation that grain was important during the hungry months of the dry season, the time when most taxes were collected (doc. 1.2), though he continued to underestimate the value Nuer placed on cultivation, an inevitable by-product, perhaps, of listening to endless cattle cases (doc. 4.1). By 1931 he saw clearly that the economic development of the Nuer would be very difficult if it was based solely on traditional methods of agriculture and herding (doc. 4.2). But he could only raise the question; he offered no solutions. In this he was no different from his successors. From the 1930s until independence British administrators in Upper Nile Province wrestled with the problem of how the Nilotic pastoralists could first pay for even part of the simple services which were gradually extended to them, and later develop beyond the subsistence economy. The introduction of cash payment for tax in the late 1930s only forced the Nuer to sell their cattle and grain at regular intervals in order to obtain money; it did not by itself stimulate production.

Coriat's comment in 1931, 'that one is uncertain, even were there a latent wealth in the Nuer country, whether economic development can be made to fit into an entirely Tribal system of control', proved partially prophetic. Since the early 1950s it has been assumed that local development can come about only through heavy investment in non-traditional means of production. Most of the money that now circulates in Nuer hands has been earned through migrant wage-labour. The discovery of oil in the very districts where Coriat once served has raised other development prospects. But for all that, the development future of the Nuer and other inhabitants of the Upper Nile remains highly problematic.

Given the Anglo-Egyptian government's inability to offer any prospect of lasting economic security, it is, perhaps, surprising that the Nuer seemed so willing to allow the government to interfere in their internal life to the extent of adjudicating disputes over cattle ownership, marriage, inheritance and compensation. Coriat's reports on the Bar Gaawar, the Lou and the Western Nuer indicate that they did show a willingness to let the government do just that. This was in keeping with a tradition of bringing in outsiders to act as arbitrators between communities (Evans-Pritchard 1940: 173–4; 1956: 292–3). Peace is important to the Nuer precisely because the pattern of feuding makes it so difficult to attain. The most effective peacemakers, Evans-Pritchard tells us, are those who exist between major political segments. Coriat records (doc. 1.2) how the Kerpeil lineage were unable to merge their neutral role as earth-masters with their politically central position as original settlers in the Gaawar migration. Some of the most famous earth-masters and peacemakers among the Lou and the Gaawar in the late nineteenth century—Yuot Nyakong, Ngundeng Bong and Deng Laka—were all foreigners to the communities which they served. Yuot and Deng Laka were Dinka. The government, and particularly Coriat and his successors, became part of that pattern.

The tradition of bringing in strangers to keep the peace, which the government unwittingly continued, affected the development of customary law. For over twenty years Coriat's administrative predecessors had operated in almost complete ignorance of the custom they were trying to enforce (Johnson 1986*a*). Coriat, through his knowledge of the language, was able to participate directly in disputes and gradually learn the principles by which they were settled. Though Jackson produced a sketchy version of 'elements of judicial life', based on conversations with and through his interpreter (Jackson 1923: 100–6), Coriat's outline (doc. 1.2) was the first written by a Nuer-speaking official. It was written as an addendum to Jackson and gave a fuller account of rates of compensation for various acts of injury and infringements of rights. Given the absence of any examples cited, and the very great potential for misunderstanding, none of Coriat's descriptions of customary law can be accepted as completely authoritative. Still, he continued to learn, and he paid the prophet Dual Diu the supreme complement of imitation in proposing to reduce compensatory payments in long-standing feuds throughout his district (doc. 1.4), as Dual had earlier proposed for the Gaawar.

If the Nuer placed Coriat firmly in an existing tradition of incorporating foreigners into the very centre of Nuer life, the government's involvement in the selection of Nuer leaders was still a matter of negotiation. In theory, and largely in practice, appointment of chiefs was supposed to be a matter of conferring recognition on leaders selected by the people themselves. But the government did set constraints by which those leaders might be selected, and gave clear indications of what sort of person might be an appropriate 'traditional' leader. The government also structured the hierarchy by which chiefs were ordered, and deposed chiefs it found unsuitable.

Coriat had a very pragmatic approach towards chiefs. Anyone who could command a following he recognized as a leader. He then encouraged those who showed themselves capable of implementing government decisions. Among the Lou and Western Nuer, Coriat advocated developing chiefly authority and autonomy, even to the point of allowing successful chiefs some leeway in the matter of collecting fines (docs. 1.5, 4.1, 4.2). Thus there were material rewards for those who co-operated with the government, and with the creation of the Chiefs' Police there were other ways of supplementing an ambitious leader's power. Competition between leaders of opposing groups was thus frequently intensified. This is more clearly documented in Coriat's reports on the Western Nuer and Lou than among the Gaawar, where government support for Dual Diu helped to control competition. But in the other two districts the government embarked on a policy of circumventing the prophets who were then the most influential leaders. This encouraged internal rivalries and led to the murder of a British DC (Captain Fergusson) in the one instance, and the death of a prophet (Guek Ngundeng) in the other.

Coriat was actively involved in the overthrow of Guek, but only because he thought Guek a dangerous and unsuitable chief. Dual Diu had been, by Coriat's account, an efficient chief, and the government bore some blame for alienating him (doc. 3.4). Among the Western Nuer, Coriat's favourite chief was Buom Diu (doc. 4.2), another prophet. But the events of the 1920s led ultimately to the exclusion of prophets and other major spiritual leaders from the hierarchy of government chiefs. Coriat's enthusiasm for strong leadership among the Nuer was not shared by his successors. Willis flatly rejected Coriat's recommendations for the Western Nuer and advocated the use of courts there to reduce the powers of individual chiefs (doc. 4.1). Throughout the 1930s the number of chiefs, representing smaller and smaller sections, increased in each of the districts where Coriat had served. As one DC among the Gaawar later put it, there were to be 'no big men—no paramount chiefs—no Dwal Dius...'[59] Rivalries were not only recognized but institutionalized, for a time, to keep the ambitions of Nuer leaders in check. It was only in the 1940s that the idea of Nuer paramount chiefs came back into administrative favour.[60] Coriat's reports must be read, therefore, as representing a phase in administrative thinking and practice, advocating a policy which was not continued in all respects after his departure, but which was never completely repudiated.

In addition to giving this grass-roots view of local administration, Coriat presents the only detailed contemporary account we have of many aspects of Nuer society in this period. His Nuer are recognizable in Evans-Pritchard's later studies, but at the same time Coriat's observations do suggest that a different emphasis from Evans-Pritchard's is possible. His reports also document the change in political terminology which followed the publication of Evans-Pritchard's earliest studies. Before Evans-Pritchard the units of Nuer political organization were only vaguely identified; after the publication of his 'The Nuer: Tribe and Clan' series (1933–5), administrators described Nuer political divisions with greater precision.

In common with his predecessors, Coriat used only two undefined terms to describe the political organization of a primitive people: 'tribe' and 'clan'. He saw

---

59. J. Winder, 'Note on the Evolution of Policy in Regard to Chiefs Sub-chiefs & Headmen', Nasir END 1.F.1 and 2 vol. I.

60. B. A. Lewis, 'The Nuer Political Problem', December 1944, SRO UNP 66.G.3/3.

the Nuer people as a single 'tribe' which was divided into 'sub-tribes' or 'clans', corresponding to what Evans-Pritchard later termed 'tribes'. The Gaawar 'sub-tribe' was divided into two sections, and within those sections were the 'shens' (*ciengs*), units which Evans-Pritchard later called lineages, segments and sections. Coriat described the shen as a family with many branches, but he tended to apply the term more to political units with territorial identities than groups of kin. For him there was no need to make administrative differentiations further than the 'sub-shen'.

Coriat did not use these terms precisely or even consistently, but neither did he assume a rigid political structure. He describes in documents 1.2 and 1.3 the great fluidity of sectional identity and draws our attention to the way in which units can expand, decline, divide or even disappear as territorial entities. The lists of Gaawar *ciengs* he gives do not correspond exactly to the lists recorded by his successors (cf. e.g. Evans-Pritchard 1940: 141); nor are they necessarily the names modern Gaawar use to identify themselves today. Coriat's tendency to identify sections by their 'chiefs' is, perhaps, mainly an administrative convenience required by the nature of the documents, which were written for the aid of new administrators. In this respect the documents might appear to over-emphasise the role of individual leaders in initiating both secession and amalgamation. But the identification of a series of personal rivalries in documents 1.3, 1.5 and 4.1 does tend to confirm the importance of personal ambition in local politics. It is this precise history of internal disputes which is largely absent from Evans-Pritchard's presentation of his theory of segmentation.

Coriat records other reasons for groups hiving off from each other. The most important, of course, and one we have come to expect from Evans-Pritchard's writings, is the feud. Coriat pays particular attention to this in his description of the Bar Gaawar (docs. 1.2 and 1.3), where we see the Bar disturbed not only by internal feuds, but by Radh Gaawar–Thiang Nuer fights. There is also passing reference to feuds among the Western Nuer in document 4.1. But fighting is not the only impetus to movement. In documents 1.3 and 2.1 Coriat gives details of the attempt of some of the Jamogh Gaawar to move southwards along the Duk ridge, a movement precipitated by the changed environmental conditions on the ridge after the high floods of 1916–18. Had it been successful it would have meant the Nuer occupation of more Dinka territory, but it was halted by government intervention. Nuer 'expansion', Coriat shows us, did not end with the nineteenth century.

In giving the details of sectional settlement and grazing patterns (see especially docs. 1.3 and 1.5), Coriat also gives us a rather different picture of inter-ethnic relations than is contained in the standard ethnography of the Nuer. For those modern anthropologists who have taken Evans-Pritchard's description of structural opposition too literally, it may come as a shock to find Dinka settlements in Gaawar territory, Dinka communities in Gaawar villages, a Gaawar section living among the Dinka, Lou grazing with the Gaawar, Shilluk living interspersed among the Dinka, and the Ballak mixing with the Jikany. It is no wonder than when Coriat's successors tried to sort these peoples out, they failed.

Coriat is an immensely valuable observer of contemporary life, and this is his real contribution to Nuer ethnography. Every year for nine years he visited some part of Nuerland, and the continuity of his visits lends weight to his observations. That he was not analytical in his description of the Nuer is evident in those sections where he makes an explicit contribution to ethnography (docs. 1.2 and 5.1). We have already seen that he was not a theoretical man. Whether he would have made a more systematic analysis of his ethnographic observations had his education not been interrupted by the war is an open question. But this leads us to the final assessment to be made about Coriat as a historian.

It is clear that Coriat the contemporary observer is very good. Coriat the historian is another matter. There is a peculiar inattention to dates, even when presenting the dates of events in which he took part. Thus we find in a 1931 letter (doc. 2.2) that he gives the date of the Gaawar–Ghol boundary settlement as 1926 rather than 1925; in 1929 (doc. 1.5) he gives 1927 instead of 1926 for the transfer of the Bar Gaawar to the Zeraf Valley District; in 1931 (doc. 3.4) he says Dual Diu was arrested in 1929 rather than 1930. None of these dates is far off, and in some cases it is really only a matter of weeks. When he deals with events which occurred before his own time among the Nuer he becomes progressively less reliable. The initiation of the Pilual age-set was delayed by the floods of 1916–18 and took place in 1920–1 rather than 1916, as given by Coriat (doc. 1.2); the last Gaawar fight with the Dinka before 1928 took place in 1918, not 1916 (doc. 1.2 and doc. 1.3); and slave-raiding against the Western Nuer began long before 1870 (doc. 4.1).

These inaccuracies are minor sins. Coriat was not a scholar, and in his later reports he was often writing from memory, without reference to earlier documents. But they are evidence that he was habitually weak on chronology. He was also rather casual in claiming time depths of 350 or 400 years (docs. 1.2, 4.1) without giving any basis for his calculations. We must bear this in mind when trying to use his own reconstructions of Nuer history. This is a particular problem when dealing with his account of early Gaawar history and the life of Ngundeng.

Coriat's account of the Gaawar crossing of the Nile, the rise of Nuaar Mer, Deng Laka's revolution, and the succession of Macar and Dual Diu (doc. 1.2) is the most detailed account of any aspect of Nuer history written by a British official from Nuer sources before the 1930s. Coriat in many cases got his information from participants in the events he described, old men whose memories may have become somewhat hazy. Coriat considerably telescopes events, and this would be expected if he heard the stories presented as a continuous narrative. Many older Gaawar today who, like Coriat himself, heard these stories from Deng Laka's contemporaries, still tend to relate this history in an unbroken sequence in roughly the same order and with approximately the same emphasis as Coriat gives here (though details do vary, reflecting the different experiences of the ancestral sources). They are, however, able to supply a longer time span between events when asked direct questions concerning the chronology of related incidents such as floods, the initiation of age-sets, and the history of neighbouring peoples such as the Lou. It may be that only a historian would think of subjecting a good story to such minute dissection, but the fact remains that the Gaawar themselves are able to provide a consistent chronological framework to their narrative history. It is not embedded in the narrative, but it is embedded in historical memory. Coriat should not be faulted for having made only a shallow excavation of the historical memory by 1923 (he extracted far more than anyone before him), but there was more to be mined.

The same weakness in chronology is apparent in his account of the life of Ngundeng, which is given here in document 3.2, and also in more detail in Coriat 1939. Here he claims that Guek was born in about 1883 and that his father's 'Pyramid' was built in about 1863 (perhaps a typographical error?). Coriat's confusion seems to arise from two mistaken assertions. The first was that Guek was a member of the Dang-gonga age-set (doc. 1.5), and the second was that slave-raiding against the Nuer began around 1870 (doc. 4.1). The Dang-gonga age-set was initiated in the 1890s, and some of its members may have been born in the early 1880s, but Guek was not a Dang-gonga. He was a Luac, the age-set after Dang-gonga, and marked some time after Ngundeng's death in 1906. It was the Dang-gonga age-set which helped to build the 'Pyramid' around the time of their initiation. Soon after its completion Ngundeng was raided by a group of 'Turuk' which we now know to have been Sudanese soldiers of the Egyptian army under the command of Major Arthur Blewitt, administrator of Fashoda District in 1902 (Johnson 1982*b*). Coriat here remarks on this raid, but attributes it to Arab slavers. Since he assumed that the Arabs first began raiding the Nuer in 1870, it followed that the 'Pyramid' must have been made in the 1860s.

It is clear that Coriat knew far more about Gaawar history than about Lou, and far more about Deng Laka and Dual Diu than he did about Ngundeng and Guek. In addition to the errors discussed above, he claims that Guek was the organizer of Lou opposition to the government in 1917 (doc. 3.2 below and Coriat 1939: 227–8). Contemporary British documents make no mention of Guek, but identify another prophet, Pok Kerjiok, as the main leader of Lou warriors at that time,[61] and this point is confirmed by modern Lou testimony. What is particularly interesting about the errors contained in his 1928 report (doc. 3.2), however, is that his 1939 article considerably expands on Ngundeng's life, and even corrects some of his earlier statements. Though he still gives Guek's birthdate as 1883 (Coriat 1939: 226), he does not place the building of the Mound in the 1860s. It would appear that much of Coriat's

---

61. See SRO UNP SCR 15.10.

subsequent knowledge about Ngundeng and Guek's earlier history was gained after 1927, not before. The only Lou who were then willing to talk to him about the prophets were Guek's enemies and the government's allies, a point made in recent Lou testimony.[62] This would explain some of the more extraordinary claims Coriat later made about Guek, such as the report that Guek was believed to be able to turn himself into a goat (ibid.). This is tantamount to an accusation of sorcery and would have been made by someone wishing to deny Guek's claim to prophecy.

There are other points of Coriat's historical knowledge which should be questioned, such as his claim that the Nuer fought the Dinka and Anuak in tribal 'alliances', or that Western Nuer 'tribal organization' remained intact because, unlike the Nuer to the east, they were scarcely raided by slavers (docs. 4.1 and 5.1). It is true that there were times when sections of Lou combined with sections of Jikany to fight the Anuak, but there does not ever seem to have been an alliance between whole tribes, nor is there any evidence that the Lou and Gaawar joined together to fight the Dinka. Individual Lou did join Dual Diu in his raid on Duk Fadiat in 1928, but there was no formal grouping together of Lou and Gaawar sections, much less all of the Lou with all of the Gaawar. We also know from contemporary sources, as well as modern Western Nuer testimony, that the Western Nuer did suffer from fairly constant, if casual, raids by Arab slavers, the Egyptian government, and the Mahdists from the 1840s until the 1890s. Such raids rarely extended far inland, but the Western Nuer seem to have suffered far more continuously from raiding than either the Gaawar or the Lou. Coriat assumed that the great territorial dispersal of Nuer clans which he observed east of the Bahr el-Jebel was a result of the sort of slave-raiding which the Gaawar recalled in their stories about Nuaar Mer. It is fairly clear from Evans-Pritchard's account of Nuer political organization and kinship that this dispersal is a result of Nuer expansion itself (Evans-Pritchard 1940, 1951).

Any final assessment of Coriat's writings must include his influence on Evans-Pritchard, beyond those comments explicitly directed to him in document 5.1. We cannot be certain how many of Coriat's reports Evans-Pritchard did read. His copy of document 1.2 is in the library of the Institute of Social and Cultural Anthropology in Oxford, and his only annotations consist of ticks against the names of 'Gaweir shens'. Coriat may have allowed him to see his final handing-over notes on the Western Nuer (doc. 4.1), but it is highly unlikely that Evans-Pritchard saw any of the other Gaawar or Lou reports. These were confidential to the administration, dealing with the implementation of government policies. Evans-Pritchard, being a civilian, would not have had free access to them. He makes no reference to government reports in his work, beyond the old numbers of the *Sudan Intelligence Report*, a preliminary census in the early 1930s, and Coriat's critique of his own paper. Coriat's transmission of

---

62. Lou texts 4.2, in Johnson, in preparation.

his knowledge of the Nuer to Evans-Pritchard was almost exclusively oral.

Given the fact that Coriat was responsible for drawing up most government lists of tribes, clans and 'shens' for the Lou, Gaawar and Western Nuer in the 1920s, it is very likely that Evans-Pritchard had Coriat specifically in mind when he devised his own terminology for Nuer political and social organization. We can see from Coriat's decision to leave 'shen' untranslated throughout most of his reports, and from his discussion of tribes and clans in document 5.1, why Evans-Pritchard had to devise a new terminology to try to divine and explain the processes Coriat was content merely to describe. In the end the only term they use in the same way in their descriptions of Nuer politics is the word 'feud'. Their 'tribes' and 'clans' are quite different. Perhaps Evans-Pritchard's primary, secondary and tertiary segments were too tailored to administrative requirements, implying a more orderly and automatic process than was always the case. But we can see from Coriat's reports why later administrators welcomed Evans-Pritchard's more precise terminology.

The one area we can identify where Coriat did directly influence Evans-Pritchard's analysis is his presentation of Nuer history in documents 1.2 and 5.1. Coriat is at his weakest in his historical reconstructions, as we have seen above. Yet it is his basic outline of the Nuer past which Evans-Pritchard accepted with the fewest reservations. Coriat's description of Deng Laka in document 1.2 corresponds almost exactly to Evans-Pritchard's later interpretation of prophets as ralliers of opposition to foreign peoples. In all other aspects of Nuer life which he was able to observe directly, Evans-Pritchard had his own qualifications to add to Coriat's interpretations. The fact that he accepted Coriat's reconstruction of Nuer history is evidence, perhaps, of how little opportunity Evans-Pritchard had of pursuing his own historical enquiries among the Nuer.

The defects in Coriat's reconstructions of Nuer history would be misleading if we had no other sources—written and oral, European and Nuer—on which to draw. They do demonstrate the need to take into consideration a broad range of materials, even if only to make the most effective use of Coriat as a source. But if there are defects in Coriat's account of the Nuer, they are a product of the fact that he was not able to undertake sustained research into subjects unrelated to the main task of administration. The conditions of his work were such that he was unable to make a systematic recording of what he did learn, a problem all administrators (and even many academic fieldworkers) faced. The quality and detail of his recorded observations can only make us regret that he did not write more, and regret most profoundly that not all of his writings survived. The survival of the main body of his reports and correspondence does add measurably to our knowledge of this crucial period in Nuer history, revealing a wealth of detail about Nuer society, and about Nuer relations with the government, their neighbours, and each other.

1. Manyel Deng, 1928 (Eastwood)

2. Guer Wiu and Deng Mayan, c.1926 (Coriat)

3. Wan Tyeir and son, 1928 (Romilly)

4. Lat Makuai, *c.*1926 (Coriat)

5. Akuei Biel, *c.*1926 (Coriat)

6. Garang Wui, *c.*1926 (Coriat)

7. Deng Kir, *c.*1926 (Coriat)

8. Them Jang, *c.*1926 (Coriat)

9. Coriat and Mayan Lam, parading Dinka chiefs' police for a bathe at Thul, S8 patrol, 1928 (Eastwood)

10. Beating two chiefs' police for lying, 1928 (Eastwood)

11. Prisoners, S8 patrol, 1928 (Coriat)

12. Coriat interrogating a prisoner, S8 patrol, 1928 (Coriat collection)

13. Nuer 'hishing' the road, 1928 (Romilly)

14. Dual Diu (in shirt on right), outside Coriat's tent, Fajilil, 1928 (Eastwood)

15. Major Wyld in Dual Diu's cattle camp, Gaweir March, 1928 (Coriat)

16. Coriat climbing the Mound, 1928 (Coriat collection)

17. Guek, with ruins of the Mound in background, 1929 (Eastwood)

18. Mayan Lam, Wyld, Coriat and Tunnicliffe with Guek's trophies, 1929 (Eastwood)

19. 'Peace treaties': Tunnicliffe, Alban, Coriat, Kerr, 1929 (Coriat collection)

Documents in Nuer History
and Ethnography, 1922–1931

•

Percy Coriat

SECTION ONE

Central Nuer

CENTRAL NUER: INTRODUCTION

CORIAT spent eight years among the Gaawar and Lou and had some brief contact with the Lak and Thiang Nuer on Zeraf Island. In administrative terms these Nuer were later classified as the 'Central Nuer', to distinguish them from the 'Western Nuer' living west of the Bahr el-Jebel, and the 'Eastern Nuer'—the Eastern Jikany—living along the eastern border of the Sudan. During most of Coriat's time the Lak, Thiang, Gaawar, Lou and some Dinka groups were contained in one large 'Southern District' with ADCs assigned to specific 'inspectorates' at Abwong, Fangak and Duk Fayuil.

Any classification based on administrative geography does not necessarily describe the range of relations existing between the different Nuer tribes. Coriat gives evidence of continuing close relations between the Gaawar and the Nyuong and Dok Nuer of the west, despite the intervening river. There are also ties between the Bar Gaawar and the Gun Lou which are not paralleled between the Gun and Mor primary sections of the Lou. The Mor were (and still are) very closely tied to the Eastern Jikany, and Coriat did not know them well.

Documents 1.1–1.3 describe the administration of the Gaawar, while documents 1.4–1.5 describe the Lou and their Dinka neighbours. They take us from Coriat's very first months among the Gaawar during the rains of 1922 to his last days among the Lou, following the Nuer Settlement in 1929. Documents referring to specific administrative problems during this period will be found in Sections 2 and 3.

Document 1.1

EASY BUT UNCERTAIN

This story relates Coriat's introduction to the Gaawar during the rains of 1922 and describes some of the difficulties he faced in imposing government order even a short distance from his headquarters at Ayod. The story is as much about an old Gaawar leader, Nyang Macar,[1] as about Coriat. A predecessor of Coriat's had complained that Nyang had so little influence that he was unable to control his young men,[2] but Coriat shows Nyang in a very different light. He appears as a man of quiet influence even in his old age, a man perhaps as eager as the government to control the younger generation. Nyang won Coriat's immediate respect and gratitude and became one of his earliest teachers of Gaawar history and customs.

This is the only complete story found among the autobiographical fragments in Coriat's papers donated to Rhodes House. It was one of the 'dining out' stories which he told his Sudan colleagues, and it was a story they used to repeat about him.

Among other legacies handed to me by my predecessor[3] was a list of 'Wanted Men'. This sounds as though it might have been a criminal dossier with photographs of gunmen and forgerers wanted by the Police. Actually it was an unexciting though interesting record of Blood-feuds. Therein were the names of Warriors from whom Blood-money was due for their victims in inter-section fights and other young Tribesmen known to be liable to a sudden rush of blood to the head.

1. See below, doc. 1.2 n. 14, and doc. 1.3.

2. W. Pollen, 'Report on Visit to Buk on the Duk (Dwal Diu's Ballad)', n.d. [*c*. October 1918], Upper Nile Province archives, Malakal, SCR 14.A.

3. C. Borradaile: see above, Introduction, n. 12.

At that time the Tribes suffered from innumerable internecine feuds and little could be done to administer the country until these had been settled. As in most cases the sections involved were unwilling for a settlement, it was necessary to enforce one. To do this the aggressors had to be caught and coerced to pay Blood-money, in the form of a payment of cattle, to the injured party. As often as not the injured party, in the hope of getting their own back on the principle of a life for a life, would refuse to accept payment and the upshot would be a peace conference by force in an anything but peaceful setting. Fortunately, provided the correct ritual was adhered to at the ceremony, it was considered an evil act and one punishable by the 'Spirits' to reopen a feud.[4] Unless however the 'killer' was present, the settlement was not a final one, thus a great deal of time was spent in chasing killers and hence the 'Wanted' list.

With one exception none of the 'Wanted' on my list lived near the Post and I knew little could be done until the dry season had set in. Heavy rains had made a quagmire of the surrounding country. Mule transport was useless under such conditions and the local inhabitants would as soon have run 20 miles across country with my Police in full cry after them, as carried a load for a 100 yards. I had perforce to confine myself to short 'treks' within easy distance of home. However it seemed possible to make a start with the gentleman referred to in an entry which read—

> Jwoi Nyang son of Chief Nyang Machar.
> Section Shodgwar.
> Killed two men of Bedak section 1921–2. Prominent in raids against Dinka. Has refused to come in or pay Blood-money. His father Nyang is a reactionary old Chief and was a noted warrior in his day. The section has been troublesome in the past and is likely to give trouble in the future.
> Village Gool.[5]

The village of Gool was only nine miles away and without giving much thought as to how I was to catch Jwoi I determined to pay a call. I was certain of one thing, that unless Jwoi was arrested and brought in to the Post the section would refuse to pay Blood-money for his victims.

The world was emerging from its shell as the Nuer describe the dawn, when I marched out of the Post one morning with my one and only Corporal of Police, two men and one Manyel who combined the duties of Interpreter, Guide and walking Encyclopaedia of the District.[6] Having left my servants behind, Manyel

---

4. These rituals are described below in doc. 1.2, and in Evans-Pritchard 1940: 172–6; 1956: 107–12.

5. See below, doc. 1.3.

6. Manyel Deng, remembered in Ayod as either a Dinka or a Thiang Nuer. The manuscript alternates between 'Manyel' and 'Mayan'. Mayan Lam was Coriat's interpreter at Abwong (see below, doc. 1.5 n. 65). This memoir was written some years after Coriat left the Sudan and he apparently confused the two names. For a picture of Manyel Deng in 1928 see Plate 1. Borrodaile described him as 'an insiduous [sic] looking senile, biblical of mien, for whom I soon acquired a

carried my lunch in a haversack slung over his shoulder and my chair perched on his head.

As soon as we had left behind us the sandy soil on which the Post was built, the going became appalling as we were either staggering or sliding through mud or splashing across pools knee to waist deep in water. It was not long before we were soaked through and covered from head to foot in a film of mud. An astonishing spectacle to present as the representatives of the mighty and powerful Government. After travelling in this fashion for three hours I was thankful to see some little way ahead, a hut partially visible behind a few stunted trees. Manyel assured me that we had arrived but I was yet to learn that a Nuer village was anything from 500 yards to 5 miles in length. Huts or groups of huts are dotted about the country haphazardly and the larger the village the greater the area covered.

For another hour we followed the path, winding our way in and out through low scrub and passed apparently deserted huts before we came to a group of buildings with signs of habitation. A few women and girls were pounding corn in a cleared space by one of the smaller huts and a young man lounged by the side of a 'Luak' (Cattle hut). Mayan [i.e. Manyel] shouted out to ask where the Chief lived but there was no response, the young warrior turning towards us and regarding us with as much interest as if we were a stray flock of sheep. The women and girls remained intent on their task and did not appear to have seen or heard us, but a second and louder shout from Mayan prefixed with seemingly uncomplimentary remarks caused one of their number to turn her head to the right and put out her tongue. A rude gesture thought I, but it satisfied Mayan as he led off again by a smaller path that led to our right. When I asked him later, I learned that it was as common to point with the tongue as with the finger, though use of the tongue was casual and a little impolite as Mayan admitted.

The path now ran through a thorn bush and after skirting a thick clump of gum trees we emerged on to a large clearing. Close by were two large huts and beyond, placed at irregular intervals about the clearing, were several smaller ones. Several young Tribesmen were standing by the entrance to one of the larger huts, the roof of which was surmounted by two ostrich eggs. Mayan pointed this out as the Chief's hut. As we came nearer numbers of young warriors came running up from all directions towards this and having reached within a 100 yards of it, Mayan decided we had gone far enough and placing my chair down told me to await him while he called the Chief.

The ground was dry and though I could have wished for a little shade as the sun was pitiless, I was thankful to be able to sit down. Mayan was soon lost in the crowd that had by that time collected at the edge of the village but I had not long to wait and shortly the gathering began to move in my direction. As they approached I noticed an old man wearing a Leopard-skin[7] in the centre

---

sneaking fancy' (Ben Assher 1928: 154).

7. The leopard-skin was normally worn by earth-masters (*kuar muon*), but others in authority

and slightly in advance of the others. When about 25 yards from my chair, the leader signalled a halt and came on alone with Mayan. I was introduced to Chief Nyang Machar, an imposing looking old man, still hale and hearty and as appeared later, in full possession of his faculties. Through Mayan who from then on interpreted our conversation, I asked the old warrior to be seated and to let his henchmen do the same, whereupon a skin mat was produced upon which he squatted in front of me, and the Tribesmen followed suit grouping themselves in a large semicircle round their Chief. After the usual preliminaries concerning cattle and crops Nyang asked me quite bluntly why I had come to his village. I explained that as the new District Commissioner, I had visited him chiefly because I wished to make his acquaintance but I added that I was also anxious to discuss with him the matter of Blood-feuds which were disturbing the peace of the country. Ignoring this, Nyang asked how long I intended to stay. I replied that I hoped not to have to return until he and I both thought the same way as regards Blood-feuds. I added that as the sun was hot I hoped we should not get as heated inside as I felt outside while we were discussing them. This seemed to amuse the old man and before long we were chatting away merrily though I fear the conversation had turned from Blood-feuds to an argument as to whether or not the crepe rubber soles of my boots were made of human skin.

Before starting out in the morning, I had confided in Manyel that I hoped to arrest Jwoi Nyang the son of the Chief whose village we were going to visit. Manyel was sceptical as to our chances of success in this line without as he put it 'asaker ketir' (many soldiers) [Arab.] but to my surprise he said he knew Jwoi quite well and would point him out to me if he saw him.

It was, I think, while we were discussing crepe rubber soles that Manyel, having interpreted some remark made to me by Chief Nyang, added, 'Jwoi is here sitting on Nyang's left. The fat young man. The third one from Nyang'. Not wishing to 'let the cat out of the bag' until I had made up my mind as to the best way of doing it, I continued to talk to old Nyang while taking stock of the fat young man on his left, whom I saw to be a large and rather stupid looking individual much bedecorated with beads and brass wire. As with his fellow warriors, of whom by then there must have been close on a 100, his spears and club were laid by his side. I was fairly certain that to ask for Jwoi to be handed over to me would have been to ask for trouble. I knew also that if I could get away with him successfully, the example would have a good effect on other sections of the Tribe and would go a long way to making my work easier in the future. The only way I thought was to try and bluff it through.

Calling my Corporal up on the pretence of wanting a drink from his water-bottle, I warned him to look steadily at me until he had heard what I wished to say to him. I then in as few words as possible described Jwoi and gave

---

sometimes also tried to assume it. Nyang was not, in fact, from an earth-master lineage (see below, doc. 1.2).

instructions for him to be arrested as soon as I gave a signal. This I would do by taking my handkerchief out of my pocket, when he and his men were to seize Jwoi and carry him off as fast as they were able to the Post. They were not to await me or to look round or to stop at all until they were well out of sight of the village. If he resisted they were to stand by him and await my orders. I had not the faintest idea what the next move would be in case of resistance but I considered it likely that the man would be so overcome with surprise that he would allow himself to be led off fairly easily.

Manyel I instructed to remain with me. The Corporal was a trusty old soldier who had served under Gordon.[8] Thick headed and very stupid, he was brave, loyal and implicitly obedient. He could be relied on to do as he was told. Having taken a pull at his waterbottle, I told the Corporal to return to his place behind my chair. Before long Nyang and I had reverted to the subject of Blood-feuds. I said that the arm of the Government was a long one, that evildoers, though they remained at liberty for years, were punished in the end. Those, I said, who wished to make peace with the Government would pay Blood-money and settle their Tribal feuds. Government would imprison those responsible for breaking the peace. Nyang as an Elder Chief should give the right lead to others. I would take his son Jwoi to Ayod with me and would keep him until Blood-money had been paid for those he had killed. I then took my handkerchief out of my pocket. My Corporal and his two men stepped forward, seized hold of Jwoi by each arm, pulled him to his feet and proceeded to walk off with him. As I had surmised, he was too surprised to do anything but follow, though he looked rather appealingly at his father as he was led off.

For an instant there was complete silence, then, 'Clack-Clack-Click-Clack!' It is difficult to describe the sound but it will long remain in my ears. The rattle of spear shafts seized by the assembled Tribesmen as they leaped to their feet. 'That finishes it' I thought to myself and then I saw old Nyang, still seated on his mat, perfectly calm and looking hard at me. The gallant old sportsman was our only chance and prodding Manyel, who was looking nervously round from side to side, I told him if he valued his life to go on interpreting. Out of the corner of my eye, I could see that every head was turned towards the Chief. I dared not look round to see how my Corporal fared. I cannot remember now what it was I said, but whatever it was Nyang, like a perfect gentleman listened to [it] with interest, heedless of a babble of talk which began to break out round us.

It must have been five minutes, though it seemed like several hours and still had there not been a move, before I concluded by hoping my host would pay

---

8. Most of the police in the Southern Sudan at this time were ex-soldiers who had served in the Turco-Egyptian army, the Mahdist *jihadiyya*, or the Sudanese battalions of the post-1882 Egyptian army. Very few served under Gordon personally either during his governorship of Equatoria (1874–6) or his governor-generalships of the Sudan (1877–9 and 1884–5). In the imagination of British administrators, however, all old soldiers were Gordon's soldiers.

me a return [visit] and grasping his hand in farewell, I motioned Manyel to pick up my chair and stalked off the way I had come. To my delight there was no sign of the Corporal or his prisoner. I could still hear the talk behind me but by an effort I refrained from looking round. Walking steadily until we had reached the welcome seclusion of the thorn bush through which we had passed in the morning, no sooner were we out of sight than we both mechanically fell into a jogtrot. We soon reached the hut, now deserted at which we had turned off to the right on our way out. There complete with two men and prisoner stood Corporal Idris wearing a large grin on his face. We were home in time for tea.

Ten days later, Nyang and his section came in with the Blood-money and gifts of bulls for the representative of Government, so there was much beer drinking and dancing.

It had been easy but [for] that Click-Clack of spears!

Document 1.2

THE GAWEIR NUERS

The following article was written after Coriat had spent over a year administering the Gaawar. He was now conversant in Nuer, though some of the information contained here was undoubtedly first conveyed to him through an interpreter. Allowing for this, we can see that it is a remarkably accurate sketch of Gaawar history and customs, given the very short time in which information was gathered.

*The fact that Coriat carried out some enquiries in Nuer, and not exclusively through an interpreter, can be seen in his section on 'kujurs'. Like all administrators of the time he used the Arabic word 'kujur' in his reports and official correspondence. Here, as in the final document (5.1), he introduces the Nuer word 'kuoth' (*kot*) and shows some understanding of the complexity of the various manifestations of 'kuoth' in Nuer society. His investigations at this point were not extensive, however. What he says under 'Laws and Customs', for instance, must be treated with caution, since, unlike Howell (1954), he gives no examples to illustrate or substantiate his description of what was customary.*

One of Coriat's main informants was Nyang Macar, with whom, as we have seen in document 1.1, he established an immediate rapport. His close friendship with Dual Diu, however, seems to have begun after this article was written. Another source of information would have been the governor of Upper Nile Province, K. C. P. Struvé, who had served as inspector among the Gaawar before the First World War and had already published brief accounts of the activities of Nuaar Mer and Ilyas Kapsun.[1]

This article was orginially published as a supplement to H. C. Jackson's SNR *article 'The Nuer of the Upper Nile Province' when the latter was reissued as a pamphlet, and it is sometimes mistakenly listed in bibliographies as having appeared in* SNR. *Jackson acknowledged Coriat as his main source of information for the Gaawar (1923: 162). An*

---

1. 'Annual Report. Upper Nile Province, 1908', GGR 1908: 656.

earlier report on Bar Gaawar political divisions[2] *is largely incorporated here in the section 'Division and Distribution'.*

History

It is related that about 360 years ago, there was a rope from heaven which reached earth by a large Ardeiba 'Kat' [*Tamarindus indicus*][3] tree in Dok Nuer country[4] and by means of which by the people of heaven used to descend to earth for recreation and in search of food.

The earth at that time was inhabited by five Nuer sub-tribes: the Jaluh [Jalogh], Kwai, Nuong [Nyuong], Rill [Reel] and Bel.[5]

There were also many cattle on earth.

One day a man from heaven called Jakar [Kar] came down by the rope in search of food and finding the earth a pleasant place and food plentiful delayed his return to heaven and made friends among the people.

His absence from heaven being noticed, his elder brother Weir [War] came down to earth and sought Jakar's return to heaven.

Jakar, however, who had by this time been prevailed upon by his friends on earth to remain with them suggested to Weir that they should make the earth their home and give up the idea of returning to heaven.

Weir would not agree to this and told his brother that they would incur the anger of God should they remain on earth.

He ordered his brother to procure a bull and slaughter it at the tree 'Kat' as a sacrifice in order that he would not be punished for his long absence.

Weir decided that he would return to heaven in the meanwhile and would rejoin Jakar after the bull had been slaughtered, when they would both eat of the meat and return to heaven.

Jakar was unwilling to leave the earth and was afraid to disobey his brother's orders or to remain on earth without him, but with the aid of his friends a plan was hit upon by which, on Weir's return to earth, he would be kept among

---

2. 'Barr or Southern Gaweir—Précis of Note by Mr. Coriat 19.01.23', NRO Dakhlia I 112/13/87.

3. The tamarind (*koat*) tree at Koat-Liec in the Jagei country. For other accounts of myths of the tree and the rope, see Fergusson 1921: 148–50; Jackson 1923: 70–1; Crazzolara 1953: 8–11, 66–8; and Evans-Pritchard 1956: 6–10.

4. On Dok Nuer country, see below, doc. 4.1.

5. Jalogh are a clan of the Gaawar which was split by the eastward migration, some remaining behind in Dok country; Kwai is a segment of the Kerpeil lineage of the Radh primary section; Nyuong, a Western Nuer tribe (see below, 4.1); Rill [Reel], the Atuot name for themselves (though Fergusson used it for the Jagei); Bel, perhaps a misprint for Bul, a Western Nuer tribe (see below, doc. 4.1).

them and would be unable to leave again.

The bull was slaughtered at the tree 'Kat' and Jakar awaited his brother some little distance away where he had prepared a fire to cook the meat.

Jakar's friends hid themselves in the tall grass close by.

Weir having smelt the blood of the slaughtered bull was soon on his way down the rope to earth and on his arrival proceeded with his brother to cook the meat and feast on it.

When he was engrossed thoroughly in this occupation, Jakar's friends slipped out of their hiding places and cut the rope from heaven.

From that day all communication with heaven was severed and Weir and Jakar perforce became inhabitants of the earth.[6]

Weir married a woman from one of the sub-tribes and eventually became a powerful and respected man.

He had three sons born to him, Padau, Yan and Twor, of whom Twor was the father of Raz and Barr, ancestors of the two sections of Gaweir, She- (Shieng) Raz [Radh] and Barr.*

* Footnote by Coriat:

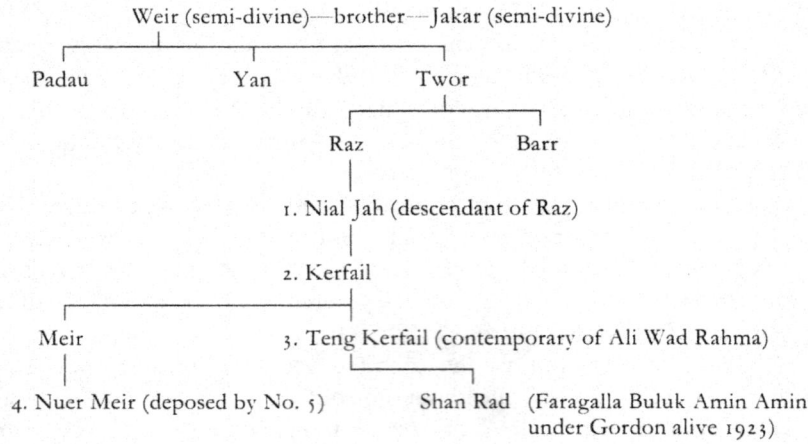

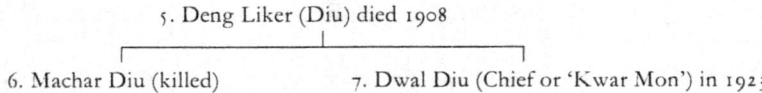

The sub-tribe founded became known as the children of Weir i.e. (Gaad Weir) Gaweir.

The earliest home of the sub-tribe is said to have been in the Rayan country

---

6. Cf. Evans-Pritchard 1940: 230–1 for other versions of the Kar and War myth.

in the Bahr El Ghazal about latitude 8° 25'N long. 30° E[7] from whence they penetrated eastwards to the country between the Bahr El Jebel and the Bahr El Zaraf by driving out the Dinka inhabitants.

From there, they continued to invade the country to the East until they occupied their present home, then in the hands of Luaich [Luac], Gnok [Ngok], Dongjol [Dungjol], Angai, and Ghol Dinkas, between latitudes 8°and 8° 30'.[8]

The last great tribal fight against the Dinkas, before the invasion of present Gaweir, took place at Fakwam [Pakuem] on the Bahr El Zaraf, when the Gaweir were under the leadership of Nial Jah [Nhial Jah] a descendant of Raz.[9]

Though the Dinka is still the hereditary enemy of the Gaweir, and raids for the purpose of filching territory and cattle from the Ghol and Angai Dinkas on the Gaweir Southern boundary had continued till as recently as 1916, this has been the action of independent Shens and the battle of Fakwam was the last concerted effort against the Dinkas by both the Raz and Barr Shens under one Chief.

After this conquest of the country Nial Jah appointed himself and became by common consent 'Kwar Mon' [*kuaar muon*] (Land Chief) of the Gaweir.[10]

This was originally the Head to whom all disputes concerning land were taken, but the position increased in importance until it eventually became that of Paramount Chief and Kujur combined.

On Nial Jah's death the position of 'Kwar Mon' passed to his son Kerfail [Kerpeil], an important Chief during his lifetime.

Kerfail became founder of the Shen called after him and the office of 'Kwar Mon' remained hereditary in the family.

Shen Kerfail consequently became the most powerful Shen in the tribe, but after Kerfail's death its supremacy was impaired by internecine warfare owing to the jealousy of Shens of the Barr section. The unity of the sub-tribe also suffered.

Teng Kerfail [Teny Kerpeil] however followed his father as 'Kwar Mon' and it was during his time that the slave raiders began to overrun the country.

When slave raiding was at its height, after the Arab Ali Wad Rahma had established posts in Gaweir,[11] the 'Kwar Mon' was Nuer Meir [Nuaar Mer] a

---

7. Near present-day Ler, then in the Eastern District, Bahr el-Ghazal Province.

8. The Luac occupied the southern Zeraf Island and the Ngok the northern half. The Angac were settled around Mogogh on the northern end of the Duk ridge while the Ghol occupied the ridge south of Ayod. The Dungjol and the rest of the Padang Dinka were in present-day Lou Nuer country.

9. Nhial Jah was neither a *kuaar muon* nor an ancestor of Kerpeil, but the companion and spokesman of Buogh Kerpeil, the leader of the Gaawar migration to the Zeraf Island. Nhial's family are said to have returned to the west.

10. It was Buogh Kerpeil who became the 'land-chief' of the Gaawar. Cf. Lewis 1951: 81. He was followed by his brother, Teny Kerpeil.

11. Kuçuk 'Ali, a Turkish trader (d. *c.* 1869), first established a *zariba* on the east bank of the

nephew of Teng.

Nuer was a Kujur and a fighting man,[12] but was more interested in amassing cattle and increasing his own wealth than in maintaining authority over his people. After forming a friendship with the Arabs, he assisted them in raids against various Gaweir Shens.

The greatest sufferers were the Barr section of the sub-tribe, though many Raz Shens and some of Nuer's own people were betrayed.

The ravages of the slave raiders split the Gaweir into small Shens and families dispersed throughout the country. Nuer was recognized as Chief by Shen Kerfail only, in which he was still able to maintain a strong following.

Gaweir remained in this condition till Deng Liker's [Deng Laka] rise to power. The story of this man is as follows:-

By birth a Dinka from Khor Filus [Fullus], Deng while still a boy was captured with his mother by the Gamok [Jamogh] Shen of Barr Gaweir.

When a young man and at the time the Barr Shens were continually being raided by the slave raiders, Deng became possessed of Kujurial powers and soon reached a position of importance among the Shensmen of Gamok in spite of his Dinka birth.

During one of the Arab raids, Deng's mother was captured and after this Deng took a prominent part in the fighting.

When not engaged in defending himself against the slave raiders, Deng led the Shens against the neighbouring Dinkas and by capturing women and cattle, made up for those lost to the Arab raiders.

Deng's influence spread to other Barr Shens and finally he attempted to unite the Barr section and organise an attack against Nuer Meir, the 'Kwar Mon'.

It is said that a day was appointed on which the Shensmen were to gather but owing to the strength of Nuer's following the idea met with little enthusiasm and Deng found himself with only a small force. This so enraged him that he left Shen Gamok then living in the country to the South of the Duk ridge and made his way to Ajwong on the Zeraf where several small Barr Shens were gathered.

On arrival at Ajwong, Deng shut himself up in a hut and refused all food and drink.

After fourteen days during which Deng had fasted the whole time, the Chiefs and Elders of Barr Shens became convinced that this was a Kujur out of the ordinary run, and collecting a small following they repaired to Deng's hut and

---

Bahr el-Zeraf (at about 8°10' / 30°46') in the late 1860s, but his son Nasr 'Ali moved it to Jambiel on the west bank (8°30' / 30°40') in about 1871. The Ghattas company had a *zariba* inland at present-day Ayod, then in Luac Dinka country, and another *zariba* was at Khandak. See Marno 1873: 130–3; 1874: 331, 394–5; and 1881.

12. Nuaar Mer was a Thoi Dinka adopted by Mer Teny, nephew of Buogh Kerpeil. The Kerpeil are earth-masters, and the only *kuoth* Nuaar was said to have was *kuoth rieng*, the tutelary divinity of earth-masters. He was not a 'kujur' in the sense Coriat uses for Deng Laka, who was a *guk kuoth* (prophet).

demanded his orders.

Deng replied that they had disbelieved in him once but would not do so again. He had been seized by Kujur during his fourteen days at Ajwong and he would remain four more days under a spell. In five days time he would set out for a spot on the Duk ridge where the Barr Shens would meet him. Beyond this Deng would say nothing further.[13]

At the appointed time and place a strong force of Gaweir met Deng, mainly owing to the efforts of Nyong Machar [Nyang Macar], a Chief of sub-Shen Shodgwar [Cotguor] of Shen Sharm [Cam],[14] who is still living, and Yor Kweth a Gamok Chief of sub-Shen Fod [Puot], father of the present Chief.[15]

These Chiefs were firm believers in Deng and later became his greatest friends.

Deng then told the Shensmen that they would march with him to Nuer Meir's 'murah'. On arrival they would find the cattle away grazing and Nuer and his men out hunting. They would however enter the central 'murah' where by a small fire they would find two gourds full of butter left there for Nuer on his return.

He (Deng) and other minor Kujurs would eat the butter when they would be seized by Kujur and fall into a trance.

A thick mist would gather in the air and the Shensmen would go forward and meet and attack Nuer's force without being seen.

In the course of the battle Nuer would be killed.

A few men had misgivings and returned home, the main body followed Deng.

The events which took place, were as had been predicted and the Barr Shens made for home the richer with cattle and women.[16]

A month after Nuer Meir's death, a Gaweir force under Deng defeated the slave raiders with Elias Kapsun [Ilyas Kapsun] at Kodni on the Bahr El Zeraf.[17]

---

13. According to modern Gaawar accounts both Deng and his mother were Ngok Dinka refugees who came to the Gaawar on their own when Deng was a small boy. When Deng was fully grown Nuaar Mer sold his mother to the slavers. It was because of this that Deng joined the growing band of Nuaar's opponents. A raiding party he joined broke up before reaching Mogogh, Nuaar Mer's home. Deng was disgusted by this and returned home to Ajuong, where he fell ill. After his illness was diagnosed as seizure by the divinity Diu, he organized the final, successful attack on Nuaar.

14. See docs. 1.1 and 1.3. Nyang lived in Mogogh with Nuaar Mer but left him, taking some of Nuaar's special cattle to Deng Laka. According to some Gaawar accounts it was Nyang, arriving with these cattle, who persuaded Deng Laka to attack Nuaar.

15. Riek Yor: see below, doc. 1.3.

16. Modern Gaawar accounts which I collected in 1975–6 mention only that Deng Laka urged his followers on to Mogogh by telling them, 'You will be up to your necks in butter tomorrow.'

17. The slavers along the Bahr el-Jebel and Bahr el-Zeraf had all been evacuated by Gordon in 1874. The battle of Mogogh took place in 1879, after the great flood of 1878. There are two possible dates for the battle near the Bahr el-Zeraf between Deng Laka and local soldiers: 1885

Deng had become by this time Paramount Chief of Gaweir and was looked upon as the rightful 'Kwar Mon'.

The heritage of the office of 'Kwar Mon' was lost to Shen Kerfail which dispersed into small Sub-shens, many of them besides other Raz Shens acknowledging Deng as Chief.[18]

Deng assumed the name of Diu, the particular Kujur spirit with whose powers he was said to be imbued.

He died about 1908,[19] after occupation of the country by the present Government, to whom he remained independent but not hostile.

His son Machar, known as Machar Diu, succeeded him, though the Kujurial spirit of Diu is said to have been inherited at birth by his brother Dwal, the present Chief.[20]

Machar was unable to maintain the authority his father had over Gaweir, and numerous feuds broke out between Shens over cattle captured from the Dinkas in various raids.

The Raz section disclaimed Machar, who occupied his time in leading Shen Gamok and others of Barr who wished to join him, in raids against the Ghol and Angai Dinkas with great success.

In 1914 a patrol was sent against Machar for his attacks on the Dinka and for his reported hostility to Government.

Machar was not captured but was later killed with two brothers by the Dinkas.[21]

Dwal Diu, the younger brother who had inherited his father's Kujur became Chief of Shen Gamok; he had at first little control over other Barr Shens, the disputes among which during Machar's time had led to blood feuds.

In 1916 Dwal led a small raid against a Gaweir Shen, Boi, which had been driven into Dinka territory by Machar following a dispute over cattle. He also attacked the Dinkas with Shen Boi, but little was gained and Dwal returned probably through fear of Government action being taken against him.

In this case a patrol was contemplated, but Dwal's brothers among whom was Gai, who was later appointed as his representative with Government, visited the Markaz Duk Fadiat in the Dinka country. He maintained that certain territory

---

(see Casati 1891: i.241, 318; Schweitzer 1898: i.184; and Schweinfurth *et al.* 1888: 488), and *c.* 1896 ('Report on March from Taufikia to Twi and Visit to Twi by Steamer, by El Kaimakam Liddell Bey, Director of Post and Telegraphs. 9th June 1904', Appendix A in *SIR* 119 (June 1904), 6). Modern Gaawar do not place it as soon after the battle of Mogogh as Coriat does.

18. Descendants of Mer Teny continued to act as earth-masters (see notes g and h to table below entitled 'Gaweir Shens'), but Deng Laka also acted as an earth-master as well as a prophet.

19. Deng Laka died in *c.* August 1907 (*SIR* 159 (Oct. 1907), 2).

20. The divinity Diu did not manifest itself in Dual Diu until about 1912–13.

21. Macar raided the Ghol and Twic Dinka once in 1908, after his father's death, and then again in 1914, following the seizure of his cattle by government troops. He and his brothers Wol and Thoi were killed while raiding the Twic Dinka on 10 June 1914 (Governor Mongalla, to governor Malakal, 15.06.14, SRO UNP 14.1). See Kulang Majok, text 2.5, in Johnson, in preparation.

captured by Machar and taken by the Dinkas, to have been the cause of the fighting.[22]

A boundary was defined and certain land captured by the Gaweir was allowed to remain in their hands.

Dwal then became friendly with the Government and no further raids were made against the Dinkas, though rumours of such, started by the Dinkas were frequent and continue to the present day.[23]

In 1921 Dwal initiated himself into new Kujurial powers and rites were held, after which he did not leave his Shen and dealt with Government through Gai only.[24]

Early in 1922 Gai died and Dwal resumed relations with Government in person.

By this time though he had not had the opportunity to gain fame as a fighting leader, Dwal had considerable influence with the Barr Gaweir as a Kujur.

His authority was supported by Government and Dwal became recognised as leading Chief of the Barr section.

He attempted to settle the blood feuds between Shens in the winter of 1922, but was then unsuccessful mainly owing to the jealousy of Shan Rad [Cany Reth] (Faragalla Buluk Amin) then a Kujur of Shen Kerfail of the Raz section employed as Interpreter at Ayod Merkaz, and partly owing to the lack of authority of minor Shen Chiefs.[25]

Since Shan Rad's appointment to Paramount Chief of Raz, Dwal has resumed his efforts in this direction.

The Raz section of the sub-tribe had had no strong Chiefs after the death of Deng Liker and had been less subject to Government influence than the Barr.

On Nuer Meir's death in the ordinary course of events the office of 'Kwar Mon' would have passed to Shan Rad, his nephew.

Shan however had been captured as [a] boy by the slave raiders and after having been released by Gordon, served in his army where he attained the rank of Buluk Amin. On the fall of Khartoum, Shan drifted back to Gaweir, by which time Deng Liker had established himself. He therefore laid no claim to his position but joined Deng as one of his fighting force.

22. The fight took place in April 1918 (see doc. 2.1 n. 8). Gai, Biel and Dual Diu made peace with the government at Duk Fadiat in August 1918 (MPMIR, August 1918, NRO Intel 2/48/408 and SRO TD SCR 36.H.20).

23. The monthly reports of Mongalla Province from 1918 to 1925 record numerous rumours of impending Nuer raids, none of which ever took place (see below, doc. 2.1 n. 9).

24. Dual, like his father before him, accumulated a number of divinities through sacrifice and dedication of cattle.

25. Dual convened a meeting of some 300 young men and chiefs from various sections in October 1922 and proposed that blood feuds be cancelled on a general payment of bloodwealth at a reduced rate of six head of cattle per death. Mayom Kuai and Cany Reth were the main opponents of this scheme, insisting on a rate of fifty to sixty head of cattle per death (see 'Barr or Southern Gaweir', cited in n. 2).

After Deng had died, Shan confined himself to his work as a Kujur and was occasionally employed by Government as Guide and Interpreter.

His influence as Kujur increased and he became much feared by the Raz section.

Shan's knowledge of Arabic and his ability to read and write were assets in his dealings as a Kujur.

In 1918 when a Government station was established on the Duk ridge at Ayod, Shan was employed as Interpreter at Awoi Post.[26]

His Kujur work was carried on in a quiet way and though he has a certain fondness for power, his main object apparently was to amass cattle and he was outwardly loyal to Government.

When Dwal attempted to settle the question of blood feuds in 1922, Shan used his influence to prevent this, from what seems to have been jealous motives and fear of losing cattle.

In 1923 Shan Rad was appointed Paramount Chief of Raz Gaweir and is now living at Moot [Mut] on the left bank of the Bahr El Zeraf, where his influence is confined to that section of the Gaweir only.[27]

The minor Gaweir Chiefs, with few exceptions have little control over their young men now that they are unable to lead them in war, but under the leadership of Dwal Diu and Shan Rad supported by Government, this should improve and the Gaweir become increasingly amenable to peaceful Government by their own Chiefs.

Division and Distribution

The two sections of Gaweir, Raz and Barr, are each divided into six Shens or families with a varying number of Sub-shens or branches of the family.

These Sub-shens alter in name and vary in strength, as some minor Chief or follower finds a Shen of his own or augments his following.

26. Cany Reth, of the Radh section, was captured as a boy sometime during the period of Nuaar Mer. He was trained as a soldier and learned to read and write, a necessary accomplishment to become a company quartermaster sergeant (*buluk amin*). He appears to have returned to the Gaawar after the fall of Khartoum (January 1885) and is also said to have taken part in Deng Laka's defeat of Ilyas Kapsun. He first came to the government's attention as an emissary sent by Deng Laka to Fashoda in 1902. He later visited Khartoum in the company of Deng Laka's son, Wol, in 1908. He began manoeuvring for government support to be made a chief as early as 1904. See SRO EHJP4, Ruot Rom, Cuol Macar, Gai Thung, 12.04.81; SRO EHJP7, Kulang Majok, 13.04.81; *SIR* 99 (Oct. 1902), 1; 119 (June 1904), 5; 163 (Feb. 1908), 2; also 'Return of Prominent Persons—Upper Nile 1909', SRO UNP (unnumbered); and Ben Assher 1928: 182–3.

27. Cany Reth was murdered on 22 October 1924 by Lel Lublub, a Jamogh-Bar-Gaawar youth who was one of Dual's own bards (see below, doc. 1.3).

GAWEIR SHENS

No.	Sub-shen	Shen	Chief	Village	'Marah'
			BARR SECTION OF SUB-TRIBE		
1	Bedeed	Bang	Won Tyeir	Gwer[a]	Akair
2	.. (sub)	..	Pong Won	Dongayo	..
3	Marinyang	..	Dol Bul	Awoi	..
4	Tod	..	Diu Bang	Kwaideng	..
5	.. (sub)	..	Fol Twop	Ajwong	Kh. Gwer
6	Gaing	..	Kor Juol	Fankor	Akair
7	Shamarn	..	Kwajen Ton	Wunlang	Kh. Dthok
8	Turwo	..	Diu Kan	Kweylek[a]	..
9	Giel	Gamok	Dwal Diu[b]	Turawo	Akair
10	Diow	..	Wol Mun Thod	Konthod	Kh. Dol
11	Fod	..	Riek Yor	Agum	Akair
12	Maen	Sharm	Pfui Yir	Wan[c]	Bek
13	Shodgwar	..	Nyong Machar	Gool	Kh. Them
14	Korar	..	Bedak Ling	Kungleir	..
15	.. (sub)	..	Mud Gien	Ajwong	left bank
16	Shuk	Dol	Biey Char	Rufshendol	Kh. Gurwel
17	Boz	..	Wal Kir	..	..
18	Ruol	..	Shakweng Jok[d]	..	..
19	Nyabel	..	Riek On	..	..
20	Kur	..	DISPERSED AMONG SHEN DOL		
21	Thoi	..	..	..	..
22	Kwad	..	..	..	..
23	Yey	..	..	..	..
24	Malair	Riah	Thalil Dah	Temrol[c]	'toich'[e]
25	Garlied	..	..	Kot	..
26	Jok	..	..	Gnol	..
27	Long	Garkwar	Gwer Weoh[f]	Bul	Kh. Gurwel
28	Nyeir	..	Lief Gaing	Maleet[c]	Bek
29	Koh	..	Lain Dar	..	..
			RAZ SECTION OF SUB-TRIBE		
30	Kwai	Kerfail	Maiyom Kwai[g]	Mogug	Kh. Famir, or Tithbel
31	Nyakar	..	Dag Meir[h]	Khandak	..
32	Rad	..	Shan Rad[j]	Moot[c]	k.175.Z.[i]
33	Bishok	..	Mut Jior	Rufkwoth[c]	Kh. Liet
34	Daiching	..	Tong Bul	Maleet[c]	Bek
35	Buh	Nyaigwar	Biey Liaf	..	Ful Yal
36	Fakeer	..	Shwol Bwol	..	Keth
37	Shon	..	Roomfut Dwos	Moot[c]	k.175.Z.
38	Liaf	..		DISPERSED	
39	Wah Farr	Yi Deng	(Bilal Yunis)	Fakwaz	Kh. Bir
40	Farr	Farr	Deng Falwal	Haad[c]	Kh. Thol
41	Liah		with Farr		

GAWEIR SHENS (continued)

No.	Sub-shen	Shen	Chief	Village	'Marah'
42	Kweer	..	Tik Bul	Haad[c]	Kh. Thol
43	Juol	Getheib	Lio Bay	Fankor	Thorol
44	Diow	..	Gnaney Kan	Shenkwon[c]	Kh. Thol
45	Mandeen	..	Wor Kolang	Ful Kir	Kh. Famir
46	Larb	..	Diu Joh	Thonakan	Kh. Dang
47	Wangjak	..	..	..	..
48	Kwoth	Nyadakwon	Gyal Nyarn	Faiyatt	k.160.Z.
49	Kur	..	Joh'w'Err	Nyongchar	Mbar
50	Beh	..	Lok Fadam	Gnwir[c]	k.160.Z.
51	Lar	..	Luah Lar	Nyongchar	Mbar & l.b.
52	Thor	..	Bil Bul	..	..
53	Giek	..	Dar Barn	Rufshenjog[c]	k.160.Z.
54	Gor	Mwanjoh	No Chief	Haad[c]	--------

a. Fasheir District.
b. Paramount Chief of section.
c. Left bank.
d. Cakuen Jok: see Introduction, above, and below, 1.3.
e. The Bar Gaawar *toic* was then the annually river-flooded grassland between the Duk ridge and the Bahr el-Zeraf/Bahr el-Jebel swamp. The Radh Gaawar *toic* was found on both banks of the Bahr el-Zeraf and inland on Zeraf island.
f. Guer Wiu: see below, 1.3, and Introduction, above. Guer's father was a Dinka, and Guer was generally on good terms with the Dinka, later playing an important mediatory role between them and the Gaawar. He was a close friend of Coriat's and sided with the government against Dual Diu in 1928. He died in June 1937 ('Personality Report no. 135' NRO UNP 1/25/182, and B.A. Lewis to governor, Upper Nile Province, 18 October 1937, SRO UNP 66.D.3). See Plate 2.
g. Mayom Kuai, one of the most prominent earth-masters of the Kerpeil lineage in the 1930s and 1940s. He was not appointed a government chief because it was felt 'he would put the clock back and run the place by the leopard skin if he could'. Two of his sons, Biel Mayom and Malual Mayom, did serve as presidents of the mainland Radh Gaawar court in the 1940s to 1960s. Mayom was accused of using magic to kill Dag Mer, the other leading Kerpeil earth-master ('Upper Nile Province Personality Report no. 34' NRO UNP 1/34/276 and 'Supernatural', n.d. [c. 1937], SRO ZVD 66.K.1).
h. Dag Mer, a younger son of Mer Teny, was an influential earth-master in his own right but also an ally of Dual Diu's until the latter's capture in 1930. Dag was the most important Radh Gaawar earth-master from that time till his death in 1937 (Lewis 1951: 81).
i. Distances along the rivers were marked by poles numbered from the Zeraf mouth southwards. K.175.Z and k.160.Z were renumbered as reference poles 34 and 31. See also document 4.1 n. 9 below.
j. Paramount Chief of section.

The name of a Shen remains the same, though a Sub-shen may increase in strength and importance until it in turn becomes the main root of various other families.

The Barr section occupies the country to the right bank of the Bahr El Zeraf, South of latitude 8° 21', with the exception of two Sub-shens of Shen Garkwar [Gaakuar] at Maleet [Malith] on the left bank (who settled there in Nial Jah's time) and Shen Riah on the left bank in the South.

The Raz, with the exceptions of two Sub-shens of Kerfail and Nyadakwon and a Sub-shen of Getheib [Jithep], live on the left bank.

The right bank Shens inhabit the country towards the Northern boundary of Gaweir.

Relations with Other Tribes

Dinkas
The history of the Gaweir has been one of raiding and invasion of Dinka territory since ancient times and the Dinka has seldom been able to hold his own against this sub-tribe of Nuers, being treated by them with the greatest of contempt.

The Nuer name for a Dinka 'Jangé' is synonomous with that of a slave.

Dinka boys captured in battle are always retained as slaves.[28]

The Dinkas themselves live in great fear of the Gaweir.

The Ghol and Angai Dinkas are neighbours to the south of the Gaweir country and the Luaich to the north-east.

These sections originally inhabited the present home of Gaweir with the Dongjol and Gnok who migrated to the north and east.

Nuong [Nyuong] Nuers
The Nuong living in the country on the left bank of the Bahr El Jebel is the neighbour of the Raz section of Gaweir and there is much intercourse between that section of the tribe and the Nuong.

Intermarriage is common and the Gaweir often loan their rifles to the Nuong, and join him in raids against the Dinkas of the Bahr El Ghazal.

Lak Nuers
The country of this sub-tribe lies to the north of Gaweir.

Relations are friendly but there is little intermarriage or trade with Lak.

Lau Nuers
The Lau are on generally friendly terms with the Gaweir though there are occasionally inter-tribal Shen fights.

Lau act as middlemen in the rifle and ivory trade between the Gaweir and Jekaing. In times of famine there is exchange of durra and cattle between the two sub-tribes.

With the exception of a few words the Nuer language is common to the sub-tribes. Dinka is related but not mutually intelligible.

28. Dinka boys, after performing menial tasks such as herding cattle (which Nuer boys also did), were usually adopted as full members of a lineage (Evans-Pritchard 1940: 221–2 and 1951: 24–5).

Economic Life

The Gaweir is entirely pastoral, growing hardly sufficient grain for his own needs in the winter months, when he is unable to fish and hunt to any extent.

Owing to the physical conditions of the country, life is more or less nomadic in character.

During the winter months, roughly from June to December, the Gaweir lives in his village, which consists of groups of mud huts scattered over a large area. Each man having his cattle hut (Lwak) and two or three small living huts (Ud [*wut*] or Dwel) surrounded by a patch of cultivation several hundred yards from those of his neighbour.

The cattle 'Lwak' is a large circular hut where the cattle are kept at night during the rains. In the centre a small mud wall about a foot high is built in a circle and kept filled with burnt cattle dung, in this and on a platform built over it the young unmarried men sleep.

The 'Ud' or 'Dwel' is a small bee-hive shaped hut with a plastered mud floor in which the married man and children and girls live.

The site of a village is moved if the pasture for cattle becomes poor. Besides cattle a few flocks of sheep and goats are kept.

Cultivation is done mostly by the women and old men.

The principal crop grown is durra, besides which there is a small amount of maize and tobacco.

Meat, fish and milk form the main diet during the summer months, most of the grain grown being kept as a reserve for the winter.

After harvest and before the Shen leaves the village for 'Marah' the grain is stored in mud jars and placed in a hut, the door of which is sealed by plastering with mud.

A village's entire crop is often placed in a hut belonging to a Chief or Elder and a bull sacrificed to some Kujur spirit as a protection against theft.

Theft of durra by parties of Jekaing on their way through to the 'Marah' with rifles to exchange for ivory is not uncommon.[29]

In the summer months the Gaweir lives on the Khors, Fulas and rivers.

The sites of these 'Marahs' vary from year to year according to the sufficiency or otherwise of water in the Khors and Fulas and the quality of the grazing.

Shens collect together during this period of the year.

Grass huts are built close together, roughly in the form of a ring, the cattle being kraaled in the centre.

This season is spent in hunting and fishing.

Fish is speared, the weapon used, 'Bith', being similar to the Arab 'Kokab'.[30]

Elephant, Hippopotamus and Giraffe are hunted with spear and with rifles by those who possess them.

29. The Jikany also sometimes traded grain, hides and cattle (Johnson 1986*b*).

30. A barbed spear.

In elephant hunting the quarry is encircled by hundreds of men and speared and shot until it falls.

Ivory is claimed by first spear and the rule regarding this is rigid.

On obtaining tusks the owner will sacrifice a bull to his particular guardian Kujur spirit, failure to do this is considered certain death.

One tusk must be given to a relative.

Theft of ivory also means death.

Should a tusk be left in the bush, a small conical shaped grass covering will be placed over it to denote ownership.[31]

The hippo is harpooned from canoes in the Shilluk manner.[32]

The harpoon is a narrow iron spike sharply pointed at the end with a barbed hook a few inches from the tip.

Giraffe are driven into swamp country when being hunted and are followed till brought to a standstill through exhaustion.

The only skilled craft known is iron working carried on by the men.

The iron, traded from the Arab, is fashioned into spears, bracelets, anklets and other articles of ornament.

Iron working is learnt from boyhood but is not confined to any sect or family.

The baskets used for all purposes, including the carrying of infants, are shaped like a long narrow box and are made by the women and old men from the leaf of the Dom palm [*Hyphaene thebaica*].

Women and men do not eat together and each man takes his food separately. Hollowed and dried marrow gourds, of which a quantity are grown for the purpose are used as bowls for food and water.

Mussel shells are used as spoons.

In a year of famine the blood of cattle is drunk, bleeding being done by an incision in the neck of the animal.

Cattle are seldom slaughtered for food excepting on occasions such as marriages, etc.

All feathered game, reptiles and the waterbuck are considered unclean feeders and are not eaten.

The waterbuck is said to eat snakes.

In war, spears, clubs and rifles are used.

Rifles are traded from the Jekaing for ivory who in turn trades with the Abyssinians.[33]

The amount of rifles in Gaweir possession is increasing.

Two types of shields are used; a shield similar to that used by the Shilluk

---

31. A more detailed description of Nuer elephant-hunting can be found in Howell 1945. The right tusk went to the first spearer and the left tusk went to the second spearer (ibid.: 100).

32. The same photograph of a 'Nuer' harpooning from a canoe, which appears on the front cover of Evans-Pritchard 1940, is in fact identified as a Shilluk in Coriat's own photo album (now in the family's possession).

33. Johnson 1986*b*.

fashioned out of crocodile or hippo hide or a stout branch of ambatch wood [*Herminiera aegyptiaca*] about four feet long with a piece carved out of the middle to act as a handle. This type is most generally used on account of its lightness.

Some of these ambatch shields are hollowed out to a depth of two or three inches at both ends and fitted with a stopper, this is for carrying tobacco.[34]

No clothes are worn but many ornaments are worn on the body, the most common being ivory and brass bracelets and necklaces of beads of various colours.

Bracelets worn by the men vary in pattern.

Some of these consist of giraffe tail hairs twined around the wrist or strips of brass bound round the wrist two or three times or round the length of the arm from wrist to elbow.

An iron bracelet with two curved prongs about three inches in length extending from it at the back of the wrist is a type sometimes worn by the men.

Ivory armlets about an inch thick and sometimes four or five inches in depth are also worn.

Charms from Kujurs, said to be protection from snake bites, illness, etc. are worn round the neck.

Hair is dyed red and worn long by the men or is plastered over with mud and cattle dung and shaped into a conical headdress brought to a point either to the front or back of the head.

This headdress is worn when the hair is in the process of being dyed.

Women wear similar necklaces to the men but bracelets worn are made of tin.

The same are used as anklets. A young girl wearing one or two and married women three or four.

The men smear their bodies and faces with the ash of burnt cattle dung.

This is not done by the women except at dances when the young unmarried girls smear the upper half of their bodies and their faces with the ash.

Married women wear skirts of plaited goat hair or two triangular shaped pieces of goat hide round the loins, the edge of which is trimmed with cowrie shells or beads or a fringe of hair is left as a border.

Both men and women wear round the waist either a single string of cowrie shells or string of beads or a strip of hide or dom palm fibre.

A deep waistband of beads is sometimes seen but this has been introduced from the Dinkas and Lau Nuer.

---

34. *Kom*: also used as a pillow or stool.

Laws and Customs

Birth

No special festivities are held on the birth of a child.

A woman will often conceal the birth of a child born to her for several days for fear of the evil eye. This means that she will not leave her hut, though quite capable of doing so.

Marriage

A marriage is celebrated by a dance and much drinking of 'marissa' at the bride's village. A bull is slaughtered by the bridegroom and the families and friends join in the feast.

On her first marriage a girl will shave the hair off her head.

A skirt is not always worn till after the birth of a child.

The 'mahr' paid on marriage is variable and is fixed by agreement between the father of the bride and her family and the bridegroom and his family.

The original amount with Gaweir on a woman's first marriage was 50 head of cattle but is now between 15 and 30.[35]

Payment is in most cases made by instalment, the last being paid on the married man receiving 'mahr' for a daughter.

The amount paid for a second wife is not influenced by the man already having one wife.

Only small 'mahr' is paid for a divorcee and none for a widow.

On marriage a man will invariably give his wife beads, anklets and bracelets which should be returned if she leaves him.

A number of relatives and friends have claim to participation in the 'mahr' received by the bride's family.

The following have first claim:-

1st claim	Father	one cow and calf and one bull or more
2nd ..	Mother	.. .. or more
3rd ..	'Wangnen'	.. .. or more
	Paternal uncles	.. ..
	.. aunts	.. ..
	Maternal uncles	.. .. and one bull or more
	.. aunts	.. ..

The 'Wangnen' are the grandfather and grandmother of the girl on the

---

35. The 'ideal' bridewealth was often claimed to be forty to fifty head of cattle. The actual bridewealth in the 1930s was usually twenty to thirty (Evans-Pritchard 1940: 20). Howell has questioned whether there was ever any fixed 'ideal' rate, or even an agreed minimum. Among the Zeraf Nuer in the 1940s seventeen to twenty head of cattle was the usual rate, but this could be reduced even further during times of severe cattle loss (Howell 1954: 98–9). Throughout the 1930s and 1940s the rate fluctuated constantly throughout Nuerland.

father's side or their heirs.

Cattle received by women are the property of their husbands or fathers.

The bridegroom will receive help in payment of 'mahr' from his father, uncles, aunts and close friends.

His friends will then participate in 'mahr' he may receive for a daughter.[36]

Divorce

If a woman leaves her husband and returns to her relatives a meeting of the families is held.

If the woman is in the wrong all 'mahr' is returned.

If the man is in the wrong the woman's relatives keep two cows as follows:-

Yang Mimni (The cow of the hair). As significant of the girl's first marriage in shaving the hair off her head.

Yang Yith (The cow of the 'Furwa' [Arab. 'hide' or skirt]) the price paid for lost virginity.

These cattle are paid only if it is the woman's first marriage.

In all cases cattle that have died are not replaced, but those eaten are made good.[37]

Adultery

The adulterer pays from two to six cows to the husband.

If a child is born it is kept by the husband of the woman but may be given to the father on payment of a cow and calf.

If a man wishes to marry and has committed adultery with a woman and by concealment of the fact has not paid 'Dier' [Arab. *diya*, 'blood money'] to her father or husband he will do so on marriage for fear of the death of his offspring.

Marriage Rights

A large offspring is the desire of every Gaweir as this means increased wealth.

If a man is incapable of producing children, he may allow a friend to have access to his wives, and will pay a cow calf for a child born.

36. Compare this with the bridewealth distribution among the Lak and Thiang during the 1940s, as recorded by Howell (1954: 102–4). Father: 2 cows, 1 ox, 1 calf; brothers: 1 ox each; paternal uncles: a variety of cows, calves and oxen; paternal aunt: 1 cow; paternal grandparents: a cow or a heifer each; father's maternal uncle: 1 cow calf; mother: 2 cows, 1 calf; maternal uncles: a variety of cows, cow calves, and oxen; maternal aunts: 1 cow calf; maternal grandparents: 1 pregnant cow each; mother's maternal uncle: 1 cow calf. Grandparents are *wangnen* (from *wang*, eye, and *nen*, see) only if they have lived to see the birth of the bride. If they have, then a share of the bridewealth is allocated to them, even if they died before the marriage (Evans-Pritchard 1946: 249).

37. Cf. Howell 1953a: 141–3, where the names of the cattle are given as *ruath miemni* (bull calf of the the hairs) and *yang yaatni* (cow of the skirt), the latter referring to the skirt married women wear as a symbol of their married status. See also Howell 1954: 149.

The child [is treated] as in the case of widows' children, being called the child of the cattle paid in 'mahr', and is considered a legal child.

Widows
When a married man dies his brother or half-brother takes the widow.

If a child is born it takes the name of deceased and is called the child of the cattle paid in 'mahr'.

If there is no brother the woman looks for another man who does not pay 'mahr' for her. Any children born take the name of deceased.

The child or children have the same rights as other children and inherit deceased's property in the event of his having had no other offspring.[38]

Seducing a Girl
If an unmarried girl becomes pregnant a deputation of girls is sent to the man concerned.

He must pay a fine of 10 to 20 cattle or marry the girl, otherwise war may result.

Inheritance
A man's eldest son inherits his property i.e. wives, sons, daughters, cattle, debts and assets.

This son looks after his brothers and assists them in 'mahr' when they marry.[39]

He also inherits the father's share of any 'mahr' paid for his sisters.

If there are no sons the brother will inherit and look after the family.

Except for a man taking his brother's widow or widows, intermarriage among relatives is forbidden to Gaweir.

Exchanges
A man wanting a sheep or bull for a feast on a special occasion and having none will get one from a friend paying a bull calf for a sheep or goat and a cow calf for a bull.

A bull may be had on loan but a cow only if in milk.

Five cows are paid in exchange for a herd bull.

Debt
In cases of dispute over debt, decision may be given by a Chief or Kujur, a cow being taken as fee where the dispute concerns many cattle. The fee is paid by Plaintiff.

38. See below, doc. 5.1.

39. A man is expected to distribute his cattle among his sons before his death. The eldest son does not get full and exclusive control over his father's property, but cattle are used in the sons' marriages according to seniority (Howell 1954: 190–4).

Theft

The following are fines for theft under tribal law:-

Article stolen	Award to owner	
Durra any quantity	One cow	
Canoe	Two cows	
Cow if killed and eaten	Five cows	
Cow if stolen and kept	Cow returned	
Cow disfigured	.. ..	no fine
Bull killed and eaten	Cow calf	
Bull stolen and kept	Bull returned	
Herd bull killed and eaten	Ten cows	
Spear	One bull	
Fish spear	Two to five cows	
Any article of ornament	One bull	
Rifle (theft or damage)	Three cows	

The above are the maximum fines.

A man has a perfect right to steal his property back or some other article in exchange, this is not considered theft.[40]

Fines are generally paid by the thief if he has been discovered.

If he refuses to pay the owner will appeal to a Kujur.

As in cases of dispute over 'mahr' a man may consider he has a right before committing a theft and will be willing to appear before a Kujur or Chief if summoned.

Where the parties are of different Shens the dispute will generally be taken before a Kujur.

If the Kujur is widely known and has sufficient influence, the defendant in the case will abide by his decision on fear of death or permanent disability by supernatural means.

Claimant pays a fee to the Kujur, but defendant may pay a larger fee in which case claimant will probably lose his case regardless of the justice of the decision.

---

40. The retrieval of stolen property was known as 'self-help' in legal language. Howell (ibid.: 198–203) notes that only certain rare items obtained in trade through the exchange of cattle used to cause litigation or retaliation if stolen, and that in many of these cases 'the damages were out of all proportion to the wrong'. Such articles included canoes and iron spears, a fishing-spear sometimes fetching six cows among the Gaawar. Many other Nuer tribes had less punitive rates of compensation.

Hurt

The following are the fines paid for hurt:-

Injury	Compensation
Beating or stabbing (no permanent injury)	Nil
Leg broken	Ten cows
Arm broken	Six cows
One bone of arm broken	Three cows
Loss of both eyes	Ten to thirty cows
Loss of one eye	Two to ten cows
Teeth of unmarried girl broken	Cow and calf

The above are the maximum awards.[41]

Procedure in Cases of Dispute

When a case is decided by some important Kujur or Chief, the following procedure is adopted:-

The general assembly is seated in a semicircle facing the Chief who may wear a leopard-skin.

The earth is scratched up into a shallow pit in front of the Chief. All parties in the case then make their speeches in rotation standing before the Chief. The man speaking has his right hand on his spear, which is embedded shaft downwards in the pit. On conclusion the presiding Chief retires with any other Chiefs that may be present and Elders and a short palaver is held after which they return and decision is given. A few minutes are allowed in discussion of the manner in which the decision is to be carried out and the case is concluded.

The significance of the pit is that a man making a false statement while holding his spear will be stricken dead on the spot or in a short time will be buried. The pit being presumably a reminder to any would be perjurer of his grave.

A man will in some cases refuse to give his evidence in this manner, in which case, though allowed to make his speech, it will carry no weight.

Manslaughter or Murder

Blood money varies from ten to forty cows the amount being determined by a meeting of the families concerned and dependent on the wealth of the murderer.[42]

This is exclusive of two payments made as a peace offering.

When a man kills another and he is penitent, he will take refuge in the house of a Kujur, where he will remain several months during which time he may not

---

41. Cf. ibid.: 69–70. A scale of compensation for bodily injury was set for the whole of Nuerland in 1945 at lower rates than those given here.

42. Howell (ibid.: 26) doubts if the rate of homicide compensation ever varied as much as this.

dress his hair or wear any ornaments.

In past times sanctuary was taken for six months in the house of the 'Kwar Mon'.

After this period has elapsed the Kujur and family of deceased meet and arrange the amount of blood money to be paid.

If death has not been the result of a Shen feud the family of the murderer will also be present.

Blood money decided on is paid and the two families then gather for payment of the first peace offering called 'Yang Toka' [*yang tuoke*] (lit. the cow of the drinking vessel).

The two families face each other and relatives of deceased assume a warlike manner. The Kujur then produces a bull 'Yang Ketha' which is his own and for which he receives a fee and holds it between the two parties. The bull is then speared by both families; after which a member of each family holds on to one side of the leg bone of the bull.

The Kujur cuts the bone through in the centre and the families gather together and cook and eat the meat and drink the urine found in the bladder of the bull out of a bowl made from the root of the 'Kuk' tree [*Acacia veruga*].

The 'Yang Toka' with a calf is then handed to the relatives of deceased and the families may again meet in friendship.

Payment of the second peace offering may not be made till years after the first.

This is a cow called 'Yang Pal Loid' [*yang pale loic*] (lit. cow of the eased heart) presumably intending to mean a clear conscience on the part of all concerned and payment is carried out as follows:-

After prearrangement relatives of deceased steal the cow from the murderer's family, who then approach as if for war.

Should proceedings be carried out without a hitch and there is to be no continuation of a blood feud which may be the case even after payment of blood money, the holders of the cow will cut the tail of the animal until it bleeds, when the relatives of the murderer will retire.

This is a final ending of the feud between the parties.[43]

Burial

Burial of a person is done by a friend of the family on payment of a bull as fee.

To bury a person without receiving a fee is believed to mean death and for this reason no Gaweir will bury an unknown body found in the bush.

No man will bury a relative.

---

43. Cf. Evans-Pritchard 1940: 172–6; 1956: 107–12, 293–7; and Howell 1954: 44–8. Ritual atonement takes place whether or not the murderer is 'penitent'. *Ruath kethe* (the bull of the gall-bladder) is sacrificed at the end of the ceremony; the *yang tuoke* is one of two *ghok pale loic*, the other being the *yang cak* (cow of the milk) which is given to the dead man's mother. The payment of the *ghok pale loic* was abolished by the Nuer Chiefs' Council in 1947 (Howell 1954: 65).

The grave of an adult is made by the door of his hut; in the case of children, inside the hut.

The body is placed in the grave feet first with the arms clasped together and tied and the knees drawn up and tied in this position to the body.

Initiation

Every boy on reaching the age of puberty undergoes an initiatory ceremony, after which he is considered to have attained manhood and enjoys the privileges of an adult.

The ceremony is an occasion for much feasting and dancing on the part of the boy's Shen.

The boy or boys to be initiated are put through an ordeal said to make them insensible to pain.

A small pit is dug in the ground by which the boy reclines at full length placing his head over the pit.

An elder of the Shen whose duty it is to carry out this operation then makes six incisions across the boy's forehead stretching from left temple to right, the blood being allowed to flow into the pit.

If the boy is the last child to be born by his mother seven incisions are made.

Cattle dung ash is rubbed into the wounds, the scars of which are visible afterwards practically during a lifetime.

The boy is then placed in a hut alone or in company with other initiates and remains segregated for a period of fifteen days or more if the wounds have not healed by that time.

During this seclusion he is only allowed out of the hut for about half an hour after sunset, food is taken him by his mother or by an old woman but he may be seen by no other women.

The boy's release is followed by more festivities and he will then take the name of his favourite bull or father's bull, which name becomes his war cry in time of war.

An adult Gaweir may not milk cattle or grind corn.

It is said that a man who milks his own cow will die and a man who grinds corn will lose the use of both his arms.

Boys initiated within a period of six to twelve years belong to the same class or sect and bear the name of that class.

The Chief Kujur living decides the time for founding and the name of the new class.[44]

Originally the class or sect of a period was said to be common to the sub-tribes of Nuers.

With Gaweir the last class was founded by Chief Dwal Diu, and named

---

44. This is normally the prerogative of the leading *wut ghok* (man of cattle). Among the Gaawar there is no separate *wut ghok* lineage, and both Deng Laka and Dual Diu were involved in the initiation of age-sets.

Pilwal, lit. the world of water [in fact, 'red water'] after the floods of that year.[45]

This class has an alternative name 'Goog', this being the name of the Kujur spirit possessed by Dwal in that year as distinct from his father's spirit 'Diu'.

All class names being significant of a particular event in the lives of the community at the time or being named after some Kujur spirit or his totem.

The following are the classes for the past 85 years:-[46]

Class or sect	Probable date	
Pi Lwal or Goog	1916	[*c.* 1922]
Dal [*sic*] [Yaal]	1906	[*c.* 1900]
Lier	?	[*c.* 1896]
Dang	?	[*c.* 1880]
Lailek	?	[*c.* 1870]
Wor [Wuor]	?	[*c.* 1860]
Thut	?	[*c.* 1850]
Lajak	?	
Tharfi	1838	

Men of Lailek may not marry the daughters of other men of the same sect.

Inter-marriage between Lier and Dang was forbidden till 1922 when Chief Dwal Diu is said to have received a Kujur spirit visitation and after sacrifice of a bull this was no longer forbidden.[47]

No woman may refuse to have intercourse with a man of the Lailek sect.

Men of the same sect are forbidden to have blood feuds, though in a Shen fight members of the same sect may be at war with one another.

In war with another tribe members of a sect must stand by each other to the death.

Kujur

The name for a Kujur 'Kot' [*kuoth*] meaning God may refer to a living person or a spirit.

All Kujurs are said to receive their powers from heaven where the existence of a supreme 'Kot' is believed in.

Kujurs may be hereditary or acquired and may have supernatural powers or may be without power.

45. *Pilual* (red water) was named after the flood of the same name, which occurred in 1916–19. The age-set's initiation was delayed by the flood, and it was not marked until 1920–1, just before Coriat arrived in Ayod.

46. The alternate dates given in brackets are calculated by relating the initiation of age-sets to datable events such as floods, battles or the deaths of famous persons. Coriat omits Karam, a set coming between Yaal and Pilual, marked by Macar Diu between 1908 and 1913.

47. This may be what lies behind a later allegation that prophets gave dispensations from the rule of clan exogamy (Willis 1928: 201), though in fact this pronouncement, while possibly concerning incest, has nothing to do with clans.

A Kujur in one man may consist of occasional fits or spiritual visitation while another Kujur may have the power to cause or heal sickness, to produce or stop rain or to cause death or permanent injury to a person.

Charms or potions are used as a medium for carrying out these practices.[48]

Charms given for protection against certain illnesses generally consist of the dried up roots of herbs or trees or pieces of bone.

All Kujurs are possessed of their own totem or totems in the form of a living animal or some inanimate object.[49]

Malakal
10.7.23

Percy Coriat
Asst. District Commissioner
Lau and Gaweir

---

48. Charms, or *wal*, were instruments of the magician (*guan wal*), not the prophet (*guk kuoth*).
49. Cf. Evans-Pritchard on totems (1956: 77–90) and Howell 1953*b*.

Document 1.3

TRANSFER OF BARR GAWEIR TO ZERAF VALLEY DISTRICT

In 1923 the Lou Nuer were added to Coriat's district, and in 1924 he transferred his headquarters to Abwong. The Radh Gaawar, who lived mainly on the Zeraf island and along the banks of the Bahr el-Zeraf, were under the jurisdiction of the Zeraf Valley District, with its headquarters at Fangak. By 1925 the difficulties of splitting the Gaawar between two districts and administering the Bar from Abwong were evident. In January 1926 Coriat handed the Bar over to Fangak and henceforth confined himself to the Lou and their immediate Dinka neighbours along the Sobat and Khor Fulluth. This handing-over note is a description of Bar Gaawar administration between 1923 and 1926. While it contains much of the same information as document 1.2, it also gives a wealth of personal and administrative detail not found there. It uses the same numbering for the Gaawar sections, and the section of each chief is indicated by a number in parentheses.

District Commissioner[1]
Zeraf Valley
Fangak

I attach a list of Barr Gaweir Shens, Chiefs and the more important villages.

---

1. G. S. Pletts: see above, Introduction, n. 5.

Tribute

The assessment of each Shen is given on the attached list of Shens. Each Sub-shen Chief is responsible for his tribute. Since the D.C. has been living at Abwong, only tribute durra has been taken to Ayod Post and the majority of tribute cattle were collected at Chiefs Dwal Diu (9) and Gwer Weoh [Guer Wiu] (27) camps.

With the formation of a Post on the Zeraf[2] I suggest that all Chiefs be made to take their cattle in there.

Durra was accepted at the rate of 2 ardebs to one bull i.e. 4 sacks.

I would suggest that a Policeman be retained at the Post who is able to read and write, not only for the checking of tribute but for sending information to your Headquarters.

You will note that I have given the tribute for the past five years on attached assessment list. A great number of Sub-shens were not registered until 1923.

The assessment is roughly one per cent of cattle [per Shen] and could be very greatly increased if a market for cattle could be obtained. Collection of tribute on present assessment gives no difficulty except with Barr Shens on left bank.

Administration

Barr Gaweir have had some years' experience of Government and there is no question of their being ignorant of Government methods. On the other hand they are a somewhat turbulent sub-tribe and require constant handling.

The greatest difficulty to contend with in the past and a source of trouble to the present day has been the Gaweir-Dinka boundary on the Southern limits of the District. The past history of this section of Gaweir consists of a long list of raids and incursions into Dinka territory and the whole of present Gaweir was originally Dinka country. A short history of these people which may be of some use is contained in the monograph published by the Intelligence Dept. 'Nuers of the Upper Nile Province' by H. C. Jackson.[3] I need only enumerate here the more recent events in Barr. The Diu family now represented by Chief Dwal Diu (9) has been mainly responsible for attacks on Dinkas.

The last raid was in 1916 when the section led by Dwal Diu attacked some of the 'Ol [Ghol] Dinkas and a section of Gaweir (Shen Kan Boi)[4] who having quarrelled with the Diu family at the time of Machar Diu were then living in

2. No additional post was established on the Bahr el-Zeraf to replace Ayod.
3. See doc. 1.2 above.
4. See doc. 1.2 and doc. 2.1 n. 8.

Dinka country near Amiel and Okak.

Since 1916 there have been no actual raids but a certain amount of trouble has been caused by Dinka intrigue and probably provocative acts on the part of the Nuer.

The Diu sections of Barr live on the south end of the Duk ridge, having lived there since the flood years 1916–17.

The ridge has now been deserted by most of the other sections of Gaweir who were living there and is becoming extremely unpopular with Sub-shen Giel (9) on account of its dryness in the dry season and poisonous grass found there in the rains. Sub-shen Giel's camp in the dry season is also situated at great distance from the Duk villages and this also is a reason for this section wishing to evacuate the Duk.

The boundary between the two tribes as it now stands (vide Shen list) was fixed by Government in 1910 after conquest of certain parts of the country by Diu (Deng Liker) [Deng Laka].[5] During the latter part of 1924, Dwal Diu requested permission to remove his villages closer to the Dinka boundary and this permission was granted on the understanding that he did not build in Dinka country. He then built four huts at Wey Tworley [Thorley], the actual position of which has not yet been determined but which was undoubtedly close to the border and possibly over the border [see Fig. 1, in doc. 2.2 below].

Shen Boi with whom there was still enmity were then some few miles south of Wey Tworley and within Dinka limits.

This move had the effect of disturbing the Dinkas and Shen Kan Boi, but there was no actual conflict until in January of 1925 Diu proceeded to cut wood in the forest south of Wey Tworley for the purpose of building more huts. This brought about a conflict with Shen Boi who attacked Dwal Diu's men in the woods and the resulting fight caused the death of two Boi Shensmen. Dwal's people suffered no casualties.

Dwal then stated his intention of living at Amiel, a centre of the Ol Dinkas, and matters became critical between the two tribes. At a meeting in that month between the D.C. Duk Fayuil[6] and Dwal Diu and the Ol Chief Mankweir Mahbub [Moinkuer Mabur][7] a fight was very nearly precipitated and was only prevented by the action of the D.C. Duk Fayuil.

5. For Deng Laka see above, doc. 1.2.

6. Major J. W. G. Wyld.

7. Moinkuer Mabur: Moinkuer's father, Mabur Ajuot, was a former slave, Arabic speaking, and an early ally of the government against the Nuer. He was the leader of Angac Dinka refugees from Awoi living among the Twic. He gained an unsavoury reputation among early administrators as a 'scoundrel' and an intriguer against the Nuer (*SIR* 119 (June 1904), 4; 153 (April 1907), 10). His son Moinkuer, however, made a very different impression on both the government and the Gaawar. He became court president of the Ghol Dinka court in the 1940s and married into the Gaawar (Marwood, 'Handing-over Notes on Bor 1938', NRO UNP 1/51/3; 'Upper Nile Personality Report no. 45', NRO UNP 1/34/276). In 1957 Dual Diu married one of Moinkuer's daughters.

The following month it became necessary to define the boundary and definitely settle the limits of the two tribes and for this purpose the D.C.'s Abwong and Duk Fayuil accompanied by Chiefs Dwal Diu and Mankweir Mahbub and other Nuer and Dinka Chiefs and Shensmen made a joint tour along the line of the boundary. Actual geographical positions were not known owing to the lack of instruments and this will require to be done in 1927 but a satisfactory division was made between the two people and Dwal Diu was forbidden as also Gaweir to proceed south of Wey Borley or Kungleir. It was also decided to order the evacuation of Shen Boi from the Dinka territory to prevent any possible cause of jealousy on the part of Gaweir and huts occupied by this section were burnt. Ground between Wey Borley and Okak was made a no-man's land. Wey Thorley is situated equally distant between these two places and building on this site was forbidden.[8]

During my recent tour of Gaweir last month Dwal again opened up the question of Wey Thorley and as I am convinced he has no desire to raid Dinkas now and is only anxious to find a good site for his villages, the matter was discussed with the Governor and District Commissioner Duk Fayuil but it was decided that the boundary was to stand.

Dwal himself if able to control his young men will not give trouble unless provoked,[9] it is however necessary to watch the border. The question of a new site for his Shen will have to be decided in 1927. There are few sites left which are considered suitable by Nuers, the main questions to be considered in choosing sites of villages being in order of importance, good grass in the rains, not liable to flood, availability of timber for building etc. and closeness to dry season 'Toich'.

Shen Boi who have not yet been taxed by this District, having had cattle plague in the last season are now settled at Awoi and Fasheir [Pacier] and should be concentrated at Awoi in 1927 if possible. Dwal Diu has stated his readiness to pay the blood money for the ten men of Shen Boi killed by his Shen and a Court should be held in 1927 for the purpose of settling this feud. Unless this is done, the feud is likely to break out again and I have found blood feuds to be the greatest obstacle in the way of peaceable administration.

Two separate Shen fights occurred during the past dry season and it is of the utmost importance that my orders given to the men concerned are carried out if the fights are not to develop into feuds and if there is to be continuity of policy.

A drunken brawl between sub-shens Gaing (6) and Turwo (8) on the one side and Bedeed (1) on the other resulted in a few casualties and I instructed the Shensmen that hurt payments should be made. I intended seeing this

8. See below, doc. 2.1.

9. This assessment was justified by the events of 1928 (see above, Introduction; also Wedderburn-Maxwell 1928; Wyld 1928; Dual Diu 1930; Gaawar texts 4.8, in Johnson, in preparation.

done in January 1927. None of the Chiefs were responsible and any further developments would be caused entirely by young men. The two Shensmen chiefly responsible are Jor Majug [Majok] and Pod Wi.

I had both these men before me and warned them, so if you wish to go further into the matter, the presence of these two men is essential. Jor Majug lives at Fankor, near Ayod and is a son of a surly individual named Majug Jwai [Majok Juc, Kulang Majok's father]. Pod Wi is a married man living at Fasheir.

A quarrel between Shens Diow (10) and Nyabiel (19) over an elephant hunt resulted in a most aggressive action on the part of Shen Diow. Shen Nyabiel are under Chief Riek On (19) but are controlled by Chief Gwer Weoh (27) who lives at Tongruop [district of] Rufshendol [Rupciengdol].

Gwer is the most efficient and loyal Chief in Gaweir.[10] This Chief was away with me on trek at the time of the incident but owing to his influence in the Shen and the presence of his brothers Shen Nyabiel refused to be drawn into a fight.

Shen Diow are a very small sub-shen living at Konthod near Rufshendol and have been somewhat neglected in the past owing to their unimportance and have never previously given trouble. I believe the sub-shen has been strengthened by being joined by a number of young men from Khandak of the Shen Raz sections. The Chief one Wol Thod is a very old and useless person and had the Shen been of any importance would have been superseded. The Shen bolted on my arrival at Konthod last month and not having the time at my disposal I was unable to deal with them. Two cows and calves belonging to the section which had been given to a Shen Dol man to hide were confiscated. The Shen I believe bolted in the direction of Shwai. All except two cattle huts belonging to old men were burnt. I give below the names of the men who require to be dealt with and suggest that if possible they be given a small term of imprisonment and a small fine imposed on the Shen. It is possible that if they think you are aware of their behaviour they will produce a fine on their own account, I should however refuse this and insist on the young men appearing before you as well as a fine being paid.

Shen Diow
Men chiefly concerned in attack on Shen Nyabiel:

    Chung Dar and son Dol
    Yey Gega and sons Garwey and Fakey
    Pui Nuot
    Yuol Duop
    Bul Rial
    Bul Wuth
    Wieh Yan

---

10. Guer Wiu: see above, doc. 1.2, note f to table entitled 'Gaweir Shens'.

Mabil Kul
Duop Nuot
Wey Yi
Pui Deng

Some of these men have the following relatives in Rufshendol with Shen Dol.

Shwol Gwath
Mud Dum
Mud Thuk Wuth a most unpleasant type of individual living with Juzz Thai of Fateng [district of] Rufshendol.

The Shen list includes the names of places where Shens camp in the dry season.

The Lau Shen under Chief Fod Gig [Puot Gig][11] occasionally camp in the Gaweir toich with Dwal Diu.

The great majority of camps are situated in the swamps south of Fasheir.

Barr Gaweir is workable from the middle of December to the end of June.

Distances

Tithbel–Fakwaz [Fakwak]	3 hours
Fakwaz–Rufshendol	3 ..
Rufshendol–Luang Deng	5 ..
Luang Deng–Bo [Biau]	4 ..
Bo–Fankor [Fankur]	4 ..
Fankor–Ayod	2 ..
Ayod–Agum	3 ..
Agum–Wau	2 ..
Wau–Shwai [Cwih]	6 ..
Shwai–Buingfor [Buonyfuot]	2 ..
Buingfor–Rufshendol	5 ..
Rufshendol–Konthod	1 ..
Rufshendol–Fasheir	2 ..
Fasheir–Awoi	4 ..
Awoi–Juai	4 ..

11. Puot Gig: see below, doc. 1.5. Puot and his section were settled on territory judged to belong to the Ghol Dinka when the tribal boundary was fixed in 1910. He moved to Gaawar country after that. He was active in trying to prevent a Nuer–Dinka fight in 1910. He had marriage connections among the Dinka, and used these to gain access to Dinka pastures (G. B. Wahab to governor UNP, 29.06.10, SRO UN GOV CRR 34 1910; L. Tunnard, inspector Bor to governor Mongalla, 01.06.13, SRO UNP SCR 14).

Juai–Luang Deng	5 hours
Awoi–Kungleir	3 ..
Kungleir–Wey Borley	1 ..
Wey Borley–Dongayo	3 ..
Wey Borley–Wey Thorley	1 ..
Dongayo–Duk Fadiat	4 ..
Dongayo–Gool [Gul]	4 ..
Gool–Turwo [Turu]	3 ..
Turwo–Dongayo (via Fagwor, Lou village)	5 ..
Turwo–Fadau	½ hour
Fadau–Dorweng	3 hours
Dorweng–Ayod	2 ..
Wey Borley–Ajwong	? common route
Ajwong–Fasheir	4 hours

The village of Luang Deng commonly known to the Nuers as 'Luak Kwoth' (House of God) is a Dinka village as is also Shwai. These Dinkas belong to the Rut group and are under an old man called Deng Gwir [Aguer]. These are the remnants of the Dinkas who originally lived in Gaweir and were not expelled from the country owing to the magical properties possessed by the hereditary Kujur of Deng Gwir's family. Luak Kwoth is the hut in which the spirit is said to repose and all elephant tusks are kept in this hut and not sold or otherwise disposed of until the spirit through the medium of Deng Gwir orders the manner of their disposal. The ground surrounding the hut is sacred and must not be defiled with refuse etc. Deng is a pleasant old man and seems quite lacking in guile. I can only surmise that he believes he has visitations by the spirit etc. This village is much revered by Nuers as well as Dinkas.[12]

A small section of Dinkas live at Awoi, the eastern end of which is known as Fadicher [Padicier] under Manyel Koi.

Awoi has increased during the past season and the sections will require to be assessed and made to pay their tribute separately unless they return to their own sections. The following live at Awoi:

Angai [Angac] Dinkas
Shen Boi (the greater part of Shen Boi. Cattle Luaks not yet built as Shen only recently arrived from Dinka country. Vide above.)
Shen Shodgwar (a few families only)
Shen Marinyang (most Marinyang families live here)
Shen Rut (really a section of Shen Bedeed (1) but should now be made to pay separately under Jok Dthor)

12. For Luang Deng, see Howell 1948 and 1961; also Struvé in Matthews 1907. Deng Aguer had been the caretaker since the last quarter of the nineteenth century. He was succeeded by his nephew Raak Yaak in the early 1930s.

The most convenient starting point for the Gaweir camps on the southern part of the Toich is Fasheir; the line of the swamp being easily followed from this village.

Game

Tiang, waterbuck, roan, cob, reedbuck, Mrs. Gray [antelope], buffalo, elephant, giraffe, Dik-Dik, rufifrons, oribi are all common particularly in the country south of Fasheir. Zebra are sometimes seen south-east of Awoi in the direction of the Toich.

Firearms

There has been a very great increase in firearms and consequently in the slaughter of game.

There is an increasing use of firearms at dances etc. and injuries in recent fights have been caused by rifle as well as spear.

Trading parties come from the Garjak [Gaajak] country generally in December and January.

Ivory is the only commodity in the arms trade.

Dwal Diu's camp has by far the greater number of arms.

During the past three years I have attempted a registration of sorts by confiscating any rifle which is not produced to me for registration, but this is an extremely slow method and has no effect on the traffic. Arms have been presented to a few responsible Chiefs.[13]

Further information is contained in the Shen and tribute lists and I should be glad to answer any questions regarding any other points you may think of.

The young men have been inclined to be [a] little unruly during the past few months owing to my absence the greater part of the year and consequent looser control. The Shen Raz Tiang [Thiang] fight during May on an old tribal scale also disturbed the Barr section and action will have to be taken before

13. A meeting of DCs at Akobo in March 1926 discussed the problem of firearms in the province. There was concern about the general increase of firearms in the rural areas, the increase in the slaughter of elephants, and the appearance of rifles in marriage payments. Since a general disarming of the population could be achieved only by force, a step all agreed could not be taken, no firm conclusions on the control of arms were reached ('Notes on a Meeting Held at Akobo, 2nd March 1926', NRO Civsec 1/2/6). The Gaawar were disarmed only during the campaigns of 1928–9.

they can realise that Government policy is to discourage violence in the way of Shen fights.

Shen Lists

1. Sub-shen Bedeed. Shen Bang. 2 bulls tribute.

A strong sub-shen under Wan Tyeir [see Plate 3] living at Fasheir. Wan has several sons, one of whom Koryom is living near Dongayo and is Chief of 2. Wan Tyeir is a pleasant old man but has no great control of the section. Tribute is paid without demur. Vide Administration [above in this document] the fight in May last with 6 and 8 must not be allowed to develop into a Shen feud.

Fasheir is a very large village or group of villages.

Cattle camp is generally situated on the Khor Gurr or swamps to the south.

A group of this sub-shen live at Awoi.

2. Sub-shen Bedeed (sub) Shen Bang. 1 bull tribute.

A small section of 1. living at Dongayo near the Dinka border. Chief Koryom Wan son of Chief of 1. Sub-shen originally under Koryom's brother Pong, a Kujur who died in 1924.

Dongayo contains a few Dinkas and a large number of huts were built there in 1926. It is doubtful whether these Dinkas pay tribute and the village should be assessed and reorganised in 1927, preferably jointly with the D.C. Duk Fayuil.

Cattle camp generally with or near 1.

3. Sub-shen Marinyang. Shen Bang. 2 bulls tribute.

A somewhat scattered sub-shen under Dol Bul.

Most of the Shensmen live in the eastern part of Awoi. Dol has a hut at Awoi and also at Fasheir. His sons, three in number live at Fasheir. Dol Bul is an old man with good control but is inclined to be lazy over tribute collection. The youngest son, Kai is by far the most intelligent and should make a useful Chief. Cattle camp on Khor Gurr area. Awoi is a very large village, containing in addition to Marinyang, families of Shodgwar (13) and 1. and some Angaich [Angac] Dinkas. This sub-shen and the Dinkas are responsible for upkeep of huts at Awoi telegraph Post, having built the huts in 1926 in lieu of paying tribute and the cost £E.15. paid by Irrigation Dept. credited to their tribute. In future they should be made to keep the huts in repair without any reduction of their tribute. Awoi contains a telegraph Post (site known to the Nuers as Fadicher being slightly west of Awoi) with a few linesmen and in the dry season of 1927 will probably also be opened as a telegraph Post to assist Irrigation parties working in the Zeraf area.

4. Sub-shen Tod. Shen Bang. 1 bull tribute.

A sub-shen under Chief Diu Bang, a strong and useful individual closely allied to the Diu family (9) though no relative. The sub-shen is divided into two groups, that under Diu Bang and the branch under Fol Twop (5).

Diu and his section originally lived at Kwaideng near Turwo, but owing to the unpopularity of the Duk ridge now, have removed to Wey Borley on the southern border (Vide Administration). A few families only remain at Kwaideng, though the crops of this section are grown chiefly at this village.

5. A small section of 5. under Fol Twop [Pol Tuop] living at Ajwong. 1 bull tribute. Section has only about 10 Luaks.

Fol Twop is very shy of Government but is considered a wiseacre by the Nuers (not a Kujur) and cases are often taken before him independently. I liked this man considerably after I got to know him. Cattle camp in Ajwong area.

6. Sub-shen Gaing. Shen Bang. 3 bulls tribute.

A strong Shen under Kor Juol, a very old but strong spirited Chief. Kor has several sons, one of whom Shwol [Cuol] is a great elephant hunter and has very considerable control over the section. He has however aversion to working for Government and has to be strongly handled. If the old Chief dies Shwol Kur must not be allowed to slide into the background.[14] Vide 1. re possible feud.

Cattle camp in the Akair area south of Awoi.

Kor and the greater part of the sub-shen live at Bo near Fankor and Shwol lives with other families at Juai. Shwol has great respect for his father and obeys him implicitly. A few of the section live at Fankor, which produces the best crops.

7. Sub-shen Shamarn. Shen Bang. 1 bull tribute.

Living at a small village called Wunlang an hour's march from Rufshendol to the south east. An unimportant group of families under a young and rather deceitful Chief one Kwajeng Ton.

Cattle camp on the Gurr and Gurwel areas.

8. Sub-shen Turwo. Shen Bang. 1 bull tribute.

Chief Diu Kun. Old and very useless. Has a lazy son called Malith. Living on the north east side of Fasheir, actual village known as Kwelek, though all part of Fasheir. A small section with many truculent youngsters. Vide 1. re possible feud.

9. Sub-shen Giel. Shen Gamok. 4 bulls tribute.

A powerful section under Chief Dwal Diu (vide Administration).

Dwal received a Sword of Honour in 1924.

Villages at present on the Duk ridge at Buk, Turwo, Kwaideng, Fagil, Fagul

---

14. Cuol Kur was eventually appointed sub-chief of *cieng* Bang and became executive chief of the Awoi B court in 1948. He was variously described by DCs as 'a thorough gentleman but lacks drive', or 'one of the best sub-chiefs and has much influence'. He was generally praised for his intelligence (Upper Nile Province 'Who's Who', UNP archives, Malakal, SCR 66.D.4). His father, Kur Juol, was reputed to have owned magic ('Supernatural', n.d. [c. 1937], SRO ZVD 66.K.1).

and cattle camp on the southern swamps close to the Dinka border.

Dwal himself lives at Turwo.

Gau Bang, a brother of Dwal lives at Fagul and has a good influence over Dwal. Another brother Biel has the reverse.[15]

Ruob Gyark [Ruop Joak] an ex-U.N.P. Policeman lives at Fagul.[16] This man had considerable influence over Dwal but is now out of the limelight. This man will have to be watched and handled without the slightest compassion. He is also a great liar.

10. Sub-shen Diow. Shen Gamok [Jamogh]. 1 bull tribute.

Village Konthod. Chief Wol Thod, a kindly old man will require to be superseded. Wol has no sons. Vide remarks under Administration.

11. Sub-shen Fod. Shen Gamok. 2 bulls tribute.

Under a young Chief Riek Yor related to Dwal Diu. Riek has not much control but can be handled with the assistance of Chief Gwer Weoh (27).

Village at Agum on the Duk ridge. Section also lives in small villages close to Agum.

The sub-shen contains two very truculent and unpleasant brothers one of whom was a wanted criminal for two years and who gave me a great deal of trouble before I was able to arrest him. These men (Lam referred to above) and Luang Yor should be watched. The sub-shen had rather bad cattle plague in 1925 but the tribute could be increased to three bulls without being felt. Cattle camp, either with 9. or just off the Duk ridge in the Lau country to the east, where wells are dug for water supply. The brothers Yor generally remain near Agum and seldom go to the Toich.

12. Sub-shen Maen.[17] Shen Sharm [Cam]. 2 bulls tribute.

A strong section whose Chief Fatai Juol was replaced owing to his old age by his nephew Pui Yir.

---

15. Biel Diu acted as Dual's intermediary when the family made peace with the government in August 1918 (see above, doc. 1.2 n. 22). He made a very favourable impression on officials from both Upper Nile and Mongalla Provinces. See J. Stevenson-Hamilton, inspector Bor District, to governor Mongalla, 03.09.18, and W. Pollen, inspector Lau & Gaweir, 'Report on a Visit to Buk on the Duk (Dwal Diu's Ballad)', both in UNP archives, Malakal, SCR 14.A; also MPMIR December 1918, NRO Intel 2/48/408 and SRO TD SCR 36.H.2. Gau Bang became the leader of the Bar Gaawar after Dual's arrest and exile in 1930. Though elected court president of the Bar Court in 1939, he saw himself merely as standing in for Dual. He died on 15 June 1948, some nine years before Dual finally returned home ('Upper Nile Province Personality Report no. 136', NRO UNP 1/34/276). Also see below, docs. 2.1 and 3.4.

16. Ruop Joak was killed in the aftermath of the Duk Fayuil raid in 1928 (see Gaawar texts 4.8, in Johnson, in preparation; and ADC Fangak to governor Upper Nile Province, 27.10.28, NRO Civsec 5/3/12). See also below, doc. 2.1.

17. *Cieng* Maen ('cinamin' or 'Shin Min' in early government reports) was the first Gaawar section to resist tribute collection in 1913, just before Macar Diu's rising (Bimbashi Tweedie, inspector Zeraf Valley to governor, Upper Nile Province, 16 June 1913 and 28 June 1913, SRO UNP SCR 14.2).

Pui has plenty of spirit but a wild group to deal with. Previous to 1923 these people had never paid tribute and it was only after I had taken strong measures that tribute was brought in. Owing to their being on the left bank Zeraf the section has been a little neglected.

Village Wan (L.B.) cattle camp in Swamps to west or on Khor by village.

This section is repeatedly having incidents with 15. who live on the opposite side of the river, but there is no feud between them.

13. Sub-shen Shodgwar. Shen Sharm. 3 bulls tribute.

Originally under Nyang Machar,[18] a Chief of very independent spirit who died in 1924, this section is composed of a number of unruly young men. On Nyang's death a younger son Giey was appointed Chief but although still responsible for tribute Giey is living away from his brothers at Kungleir having quarrelled with the family over division of their father's riches. Giey is a pleasant lad and far in advance of an elder brother Jwoi.[19]

The sub-shen lives at Gool just west of the Duk ridge, a few families being at Kungleir and Awoi.

This section is apt to give trouble and are constantly moving to and fro.

Cattle camp generally in the Akair area on Khor Gurr and other tributaries.

14. Sub-shen Korar. Shen Sharm. 3 bulls tribute.

Chief Bedak Ling, an old man. Chag Lam is acting Chief, Bedak's young son Mut being quite unsuitable.

The section is fairly strong and lives at Kungleir on the Dinka border. Cattle camp due west of Kungleir on the Khors.

15. A sub-section of 14. of fairly large families under a strong and useful Chief Mud Gien living at Ajwong on the Zeraf. Tribute 2 bulls.

16. Sub-shen Shuk [Cuk]. Shen Dol. 2 bulls tribute.

Under Deng Biey and living in the quarter of Rufshendol known as Torkey.

This section assisted Government in the capture of Fathot Shakweng [Pathot Cakuen] who was responsible for the murder of a merchant in 1924. Fathot was actually shot by a relative of his, living with this section at the time and since removed to the Tiang country, consequently the relations between this section and Fathot's section 18. are somewhat strained. The question of Fathot's blood money was raised but was naturally disallowed, Fathot being a criminal outlaw at the time of his death.[20]

Cattle camp on the Khor Gurwel.

17. Sub-shen Boz or Buth. Shen Dol. 1 bull tribute.

A very small section under Wal Kir living at Rufshendol in the village known as Nurborau.

---

18. See above, doc. 1.1, and doc. 1.2 n. 14.
19. See above, doc. 1.1.
20. See above, Introduction.

Cattle camp generally with 19. on the Gurwel.

18. Sub-shen Ruol. Shen Dol. 3 bulls tribute.

Living at Jongshol. Rufshendol. Chief Bang Shakweng appointed on the death of his father Shakweng Jok.

Shakweng died in 1924 while in prison when his son Fathot was outlawed.[21] Fathot was mortally wounded by a Shensman of 16. and died after being captured by the Government. Bang Shakweng is a useful young Chief and realises that the question of his brother's blood money cannot be raised but some of the young Shensmen are inclined to resent sub-shen Shuk's action.

Camp at Gurwel.

19. Nyabiel. Shen Dol. Tribute 3 bulls.

Under Chief Riek On nominally, practically run by Chief Gwer Weoh (27) who is also largely responsible for the whole of Shen Dol.

Cattle camp on the Gurwel and village Tongruop. Gwer Weoh also lives at Tongruop with his brothers. (Vide Administration re affair with sub-shen Diow (10).)

20 (Kur) 21 (Thoi) 22 (Kwad) 23 (Yey) all non existent and dispersed among Shen Dol.

Shen Riah	24. Sub-shen Malair village Temrol left bank Zeraf	All under Thalil Dah and all Shen Riah
	25. .. .. Garlied .. Kot	
	26. .. .. Gok .. Ngol	

Thalil is an old man and the Shen is somewhat ungetable, moving in the dry season towards the Nuong [Nyuong] swamps. Tribute is seldom brought in voluntarily and the Shen has much in common with the Nuong.[22] Requires more visiting than other Barr sections, but gives no trouble. Owing to very loose administration assessed at 3 bulls tribute for whole Shen.

27. Sub-shen Long. Shen Garkwar. Tribute 2 bulls.

Under Chief Gwer Weoh, awarded Sword of Honour 1926. This Chief is the most enlightened and useful Chief in Gaweir and was chiefly responsible for the submission of certain Shens after the Gaweir patrol in 1914 and for the information which led to the arrests of Leil Luflug [Lel Lublub] (murderer of Shan Rad [Cany Reth] (Faragalla Buluk Amin))[23] in Dok and Fathot Shakweng (murderer of merchant Ibrahim Hassan). The section lived on the Duk ridge at Bul and Wonkwil and also at Buingfor on the Tithbel-Ayod road, but Gwer himself lives at Rufshendol. He also has a Luak at Buk.

This section also has a few families at Fakwaz and at Fangak (near Luang Deng).

21. See above, Introduction, and doc. 1.2.

22. See above, doc. 1.2.

23. See above, doc. 1.2 notes 26 and 27.

One Juz Thai of 19. is extremely jealous of Gwer's authority and is an individual who requires watching.

28. Sub-shen Nyeir. Shen Garkwar. Tribute 3 bulls.

Living at Maleet on the left bank Zeraf. Chief Lief Gaing [Liep Gany]. Lief has little authority but is able to produce his tribute when reminded by Gwer (27). This section has much in common with Dok and Nuong. Trouble occasionally with 15.

29. Sub-shen Koh. Shen Garkwar. Tribute 1 bull.

A left bank section who were under Diu Bar. Since his death I have been unable to visit the Sub-shen and appoint a new Chief. The group is small and scattered. I suggest Lain Dar, a nephew of Diu to be appointed.

27. have their cattle camp at Gurwel and 28. and 29. in the left bank swamps.

Above completes the list of the 29 sub-shens of Barr Gaweir. The following information may be of use for 1927:

One Wan Kwoth [Wuon Kuoth], said to be a Chief of Dok has visited Fasheir and will probably settle there.[24] D.C. Nuong[25] informed.

Several Nuong and Dok are living with Shen Riah and sub-shens Nyeir and Maen.

1. paid the one tribute bull for 2. in 1926, therefore 2. will pay one of 1.'s bulls in 1927.

Shen Diow (10) may possibly try and settle with the Dinkas at Shwai; if so they must be ferreted out.

Shen Boi (vide Administration) are under Lam Kan son of the late Kan Boi.[26] These people have not yet been listed.

Dinkas at Awoi are under Manyel Koi.

Dinkas at Shwai and Luang Deng are under Deng Gwir and pay 2 bulls tribute (Rut section Dinkas).

---

24. See below, doc. 4.1 n. 27.

25. Captain V. H. Fergusson: see above, Introduction, n. 4.

26. Kan Boi, who first fled to the Angac Dinka of Mabur Ajuot, died in c. May 1922 (MPMIR May 1922, NRO Intel 2/48/408 and SRO TD SCR 36.H.2). His son Lam became the main negotiator with the Gaawar in 1925 and was persuaded by the government to return to his old home. See below, doc. 2.1 n. 5.

Settlement of Gaweir Nuer Duk Fadiat boundary 1910

At Wirfwoi on 13.3.10 by Struvé, Owen and Fox.[27]

The [Lou] Nuers were ordered to move East of Khor Fulus [Fulluth].

The Gaweir were definitely confirmed in possession of territories captured by Diu.

The Ol and Angai Dinkas were repatriated.

Struvé wrote—

> I therefore request that no application for a Southern move on the part of Luaj [Luac], Thoi and Duar [Duor] Dinkas[28] ever be considered unless when confidence and complete tranquillity shall have been restored it may be possible to allow Dinkas and Nuers to live together in the Duk and Awoi territory by mutual consent. Bimb. Fox was to complete the exact delimitation of the boundary which runs west of the Khor Kabaij and East to the Khor Fulus. North of this line the Gaweir Nuers retain all the country which they have made use of since Diu's invasion.

Owen wrote—

> We decided to make the boundary from the West Fula on Khor Kabaij and thence in a line parallel with the meridian to Kh. Fulus we tied a long pole from bough to bough of the prominent Higlig trees [*Balanites aegyptiaca*] about two miles North of Duk Fadiat to fix the boundary. The representative of Machar [Macar Diu][29] was entirely satisfied with the boundary.

The East to West boundary line approximately is as follows: Mankwaka–Fatitet–Juat–Fanyok–Warawar–and Duk Warawar.

This was settled in 1918 by Godwin and Stevenson-Hamilton.[30] In 1925 by Wyld and Coriat, the village of Wey Borley was fixed as the most southerly point in Gaweir and Okak as the most northerly in Dinka territory.[31] The country in between which includes a site known as Wey Thorley was proclaimed a No-man's land.

---

27. K. C. P. Struvé: see above, Introduction, n. 9. Lt.-Colonel R. C. R. Owen CMG, OBE: governor Mongalla Province 1908–18. Captain C. V. Fox, junior inspector Mongalla Province 1910–13.

28. The Luac, Thoi and Duor Dinka were then living on the Khor Fulluth, to the north of the Gaawar. As part of the Nuer Settlement of 1928–9 attempts were made to repatriate them to Ghol and Nyareweng country (see below, docs. 1.5, 2.2).

29. Macar Diu: see above, doc. 1.2 n. 21. A more complete account of the border settlement will be found in Struvé 1909, Wahab 1910, Owen 1910, O'Sullivan 1910.

30. Bimbashi C. C. Godwin, second inspector UNP (Nyerol) 1917–18. Bimbashi J. Stevenson-Hamilton, second inspector Mongalla Province (Bor) 1916–19. The border settlement took place in June 1918 (*SIR* 288 (July 1918), 2).

31. See below, doc. 2.1.

DOCUMENT 1.3

BARR TRIBUTE
(Figures alone refer to number of bulls)

No.	1922	1923	1924	1925	1926	Remarks	Asst.
1.	1	2	2	2	2	very light	2
2.	nil	2	2	1	1	light	1
3.	1	2	2	2 (in durra)	2	..	2
4.	1	2	2	2	2	.. 1 to be collected	2
5.	nil	1	1	1	1	medium	1
6.	2	1275 rtls durra	2 & 600 rtls durra	2000 rtls durra	1 & 1200 rtls durra	..	3
7.	nil	1	1	1	1	light	1
8.	..	1	1	1	1	..	1
9.	2	1 & 1650 rtls durra	1 & 1200 rtls durra	4	4	light?	4
10.	nil	1	1	1	1	medium	1
11.	2	1 & 1200 rtls durra	1 & 800 rtls durra	1 & 1000 rtls durra	1 & 1200 rtls durra	medium	2
12.	nil	2	1	2	2	light	2
13.	2	1500 rtls durra	1 & 1200 rtls durra	2 & 900 rtls durra	1800 rtls durra	medium	3
14.	1	3	3	3	3	..	3
15.	nil	2	2	2	2	medium?	2
16.	1	2	2	2	2	medium	2
17.	nil	1	1	1	1	..	1
18.	3	3	3	3	3	..	3
19.	3	3	3	3	3	..	3
20, 21, [22], 23	nil nil	nil nil	nil nil	nil nil	nil nil		
24. 25. 26.	nil	1	nil	3	2	..	3
27.	1	1200 rtls durra	800 rtls durra	2	1 & 600 durra	..	2
28.	nil	2	2	3	3	..	3
29.	..	1	nil	2	nil	v. light	2
						Total[a]	49 bulls

a. Not including Awoi and Luang Deng Dinkas and Shen Boi [Coriat's own annotation].

4800 rtls durra paid in durra for 1926 according to number of sacks reported paid in by Chiefs to Ayod. Police at Ayod illiterate and correct amount of durra paid unknown but above is probably right therefore cost at 90 P.T. per 300 rtls to be collected equally from four Policemen.

Percy Coriat
ADC
Lau

Malakal
9.7.26

Document 1.4

BLOODWEALTH PAYMENTS

The settling of feuds was the main preoccupation of Nuer administration in the 1920s. This led administrators into the realm of compensatory payments which Nilotes employed in the settlement of feuds. The aim of such payments was to reconcile the parties involved, rather than impose punishment on a guilty party. Nilotic justice was sought through negotiation, rather than through judicial sanctions as practised in the Sudan Penal Code.

Coriat had already given a list of some compensatory payments for hurt, theft, death, etc. He noted that the rates of various payments, whether bridewealth or compensation, were not fixed but varied widely according to a number of circumstances,[1] not the least of which were the availability of cattle and the degree of political and social closeness between the parties involved. In 1926 Coriat, now dealing exclusively with the Lou and their Dinka neighbours, proposed to regularize compensation payments among the Nuer and between adjacent Nuer and Dinka communities. This was the first government attempt to reduce the complexity of compensatory payments. It was not the last, and efforts to expand and reform the principles of compensation continued for over twenty years.[2]

As in document 1.2 we must be cautious about accepting Coriat's reconstruction of what was customary in the past. Here also he presents a much simplified version of the Sudan Penal Code's own definitions of culpable homicide.

It should be noted that in discussing compensation between the Lou and Dinka, Coriat was referring mainly to the Ngok and Nyareweng Dinka, with whom the Lou had intermarried. There were, therefore, a number of active and growing social and economic ties between them. The procedure of payment between the Lou and the Nyareweng and Ngok, which Coriat refers to, had existed before the arrival of the Anglo-Egyptian government in the area.

1. See above, doc. 1.2.

2. Later attempts were aimed more at regularlizing procedure than codifying law for the whole of the Nuer (Howell 1954: 1). See also Johnson 1986a: 75–6.

Coriat's recommendations were accepted by both the governor of Upper Nile Province and the district commissioner of Duk Fayuil District, the Dinka district bordering his.[3] *They formed the basis of the first intertribal court meetings which began the following decade. No standard set of payments for all Nuer districts, as proposed in his final paragraph, was ever introduced, or even seriously considered, by his successors.*

———

Governor
Upper Nile Province
Malakal

I beg to submit for your approval that the following rulings relative to administration in the Nuer and Dinka Districts should be regularised and enforced.

1. Blood money payable between members of the same sub-tribe to be 20 head of cattle for each life.[4]

2. Blood money payable for a member of a different tribe or sub-tribe killed before 1918 to be 10 head of cattle for each life, except when past custom has been to make similar payments to another tribe as for blood payments between members of the same tribe. i.e. LAU and GAWEIR.[5]

3. Blood money payments to be equal for all tribes for all cases after 1918 (flood year) i.e. 20 head of cattle.[6]

4. Causing the death of a person other than in a tribal war or Shen fight to be dealt with under the Penal Code as murder.[7]

5. Action to be taken by Government in all cases of Tribal, Section or Shen fights.

With regard to 1 & 2. These have been in force in this District for the past 18 months and are definitely adhered to in all awards made by Chiefs Courts

---

3. K. C. P. Struvé to district commissioner Duk-Faywil, 10 July 1926, and J. G. Wyld to governor, Upper Nile Province (n.d.), both in SRO BD 66.B.3.

4. Coriat's reduction here is a response to the recent loss of cattle among the Lou and others, as well as for the reason given below. However, in the 1930s the government proposed to keep the bloodmoney rate at its past high level to act as a deterrent to murder. In 1945 the rate was fixed at fifty head of cattle, of which ten were paid to the government (Howell 1954: 63).

5. Evans-Pritchard (1940: 156) noted that where two groups had intermarried extensively compensation was usually agreed on and paid easily. Howell (1954: 24) noted that 'the closer the structural relationship of the parties involved, the more likely is the wrong to be rectified, but the smaller the idemnification required to do so. Conversely, the more remote the relationship the greater the idemnification necessary but the smaller the likelihood that the wrong will be rectified at all.'

6. It was also the year following the 'Lau patrol', after which administration began in earnest.

7. The Sudan Penal Code was modelled on the Indian Penal Code and was enacted in 1899 (Warburg 1971: 124). For early applications of the Sudan Penal Code to the Nuer, see Johnson 1986a: 62–7.

and Councils.

My reason for submitting that these should be generally adopted is that there are occasionally varying amounts of blood money paid in different Districts and tribesmen are apt to resent some decisions as a consequence, being unable to see any reason why there should be any difference in blood money payments in different Districts.

These rulings were the outcome of both Nuer and Dinka Councils in this District.[8]

The original payments made for a member of the same tribe in the old days were not less than 40 head of cattle, but this was generally agreed to be an excessive amount and was apt to aggravate the feud between families; the amount of cattle to be paid falling not on the murderer alone but on his family.

Chiefs were in favour of only 6 head of cattle being paid for members of a different tribe, the old custom allowing only this amount in blood payments between Nuers and Dinkas and in some cases no blood money was paid between tribes, but I considered this one of the Laws in the Tribal Code which it was necessary to abolish.[9]

My only reason for not allowing the full 20 head under 2 is owing to the number of outstanding cases for which blood money is due for men killed before 1918.[10]

I believe the tribesmen have reached a stage of administration when cases of cold blooded murder should be dealt with under the Penal Code and I consider this and action by Government against Shens in the cases of section or tribal fights is imperative if violence by young tribesmen is to be stopped.

It necessarily follows that the above should be general and not confined to one District.

Malakal
30th June 1926

Percy Coriat
Asst. Dist. Commissioner
Lau

---

8. The Dinka were mainly Ngok and Nyareweng, but also some Luac.

9. Evans-Pritchard (1940: 217–18) recorded the rate of six head of cattle for an unadopted Dinka among both the Jikany and Lou.

10. This proposal is in clear imitation of Dual Diu. See above, doc. 1.2 n. 25.

DOCUMENT 1.5

SOUTHERN (ABWONG) DISTRICT HANDING-OVER NOTES

Coriat administered the Lou Nuer from 1923 to 1929, being based at Abwong on the Sobat river, in Ngok Dinka territory, from 1924. During 1927–9 he was involved in the various patrols against the Lou and Gaawar prophets (see Section 3 below). After the death of Guek in 1929 he was posted to the Western Nuer District, following its transfer from Bahr el-Ghazal to Upper Nile Province. This handing-over note on the Lou was written after he left Abwong and had taken up his duties among the Western Nuer. It gives the same sort of detailed, personal information which he had written for the Bar Gaawar in 1926 (document 1.3 above). It should be noted, however, that the most substantial information concerns the Gun Lou and the Dinka living along the Sobat. Coriat had relatively little contact with the Mor Lou, who did not come under close administration until after 1930.

This document gives a fair summary of Lou Nuer administration and Lou society immediately after their defeat in the Nuer Settlement campaign. As such it gives useful background information on the condition of the country at the time Evans-Pritchard began his fieldwork.

No copy of this report has yet been found in the Sudan. This copy, minus two pages of appendixes, was found in Coriat's personal papers, now in Rhodes House, Oxford. It follows the form for handing-over notes required in all districts of the Sudan whenever there was a change in administrators, but this document and document 1.3 are the earliest handing-over notes to survive for any Nuer district, and are among the oldest to survive for any southern province.

Capt. A. H. A. Alban D.F.C.[1]
Abwong

Much of the matter contained in these notes should be sent in as additions and corrections to 'General Information in respect of District' report 57/B dated 22.5.26.[2] The various corrections etc. should be sent as addenda under their respective headings in the report.

The causes and results of the Lau Patrol 1928 are contained in the report File 5.[3] A summary of these should be written in heading 'History' in report referred to above.

After the Patrol and in the latter part of 1928, Gwek remained a fugitive in the Jekaing [Jikany] country at Faweng [Paweng] on the Sobat, where his mother's relatives lived. He returned just before my departure on leave in August and built himself two huts by the site of the Pyramid [Ngundeng's Mound]. His further history and the causes and consequences of the Nuer Settlement 1929 will be sent under a separate report on the Nuer Settlement.[4]

In 1927 [in fact, 1926] the Barr Gaweir were taken over by Zeraf Valley District; the Gaweir thus becoming administered as a Tribe by that District.[5]

The District boundary to the west now running from Fulus [Fulluth] mouth east bank to opposite Wuthol on west bank, thence across the Fulus and including Wuthol to E. long. 31° 30′, thence south following this longitude to Southern boundary. East of this line from its northern point south to approximately N. lat. 9° live Shilluks and Rueng Dinka.

Between Gobjak on the Sobat and Fulus mouth is Shilluk country and although included within the District boundaries, these people are under Central District for purposes of administration and taxes.

This is unsatisfactory owing to cases between them and the Dinka and the difficulty of arranging for roads to be cleared in that area. The Shilluks slip over the boundary when it suits them.[6]

Cann (1927)[7] agreed that all those within the boundary not living in proper concentrated Shilluk villages, could be ejected and their houses burnt, but this is difficult to carry out from this District. These Shilluks live for the most part

1. Captain A. H. Alban: see above, Introduction, n. 5.
2. Not yet found in any office or archive.
3. See below, doc. 3.2.
4. See below, doc. 3.3.
5. See above, doc. 1.3.

6. Central District (Shilluk) at this time had one DC at Kodok (the Shilluk Resident), one at Malakal (the province capital) and one at Tonga. The Shilluk colonization of new areas generally began with isolated barns and huts (Howell 1941). There are still settlement disputes between the southern Shilluk and the Dinka of this area.

7. Captain G. P. Cann, Shilluk Resident (DC Kodok) 1923–30.

like Nuers and Dinkas, i.e. isolated luaks and huts containing individual families and not, as with other Shilluk, in group villages.

I suggest a meeting with D.C. Shilluk when possible.

It is proposed as an outcome of the Nuer Settlement that the three Lau sections in the south (Shiengs Maikieir [Maiker], Kwaijien and Dung, all of Gun), should remove to new homes within this District, they being at present administered by Duk District.[8]

There are three alternatives for them, either they can live in present Jureir[9] country, or between Fanyangluel [Panyanglual] and Nyerol on the Fulus and westwards between these two points, or within Lau proper with the consent of the respective Lau Chiefs concerned. The Chiefs of these sections have been given definite orders to move in 1930. So far they have elected as follows; Shiengs Dung and Kwaijien move their southernmost villages to the unoccupied area north of their present homes. Actual position and details with D.C. Duk District.[10] Shieng Maikieir to live in Khor Kunjur (Kwanjor) country with villages at Ayau, Fagau, Ngok, Yo etc. Fagau is inhabited by Shieng Dul (Chief Biey Rieg 27) but the section will move in 1930 to the home of the remainder of their section (28) at Jokrial.

The Chiefs concerned have agreed to the above but are quite likely to change their minds by 1930 and the D.C. Duk and yourself will have to arrange these moves as you may find the circumstances.[11]

The Jureir Dinka, also conforming to the Nuer Settlement, will be repatriated to Duk District (their ancestral home) in 1930. The majority are willing and the rest unwilling, but they will all go when told to, with the possible exception of the Thoi division living at Wuthol and vicinity. These may require pressure.[12]

The Jureir is not a cattle country but is a home of plenty as regards durra. The Nuers loath the very name of it.

If you can, it would facilitate road work to get the Rueng Dinkas[13] of the Central District to occupy Jureir, otherwise you will have to make special arrangement to clear some 39 miles of road. As you will see from Shieng

8. The original reads 'Shiengs Maikieir, Kwaijien and Dung. All of Gun.' The Maiker, Kuaijien and Dung sections of the Rumjok Lou were ordered to evacuate the Lang area in 1931. They never completely abandoned the area and were allowed to return in 1933 (see below, n. 11).

9. Jureir, or 'outlander', the nickname of the various Luac, Thoi and Rut Dinka groups settled along Khor Fulluth, refugees from the Gaawar raids of the nineteenth century.

10. Major Wyld: see above, Introduction, n. 25.

11. These moves were never carried out due to Lou Nuer opposition.

12. The Luac arrived in Bor-Duk District just in time to be hit by rinderpest, floods and locusts. Having lost nearly all their cattle they were allowed to return to their homes along the Khor Fulluth in 1933 (Johnson 1982a: 200).

13. The Rueng Dinka living along the Khor Adar between the mouths of the Bahr el-Zeraf and Sobat were then part of the Central District, administered from Tonga. They were later transferred to the Zeraf Valley District and placed under Fangak.

Book,[14] a few Ngok sections live in the Jureir country to the east bank Fulus and they are responsible for their respective sections of the Malwal (Fulus mouth) Mwot Dit road. It would be a pity if the greater part of Jureir was uninhabited waste land.

Fanyangluel on the Fulus is the boundary between Nuer and Dinka.

The Dinkas have given up growing cotton and have been encouraged to cultivate more durra. The demand for durra during the past 3 years and prices ruling have resulted in a considerable increase in grain cultivation and approximately 5000 ardebs of durra are exported in a normal year from Sobat and Fulus markets.

The estimate of population of the Lau Nuer must be revised and the figures obtained from census taken during Nuer Settlement plus 10%.[15]

A list of the more prominent Chiefs and persons with Personality reports was sent to the Governor in August 1928. Copies were to have been typed for Governor's Office, Intelligence Dept. and District Office. These have not yet been returned and there is no copy in District Office.[16] I attach Personality reports on Chiefs and other persons in brief.

Lau Nuers

1/ Gwet Thi [Guet Thie].[17] A Kujur. Has been of great assistance to

---

14. The 'Shieng [*cieng*] Books' were census books listing male taxpayers by village, and sometimes giving the numbers of wives and dependants. None of the Lou Nuer District Shieng Books from this period are known to have survived.

15. Population figures at this time were highly unreliable, being rough guesses based on incomplete counts.

16. The originals of these reports have not been found, but some of Coriat's comments on individual chiefs were copied into later, updated versions which are now in Khartoum, Juba and Malakal (NRO UNP 1/25/182, SRO ZD 66.K.1, and Malakal SCR 66.D.4). It is clear that not all those names appearing on the original personality reports are given here, and this explains the gaps in the numbering. Of the Lou chiefs listed below, numbers 2, 4–7, 9, 12–15, 20, 21, 24–26, and 30 were no longer listed as chiefs by the mid-1930s. The sub-sections (both tertiary and secondary) of each chief, where known, are given in brackets at the end of each entry (from 'Chiefs and Headmen Lau Nuer District', n.d. [*c.* 1936], SRO LND 66.B.3).

17. Guet Thie: (b. *c.* 1885), an earth-master and son of Thie Rue, one of Ngundeng's rivals and antagonistic towards Ngundeng's family. Guet was one of the first Lou chiefs to welcome the new post at Nyerol at the end of the Lou patrol in 1917. He continued his father's antagonism to Ngundeng's family, partly because he was a magician (*guan wal*). He was described by Jackson in 1921 as 'a Kujur touched in the head' but rapidly became 'an "old pal" of Coriat's' in the late 1920s. He retired as chief in 1949 and was still alive in 1954 (Godwin, Nyerol 23.04.17, SRO UNP SCR 15.10; 'Diary–Nyerol–April 1917', UNP archives, Malakal SCR 14.A; H. C. Jackson, 'Safaria Notes, January–February 1921. Lau Nuer Country', SAD 465/4; 'Upper Nile Province

Government since 1927, before which he had various Kujur seizures. Loyal and intelligent enough to realise that Government wins in a long course. Inclined to shirk responsibility occasionally. Should prove a prominent Chief if he can be bolstered up sufficiently and at the same time kept on the right side and when he finds that it will pay him (materially) to assist Government. [Sub-section Cic-Gaadbal]

Age Makeir [Maker] class.[18]

2/ Kwainien Thi [Kuanyen Thie]. A brother of Gwet. Dealt with Government when Gwet was doing conjuring tricks. Intelligent and out for a peaceful life. Has slid into backgound since Gwet took over section but always a useful ally.

Age Makeir class.

3/ Gwek Wundeng [Guek Ngundeng] killed January 1929. Section dispersed. Gwek's age was Dang Gwonka [Dang-gonga] class.[19]

4/ [Kwoin Mal][20] A young Chief inseparable from Lam Wel No. 7. Works well, not afraid of his men and acts as number two to Lam. [Sub-section Pälker-Rumjok]

Age Luaich [Luac] class.[21]

5/ Pur Kui. A useless old man. Ding Twil Kwoth acts as Chief of section. Ding has considerable authority over the section but is jealous of Lam Wel. Prevented a Dinka raid in 1928 by challenging Gwek and Dtho Dieng.[22] Vide report File 57/B. [Sub-section Pälker-Rumjok]

Age Luaich class.

6/ Kong Wuth. Characterless and pretty well useless. Obeys Lam Wel. Has no control. [Sub-section Pälker-Rumjok]

Age Luaich class.

7/ Lam Wel. Possibly the most prominent of the younger Chiefs in Lau. Has complete control over Fulkir [Pälker] (one of the largest Shiengs) and great authority. Was a rebel in 1928 and the first to come in with entire section for the concentration during Nuer Settlement. Does not fear his men and now realises power of Government and benefits of a peaceable administration. Was a prominent fighting leader. Should be encouraged.

Personality Report no. 5', NRO UNP 1/34/276; P. L. Roussel, 'List of Notables and Chiefs now Retired or Dismissed', 02.11.54, SRO LND 10.A).

18. The Maker age-set was marked in about 1887.

19. Guek was not a Dang-gonga (marked c. 1895), but a Luac.

20. He appears as Kwek Mal in documents from the mid-1930s to the 1950s. He became president of the Dak-Rumjok court in 1942.

21. Luac were marked in c. 1908.

22. Ding Twil Kuoth is now remembered to have opposed this raid because it was aimed against the Dinka, among whom he (and other Lou) had many relatives.

Age Dang Gwonka class.

8/ Rial Mai. One of the oldest of Government Chiefs.[23] Has always been pro-Government but has lacked support and is too old to be of much use with the young men. Had difficulties with his section in the past but has never himself supported anti-Government tendencies. Is now assisted by Chag Gaing [Cak Gany] (10) who is one of the younger leaders. [Sub-section Nyajikany-Rumjok]

Age Makeir class.

9/ Chokwel Dthwor [Cokuel Dhoar]. Ignorant, useless and unable to realise meaning of Government. Absconded in 1928 and arrested early 1929 when he served a term of imprisonment at Mwot. Never likely to improve. [Sub-section Nyajikany-Rumjok]

Age Dang Gwonka class.

10/ Chag Gaing. Appointed a Chief in 1927 on death of his brother Yuai Lith Gaing. Young, energetic, is gaining increasing control over young men of Shieng Nyajakan [Nyajikany] and should eventually replace Rial as Head Chief.[24]

Age Luaich class.

11/ Warweng Tudel. An amiable young Chief without much character and is timid. [Sub-section Nyajikany-Rumjok]

12/ Thiep Ruai. Aged and infirm. Warweng acts for him. [Sub-section Nyajikany-Rumjok]

13/ Pur Tiop. An old rascal who has more influence with his section than he is inclined to admit. Reactionary tendencies and shirks responsibility but has a broad sense of humour, which helps a lot. Bolted annually in past. Afraid and suspicious of Government in the past. [Sub-section Nyajikany-Rumjok]

Age Makeir class.

14/ Goy Thuin Bey. Hereditary Land Chief of Lau ('Kwar Mon' [*kuaar muon*]). Father died in 1928.[25] A loyal young Chief, not sufficiently forceful but has a pleasant manner and is generally liked. Influence as regards spiritual position now practically negligible except as concerned with the determining of age class names and times of initiation. [Sub-section Mathel-Rumjok]

Age Karam class.[26]

---

23. Rial Mac, first mentioned in government reports in 1918 (J. Stevenson-Hamilton and C. C. Godwin, 'Boundary between Lau Nuers (Upper Nile) and Bor District (Mongalla)', 25.07.18, SRO UNP SCR 14.4).

24. Cak Gany was still only a sub-chief under Rial Mac in the mid-1930s.

25. It was erroneously reported in 1927 that Tony Begh died after criticising Guek (Lee to governor, Malakal, 16.10.27, NRO Civsec 5/2/10 and UNP 1/5/27). Tony Begh, in fact, sided with Guek. He was a *wut ghok* (man of cattle), not a *kuaar muon*.

26. The Karam age-set among the Gaawar was marked between 1908 and 1913. There is no separate set called Karam among the Lou, but it may have been a sub-set of Luac.

15/ Thain Pin Dul. Outwardly meek and timid but lying and treacherous. Fled in 1928 but gave himself up after [S8] Patrol. Thoroughly unreliable. [Sub-section Mathel-Rumjok]

Age Dang Gwonka class.

16/ Fod or Pod Gig [Puot Gig].[27] A pleasant old fellow who threw his lot in with Gwek in January 1929 and has not been seen since. Lived with his section in Gaweir at Kwaideang and was told to return to Lau when this area was handed over to the Dinkas in 1928. He probably joined Gwek because of his home having been taken from him. Went to Gaweir when this part was invaded and captured from the Dinkas by Machar Diu in 1914. Chiefs Policeman Tut Roa is at present acting for section. [Sub-section Nyajikany-Rumjok]

Age Makeir class.

17/ Nuer [Nuaar] Ganur Wor son of Ganur Wor. His father is a high spirited old man who cannot recognise that a Dinka is anything but a slave and who has only recently become friendly to Government. Nuer is a powerful young Shiengsman who should do good work if he finds it worth his while.[28] [Sub-section Yuong-Gaadbal]

Age Luaich class.

18/ Yik Turog [Turuk]. A young supporter of Nuer without character. Was appointed because his father had become too old. [Sub-section Yuong-Gaadbal]

Age Luaich class.

19/ Lem [Lam] Thon. A young Chief rather like Nuer and a very decent fellow to boot. A typical young blood. [Sub-section Yuong-Gaadbal]

Age Karam class.

20/ Rueh Kuh. Rapidly becoming senile. In 1924 and until that year he was the cause of a great deal of trouble. Had never paid tribute and raided Jekaing [Jikany] parties passing through Lau. Was caught with his section after a ten day chase in 1924. Son Changath [Cangac Ruei] acts as Chief; a young blood but bone lazy. [Sub-section Yuong-Gaadbal]

21/ Dtho Dieng [Dhiew Dieng].[29] I have been unable to fathom this Chief. Was first appointed in 1923 when he walked into the office at Ayod. He produced two bulls with him and stated he had never paid tribute before. He was then made to accompany me to Malakal. Became a most prominent personality at Courts but would not live either with his section or elsewhere

---

27. Puot Gig, see doc. 1.3 n. 11. Puot settled with the Gaawar before 1914.

28. In 1918 Ganur was described as a minor chief 'capable of causing local trouble', but with no real authority ('Notes for Inspector Lau Nuers' [1918], Malakal, UNP SCR 14A. By the mid-1930s Nuaar Ganur was chief of the Yuong-Gaadbal section (see 'Chiefs and Headmen', cited in n. 16).

29. See below, doc. 3.1 n. 32, and doc. 3.2.

where there were others living and built himself a house near Nyerol. Warned Government before the Gwek trouble in the latter part of 1927 and then bolted clean away when the Patrol took place. Gave himself up at Abwong after the Patrol. Attempted to lead a raid against the Dinkas during the rains of 1928 and was only stopped by action of other Chiefs. Came into Abwong while I was away on leave and said his only reason for attempting to lead a raid was because a case he had against the Dinkas of Duk in 1924 had been wrongly awarded against him. Vanished during Nuer Settlement when he played about a little at Mwot Tot and when the place became too hot to hold him, crossed the Sobat and made his way to Tayabur on Garjak [Gaajak] swamps. Gave himself up at Abwong April 1929. His explanation both times was that he could not go with the herd and wished to avoid Government while there was trouble. Was imprisoned and sent to join prisoners at Malakal.[30] It may be he runs with the Hare and hunts with the Hounds or possibly it is that he is never sure which is the winning side. He has a very winning personality, is cheerful, uncommonly intelligent for a Nuer and has a very straightforward manner. The only native I have known who can be effectively ironic. Had a dog he called 'Kai Lora' (All Lies); the other Chiefs now say that the dog was the only person who knew Dtho's mind and that it was 'All Lies' anyway. [Sub-section Manthiep-Gaadbal]

22/ Kol Gai. Half his face was chewed off by a Hyena when he was a child hence 'Hyena Face'. Was a great fighting man. Is a fairly good Chief I believe but is always prowling around and one is never sure of his intentions or movements. [Sub-section Manthiep-Gaadbal]

Age Dang Gwonka class.

23/ We[t]h Turial. Son of Turial Nyit. A talkative young fellow. [Sub-section Macok-Gaadbal]

24/ Witong Tong. Has a few families of Jadul (14) to whom he belongs, under him and lives with Kol at Ful Bar in the Mor country. Missing since 1928. [Sub-section Jadul-Rumjok]

25/ Malo Tur was Chief and a note about him follows. Present Chief Gwel Poy. An uncertain individual who was appointed in 1927 with Malo Tur's brother Chag [Cak] to help him. Chag is a very decent fellow. A number of Gwel's people were with Gwek at the battle of the Pyramid in January 1929.[31] [Sub-section Leng-Gaadbal]

26/ Luak Lam.[32] A young Chief of an unpleasant type. Ignorant and possessed of a low cunning. Age Luaich. Most of his section were with Gwek at battle of Pyramid. [Sub-section Leng-Gaadbal]

30. Note in margin: 'No at Abwong'.

31. See below, doc. 3.3.

32. See below, doc. 3.3. Luak Lam died in December 1935 (UNPMD December 1935, SRO BD 57.C.1).

27/ Biey Rieg [Bie Riek].³³ A poor type of Chief with an unruly section living at Fagau on Gaweir border. [Sub-section Dul-Rumjok]

28/ Maikier Thijok [Maiker Thijoak].³⁴ Was an ally of Gwek's. Sister married Gwek in 1929. Now in prison at Malakal. [Sub-section Dul-Rumjok]

29/ Ngwoth Kuin [Nguth Kuny].³⁵ Newly appointed. Brother Kwaigur was Chief and died in 1928. Not a pleasant fellow. Liglig the second brother was appointed and died at Gwek's side in 1929. Ngwoth may prove satisfactory now. He returned that Sparklet bulb I told you about. [Sub-section Nyarkuac-Gaadbal]

30/ Bul Kan.³⁶ A loyal old Chief who never gives any trouble. Neither does his section. Jok acts and is a cheery young Nuer. They live on the Sobat and are the best Nuer section. Bul has a feud with the Kuin family of 29. [Sub-section Nyarkuac-Gaadbal]

The remaining Lau Chiefs are Mor and I do not know as much about them.

Herewith notes on the more prominent ones and the Chiefs one normally deals with.

33/ Kong Pan.³⁷ A promising Chief if only he had control over Shieng Buth. He wants to go and live on his own on the Pibor which must not be allowed. [Sub-section Buth-Mor]

Dang Gwonka class.

33. Bie Riek, b. *c.* 1890, sub-chief of Dul-Rumjok *c.* 1917–49. Still alive in 1954 when it was noted that he had good relations with the Gaawar and was a friend of Dual Diu (only recently allowed home). Even though retired from his chiefship it was thought he might still be useful in future Lou–Gaawar relations (see Roussel, 'List of Notables', cited in n. 17).

34. Maiker Thijoak's father, Thijok Dul, was a minor prophet under Ngundeng. He died in the mid-1920s, and the government subsequently alleged that Guek's settlement of compensation claims following Thijok's death constituted a perversion of custom (Johnson 1985*a*: 142–3).

35. Nguth Kuny: Luac age-set; sub-chief of Thul court (*cieng* Nyarkuac-Gaadbal); was considered 'uncouth... pig-headed... obstructive...' and 'unco-operative' by Coriat's immediate successors, but 'improving' and 'a rascal but a likeable one' by later DCs (see Roussel, 'List of Notables', cited in n. 17). He died in 1975.

36. Bul Kan was one of Ngundeng's contemporaries (Johnson 1982*b*: 124). He was a renowned magician, and in 1931 Evans-Pritchard found him settled at Kurmayom, on the border between the Ngok Dinka and the Lou. Bul's genitor was a Ngok Dinka, while his pater was Kan Kwoth, a Lou Nuer. Bul traced descent to the dominant Jinaca clan, who owned the village, through his maternal grandmother, not through his pater, who was of the Kiek clan (Evans-Pritchard 1935: 72–3; 1950: 384–5; 1951: 21–2). The ambiguities in Bul's kin affiliation remind us how political attachments were often more complex than Coriat and his successors allowed in straightforward lists such as this.

37. Kong Pan: chief of Buth-Mor. Both his father and grandfather were warrior leaders against the Anuak (see Roussel, 'List of Notables', cited in n. 17). He imitated the manner of a prophet during Guek's lifetime but abandoned any public display of seizure after Guek's death (A. H. A. Alban, 'Note on the Indigenous Basis of the Present Administrative System', 26.06.35, SRO UNP 32.B.1).

34/ Wey Twor Bey [Weituor Begh].[38] An old man with a lot of authority but extremely suspicious of Government. Bolted during concentration 1929 but should be tried again. Is now in prison at Malakal. [Sub-section Buth-Mor]

38/ Kwil Rueh. Has complete mastery over his section of Buth but anti-Government. Missing since 1928. Probably on Gila river. Related by marriage to Gwek vide reports.[39] [Sub-section Buth-Mor]

41/ Gwem Kur Bum.[40] Utterly useless but is supposed to run Jegar [Jajok] for lack of a better. [Sub-section Gaaliek-Mor]
Age Luaich class.

46/ Mut Shan Poich [Mut Cany Poc]. Not prepossessing but is gaining mastery over his section and is well meaning. Must be dealt with patiently. Age Lith Gai class.[41] [Sub-section Jajok-Mor]

53/ Pey Ruai Thit [Pec Ruac Thit]. A very promising young Chief who lives at Kaibui near Akobo. His father Ruai Thit lives with the remainder of the section at Kaikwi and Kurwai in Lau. Pey loses his head very easily. [Sub-section Can-Mor]
Age Lith Gai class.

62/ Diu Muk. A good steady Chief who runs the whole of Shieng Maroa and was discovered in 1926. For some inexplicable reason, did not put in an appearance at the Wegin concentration. Neither did his section who were absent in toto. [Sub-section Kun-Mor]

67/ Tut Lam. The most prominent of the Mor Chiefs with a wild section. A determined fellow who, with his section, assisted Gwek in 1928. Now a loyal Government Chief. Brought section and other Jemaish [Jimac] Chiefs into Wegin.[42] [Sub-section Jagueth-Mor]

73/ Red Ruathdell [Ret Ruathdel]. Means well but has not the character or influence required to control his section. Shieng Belyu [Biliu] near the Geni are the farthest Lau. [Sub-section Biliu-Mor]

The following leopard-skins are those chiefly dealt with by Government:

---

38. In the manuscript the number is handwritten and appears to be '31'. Weituor Begh was released from prison on 09.07.29 ('Detail of Political Prisoners Taken by Morcol', NRO UNP 1/6/43). He eventually became court president of the Faddoi B court. His sons Cuol and Rau Weituor succeeded him in that position. Cuol Weituor was murdered during the first Sudanese civil war; Rau Weituor died during the second civil war.

39. Though an ally of Guek's, Kwil actively supported a number of Rumjok chiefs who were protecting Dinka cattle from other Lou, following the August 1928 raids (J. W. G. Wyld, 'Report on Dinka of Duk District', NRO Civsec 5/3/12).

40. Guem Kur was chief of the Gaaliek-Mor by the mid-1930s (see 'Chiefs and Headmen', cited in n. 16).

41. Lithgai were marked in 1913–15.

42. See below, doc. 3.3. One of Guek's wives was a Jimac.

Jok Diang[43] of Yarkwaith [Nyarkuac] on the Sobat. Gun Lau. He is at enmity with his brothers who live at Shwil on Sobat. All Diang family are hereditary leopard-skins. One brother Thung is a Chief's Policeman.

Pui Majug [Majok] of Faddoi. A friend of Chief Kong Pan. Has been of assistance in dealing with Shieng Buth.

Nyang Keth of Faddoi. Related to Chief Nuap Turog of Shieng Niag. A good influence with Nuap Turog.

Among the Mor Chiefs I omitted Nuap Turog [Turuk][44] who is untrustworthy and a bad type.

Other Persons

Pok Keirjok. A Kujur of Shieng Nyajakan, vide Report on Patrol S8. Pok was at the battle of the Pyramid and was last heard of going over to the Mor country with a pipe and a bag of charcoal in his hand. He is said to have received three outers during the battle, in the head, arm and chest. It is probable he went over to Kwil Rueh.[45]

Malo Tur. Until 1924 was with Rial Mai, one of the oldest of Government Chiefs. He had control of Shieng Lang. In 1924, Malo believed he had been bewitched by one of his Shiengsmen and he consequently moved from Majuk in the Lang country to Dik Mareng on the Geni, a village occupied by oddments and Gogo Wel of Shieng Belyu and his family. He was ordered to return to Gun but protested that he would run his section if he was allowed to remain at Dik until the sickness he had left him. This was granted and until the end of 1927 he continued to be responsible for tribute and administration of his section. When Gwek rebelled he disappeared and was heard of at various places on the Pibor, including Dengjok. His brother Chag was sent to him during the rains of 1928 in order to find out what his intentions were. He met his brother and told him he would return in the dry season of 1929 and would come to see me. He did not come in and the last heard of him was that he was living among the Jekaing on the Pibor, had become a Kujur and that he had caused the death of

---

43. Jok Diung, of the Beegh clan and Luac age-set, was one of Evans-Pritchard's sources and is mentioned by him several times (Evans-Pritchard 1934: 48; 1935: 48; 1936: 260; 1950: 378).

44. Space for a number appears before Nuap Turog's name, which may have been filled in on the original, but there is no indication of this in the remaining file copy I used in preparing this document.

45. Pok Kerjiok became possessed by the divinity Gär in *c.* 1914. He organized the 1916 Lou raid into Bor district, which ended with the annihilation of a detachment of Sudanese soldiers. He was defeated in battle by government troops in 1917 but was never captured. He finally surrendered at Abwong on 5 August 1930 and died in exile.

a Jekaing by witchcraft. It seems that he has found an easy way of increasing his wealth in cattle and will probably remain on the Pibor until he falls foul of the Jekaing or gets caught.[46]

In 1930, the Political prisoners arrested during the Settlement will have to be returned to their sections. I suggest that instead of being released at Malakal, they are handed over by you in person to their respective Chiefs.

Dtho Dieng, should I suggest be given another chance, but must be made to live with his section.

Chamjog Chai now living at Kwemdthol is to be appointed Headman of Shieng Lam (a new section). Chamjog recently came over from Gaweir (1928) with his family and others and the remainder of the section were living among Shieng Lang. They dispersed after a blood feud. This feud with Reth Dar of Gwet Thi's people will need to be tackled in 1930. Shieng Lam wish to live at or near Fanyang of Gwet Thi's. They would come under Gwet as Head Chief. The present Policeman, a brother of Chamjog's should be exchanged for a member of some other branch of the family or it would be better still to appoint Jok or his brother Luk Tulshieng as Headman with Chamjog as Policeman.[47]

The Gwek family and relatives should if possible be deported or failing that give them a settlement on the Sobat, but you would have to see that they stuck to the Settlement.[48]

One Shwol [Cuol] Kur is a Political prisoner at Malakal. Vide file Political prisoners. He should be deported to Jekaing when, and only then, his brother Kuin Kuin turns up. There is another brother a fairly decent [chap] whose name I have forgotten who is always hanging around and unless you are wary will try and cajole you into releasing Shwol without further ado. Shwol is a Kujur. Kuin Kuin the elder brother is merely a bad hat. They live at Thieylang just inland from Wegin and are mixed Dinka-Jekaing. They harboured Gwek, have never paid taxes and do not appear to be known by Eastern District. Turn them out of Thieylang as this was to have been done for the past two years but I have not yet had the time. They go over to Jekaing for dry season cattle camp. The Ballak Withiel and his brother Torkai Ngor are friendly with them.

Subshieng Rueh. Ch. Rueh Kuh 20/ Old Rueh wants to go and live on his own at Wunbil (Shieng Tiang) and is there now. He says Wunbil is his ancestral home and Leet does not agree with him. You will have to try and get him to live with his section somewhere. They need not necessarily stick to Leet but

---

46. Malo Tur returned briefly to Lou in 1930 but went immediately to the Khor Geni and then to Dinka country (A. H. Alban to DC Nasser, 16.01.31, Nasir END 66.B.3/1). He appears on no subsequent list of Lou chiefs.

47. Camjok Cai was still chief in the 1930s, with Jok Tulcieng as a sub-chief under him (see 'Chiefs and Headmen', cited in n. 16).

48. Guek's brother Lel subsequently settled in Nasir, while most of the rest of Ngundeng's grandchildren settled around Weideang.

they must be together.

Subshieng Manthiep. Ch. Dtho Dieng 21/ One Gung Wil runs the section or what he can of it. Dtho can go back when he comes out of prison but they must concentrate somewhere. Preferably at their old home Gweirthar and vicinity. The families at Milkeir under Bum Kai [Buom Kac][49] must be turfed out. Gung Wil is a very decent fellow and so is the C.P. [Chiefs' Police] Nyith.

Shieng Dul 27/ & 28/ Biey Rieg can come out of Fagau which may be going to Shieng Maikieir of Duk vide above and can live at Jokrial running both the Maikieir subsections.

Thijok 28/ should go and live with the Gwek family.

Shieng Matchok 22/ & 23/ These people of whom half are at Fulbar in the Mor country should join up and live at Limkuntchik and vicinity where 22/ is. 23/'s father Turial Nyit is still alive and is really Head of the section.

The Mor did not concentrate because they were too far away from their homes and did not know what they were in for. I suggest they concentrate between Kaibui and Mangong or Ful Geni on the Geni. They can hish [Arab., 'to weed', i.e. clear; see Plate 13] a road along the area and from Kaibui to Akobo, which road will be wanted in any case. They should stick to one side of the Khor. Supplies can be taken up to Akobo during the rains, including motor transport. You will require a post of a Platoon or perhaps less at the Geni or southern end and a troop of Mounted Police or Cavalry for any chasing there may be. Done this way and particularly after they have seen the results of Guncol,[50] I am pretty sure you will get them to concentrate easily. When that is done they will want a lot of reorganising as to village and camp sites for the future. Luckily the Chiefs' Police were appointed for the most part, while I was at Wegin. Gun can do as they please, that is they can have their Courts and will camp by Sections or Subshiengs as they please, provided they do their roads and you know where each Subshieng is camped. They cannot all camp in Shiengs as [ordered] during the Settlement as there is not normally enough water or large enough water holes in Lau for this.

When and if the Mor concentrate properly, they can be sent off in batches to do the particular piece of the Akobo road allotted them. Vide below re roads [Appendix B to this document, now missing].

The Chiefs' Police have been given instructions to report every month till December when they all come in for orders. One Policeman from Gun and one from Mor only will report at the full moon of each month. In the event of sickness they are responsible for finding their own substitutes.

---

49. Buom Kac became head chief of *cieng* Manthiep in the 1930s.
50. For Guncol, see below, doc. 3.3.

The following is the scheme:

Month	Nuer Month	Chiefs' Policemen to report
January	Tiup 2nd [Tiop Intot]	—
February	Pet	—
March	Dwong	—
April	Gwag [Gwaak]	—
May	Dwat	Red Bidong (52) Gun. Char Poi (53)[51] Mor.
June	Kurnuot [Kornyuot]	Reth Moin (77) Gun. Banang Nuon (75) Mor.
July	Pai Yetni [Paiyatni]	Bayak Tutyil (71) Gai Tong (74) Gun. Luai Muinlau (108) Mor.
August	Thur [Thoor]	Lul Thiankan (80) Gun. Mun Gai (104) Mor.
September	Teir [Teer]	Tutjieh Pan (92) Gun. Luak Nuon (64) Mor.
October	Labur [Lath Boor]	Wanjang Niag (95) Gun. Wanjang Weytwor (78) Mor.
November	Kur	Tob Rih (94) Gun. Butbut Korwal (2) Shwol Balang (4)[52] Mor.
December	Tiup 1st [Tiop Indit]	All Police to report.

Allow them a few days' latitude each way as regards the full moon.
Note. The numbers above 100 are incorrect but the Chiefs' Police roll will give you the correct numbers.

Herewith notes on the [Ngok] Dinkas.[53]

81/ Ajiak Thon. A pleasant young Ngok without much control. [Sub-section Deng-Jok]

82/ Fadwom [Paduom] Manyang. A bit of a Wizard in curing sickness. Quite honest but not of much use as regards Government. Lazy. [Sub-section Deng-Jok]

83/ Deng Awok. A good Chief with authority. [Sub-section Ajuba-Jok]

84/ Munkal Kir. Not much use.

---

51. Char Poi [Car Poc] became a sub-chief of the Jagueth Mor under Tut Lam in the 1930s (see 'Chiefs and Headmen', cited in n. 16).

52. Shwol [Cuol] Balang was a political prisoner in Malakal in 1929 (see 'Detail of Political Prisoners', cited in n. 38).

53. Of the following Ngok Dinka chiefs, numbers 86, 91, 94, 112, and 113 no longer appeared on the list of chiefs by the mid-1930s (see 'Chiefs and Headmen', cited in n. 16). The Ngok were administratively divided into two major divisions and ten sections: Jok (Ngau, Abi, Deng, Acak, Adong, Ajuba), and Yom (Baliet, Awir, Dud, Diak). The section of each chief, where known, is given here in brackets at the end of each entry.

85/ Thon Lual Akon. Lazy, deceitful and has the worst section of Ngok. They live at Wunarual on the Fulus not far from Fanyangluel. [Sub-section Ajuba-Jok]

86/ Marial Jok. Efficient and quiet.

87/ Shwol [Cuol] Deng Dau. Does what is required of him. [Sub-section Abi-Jok]

88/ Kir Lual Kir. Lives at Gobjak near the Shilluk border. Rather a young shirker. His section has much to do with Shilluks. [Sub-section Ajuba-Jok]

89/ Dey Kir. Truculent, dishonest and shirks responsibility. A thoroughly bad hat. Now in prison. Should not be reappointed. Section can come under Deng Gai. [Sub-section Acak-Jok]

90/ [Unidentified] A fairly useful Chief in the past. For two years (1926–27) believed himself to be suffering from a spell and was semi-paralysed from waist down. Spent 6 months in Malakal Hospital and recovered. His ailment was not diagnosed. Has never fully recovered his strength and has become rather a wheedler.

91/ Angun Akai. Lives close to Station. Has good control over section. Runs ramps [i.e. 'swindles'].

92/ Awol Ashwol acting for Makeir Amoryal whose sons both died as Chiefs and whose third son Pok is one of the District motor drivers and will never make a Chief. Makeir is senile and completely brainless. Awol is a nonentity. There is another son of Makeir whose name I have forgotten. This fellow has never had much to do with Government but may be worth trying.[54] The section is large and although living close to the Station is a nuisance particularly as regards taxes: this is for want of a Leader. [Sub-section Ngau-Jok]

93/ Dau Deng. Appointed in place of Thoi Shan in 1926. Very litigious but can tackle his people. [Sub-section Ngau-Jok]

94/ Awan Ajin. The worst headman in Ngok. Dishonest, cowardly and utterly incapable of doing anything with his section. Should follow Dey Kir when there is an opportunity.

95/ Awol Majuk. An intelligent hardworking Chief. Has authority. Looks young but is well over middle age. [Sub-section Ngau-Jok]

96/ Akey Datwil. Appointed on death of Chief in 1929. Chief died without heirs. Akey looks alright. [Sub-section Awir-Yom]

97/ Bul Agwet. Old and thoroughly useless. Run by his wakils who quarrel with him and amongst themselves. [Sub-section Awir-Yom]

98/ Gai Kir. A very forceful fellow. Ramps [i.e. 'swindles'] but is one of the few Ngok who really is a Chief. Uncommonly intelligent very fond of litigation and sways the other Chiefs by a flood of oratory of which he is master. Has

---

54. Abiel Makeir, headman in the Ngau section by the mid-1930s (ibid.).

only a small section. [Sub-section Awir-Yom]

99/ [Left blank in text]

100/ Keid Ayey. An intelligent old Chief with authority and a good influence over other Chiefs. [Sub-section Awir-Yom]

101/ Deng Duop. Has a small section of Adong and does well. [Sub-section Adong-Jok]

102/ Deng Bul Ayik. Quiet and reliable. [Sub-section Adong-Jok]

103/ Deng Shwol Fiot. A useful Chief. Extremely litigious. Mixes overmuch with Jellaba and involves himself in dubious transactions. [Sub-section Adong-Jok]

104/ Shwol Dau Abak. Young but very stupid and useless. [Sub-section Adong-Jok]

105/ Akol Ajok. Untrustworthy and lazy but a fairly pleasant manner. [Sub-section Adong-Jok]

106/ Muntong Dabul. A hard working Chief with influence. He and his people foully murdered one Ajang Ballak who had killed Muntong's brother Ago. Ago was a Chief and died of his wound at the Station where he is buried (1925). [Sub-section Diak-Yom]

107/ Shwol Ajal. Stupid and a shirker. [Sub-section Dud-Yom]

108/ Awan Ayom. The most able of the Ngok Chiefs. A strong influence and has complete control over section. Friendly with the Nuers particularly Bul Kan near whom he lives. [Sub-section Baliet-Yom]

109/ Deng Ayey. A decent and reliable Chief but disinclined to take much part in Courts except as an onlooker. [Sub-section Baliet-Yom]

110/ Shigai [Cigai] Deng. Hardworking but timid of his people. [Sub-section Baliet-Yom]

111/ Riak Deng Mayan. Hereditary Paramount of Ngok. Has not yet attained much influence outside his section. Retains his father's privileges as a foil to Ateir Kur and family. Father[55] was murdered in 1926 by a brother of Ateir Kur 112, with whom there had been and still is an agelong feud, though parties are now quits. Murderer of Deng Mayan was killed as a result of Government action taken vide reports.[56] Riak has a fiery temper which he must learn to control. Has quarrelled with his brother Awan Ajin and unless watched section

---

55. Deng Mayan (sometimes spelled 'Deng Maiung') was made *omda* (Turk., 'head chief') of the Ngok Dinka at Gobjak on the Sobat in 1903, but he 'gradually lost influence, his people considering him too zealous in collecting taxes & on behalf of Government generally. Finally he petitioned to resign, as he was afraid of his people. As it was realized that he had lost all influence he was relieved of all responsibility' in 1909, but retained the 'chiefship' since no one else was willing to take it up ('Return of Prominent Persons in Upper Nile—1909', SRO UNP unnumbered). See photograph of him on Plate 2.

56. No official account of this feud has yet been found in Malakal or Akobo.

is likely to become divided. Awan is jealous of one Bang who is inseparable from Riak. Riak was shy and very quiet when first appointed but does not know himself now. Should make a strong paramount when he is older and all going well. [Sub-section Baliet-Yom]

112/ Ateir Kur. Father was Paramount during time of Slave-raiders, hence feud with Mayan family. Brothers Faleig and Athoai are unpleasant fellows, particularly Faleig who has much to do with Shilluk Kujurs.[57] Section lives on Shilluk border at Gobjak. Ateir is a pleasant enough old man but is getting past his working days.

113/ Wal Kir. A young Chief. Reliable and well mannered.

114/ Lual Kir Jumka. Has no real section of his own. Would make a strong Chief if he had a large section. Good on Courts. [Sub-section Ajuba-Jok]

The following Jureir Chiefs, who will move to Duk District in 1930:[58]

115/ Kor Akwey [Akuei]. Mediocre. [Luac Dinka tribe]

116/ Shwol Akwey [Cuol Akuei] for whom son Lam acts. Both are stupid and of little use. [Duor Dinka tribe]

117/ [Unidentified] At Duk Dist.

118/ Diu Ngor. A thorough ass but works hard. Assisted by one Muinlek. The old Chief Mabiur [Mabior] Lual who died in 1927 was an excellent fellow. Mabiur had no grown sons. [Rut Dinka tribe]

119/ Lat Makwai [see Plate 4]. Useless as is his section.

120/ Ayang Awan. Is not much use. Has a very small section.

121/ Akwey [Akuei] Biel [see Plate 5].[59] With Garang Weo, runs the Jureir. Very able and intelligent and has been known to Government since the early days. A great humourist. Useful as intelligence agent among the Nuers and commonly known as 'Bashom'. Garang Weo is very jealous of him and Akwey hates Garang Weo. They are supposed to be friends now. [Luac Dinka tribe]

122/ Garang Weo [Wiu] [see Plate 6]. Able and complete control over Luaich. Runs the Jureir with Akwey. Very jealous of Akwey.

123/ Deng Kir [see Plate 7]. Does his work fairly satisfactorily. [Luac Dinka tribe]

124/ Dag Them Jang a young fellow without much character who acts for his

---

57. For the 'Shilluk kujurs', see Johnson 1985*a*: 142.

58. Of the following Dinka chiefs, numbers 119, 120, 121, and 122 were no longer listed as chiefs by 1936 (see 'Chiefs and Headmen', cited in n. 16). Their specific tribes, where known, are given in brackets at the end of each entry.

59. Akuei Biel was appointed chief of the Luac Dinka by Coriat. He agreed to lead his people to Bor District, but when they returned to Khor Fulluth he resigned his position as chief and remained behind. Even as a very old man he used to give a fair imitation of Coriat speaking Nuer.

father Them Jang [see Plate 8]. Them [i.e. the father] was a great deal of trouble at one time and the last of the Jureir to become amenable to Government. He still runs his section but is becoming old. [Luac Dinka tribe]

Of the Ballak Chiefs none are worth mentioning except Deng Aiwel Agot 131/. I have been trying to get this Chief to run the whole of Ballak. He is a determined fellow with influence over the others, none of whom are worth calling Chiefs.[60]

Other Dinkas of note are:

Thoi Shan a very cunning rogue with a Kujur wife who was a Chief until 1926 when Dau Deng was appointed in his place. Lives near Abwong.

Koi Athon Ator. A determined and forceful Ngok who would make a good Chief and who is trying to oust Wal Kir. Will have to be watched that he does not give trouble.

Dinkas love litigation.

All the Dinkas have too many Chiefs and they must be got rid of by degrees i.e. the death of a Chief need not mean a new appointment. I have not done anything about this in the past as I have been too occupied with Nuers. Their problems are not the same as those of the Nuers. The young men are easy to handle and the plethora of Chiefs is a nuisance in that you have to deal with more persons and not that the young men will not obey their appointed Chiefs. The scheme I suggest would be to retain the present Chiefs as Headmen and they in turn would be responsible to one Chief from each of the respective divisions, about 6 in number. This will simplify Riak Deng's position as Paramount at some future day.[61]

The Ballak are a cause of unnecessary trouble. They are always mixing themselves up with Jekaing and always having trouble with them over fishing and grazing rights. A fortnight on that border with the D.C. Eastern District[62] would do a lot of good.

Both Nuer and Dinka Courts function well but the great and lasting drawback is lack of Clerks. This can only be overcome when the Mission[63] produce literate youths.

The Dinkas have only two Temargia and they must produce more boys.

Both for this and schooling, you require to use a little pressure but they are perfectly contented when they realise their boys are not going to be taken away from them and are going to be of use to them.

60. Ballak Dinka: a group of mixed Dinka–Anuak–Nuer fishermen who inhabit a short stretch of the Sobat. Deng Aiwel was listed as head chief of the Ballak by the mid-1930s (ibid.).

61. The number of Dinka chiefs increased to seventy by 1936 (ibid.).

62. John Lee, DC Eastern District (Nasir) 1921–9, replaced by C. L. Armstrong, DSO, MC, in December 1929.

63. The American Protestant Mission, Nasir.

It is no use getting Dinka boys for schooling as there is no place you can send them to. I suggest you obtain permission to send them to Malek Mission[64] otherwise it looks as if you will never have Dinka Clerks.

The Hospital should be enlarged in 1930.

Mayan Lam is a good Interpreter and honest [see Plates 9 and 18]. Personally I think he is the best in the Province but you will have to keep him up to scratch. If you give him a day's leave, he may take two and come back full of excuses but that's roughly the only sort of crime he ever commits. He will report to you when anyone wants to see you at any time of the day or night and whoever the person is. I have insisted on his doing this. It does not follow you will see the nas [Arab., 'people'] at odd times but he has to report. I avoided fining him as he needs all his pay but if necessary you can generally find a punishment to fit the crime. He has never yet had anything to do with the usual Interpreter type of ramp.[65]

The A.M.O. Awad Bakheit is the best I have had in the District. He knows both the Nuers and Dinkas and works hard and can run his Temargis. When he is out on trek with you the Temargis do the work in the Station. They cannot yet give injections. Nothing is charged for Medical treatment unless taken away or injections given in the Station are 10 PT each unless there is a chit from you.

The Felucca crew are used on the Garden when not otherwise required. They receive extra pay for this.

The Herdsmen are all Tribal and are never allowed to wear clothes. There is a large Station herd. The nucleus of the herd were fine cattle. The Friesian bull is not yet doing very well. One died last year.

It would be a mistake to hand over the Friesian to a Chief. There would never be any apparent result and it would be a drop in the ocean. It is better to grade up a Station herd and the Chiefs can then be asked to look at it when there are some cows worth having.[66]

There is also a small sounder of pigs & a flock of goats & sheep.

The General Book[67] referred to in General Information in respect of District report, now contains in addition, the following:

---

64. The CMS school at Malek in Bor District.

65. Mayan Lam was the son of Lam Tutthiang, the Lou chief who was arrested and imprisoned in Malakal in 1911. Many of Lam's children learned to speak Arabic there, and he subsequently became a staunch ally of the government, coming to settle near Abwong. Mayan's main job was to translate from Nuer into Dinka. While employed by the government he was sent to the American Mission school at Nasir to learn to read and write. Alban praised him highly and even proposed to make him a chief (A. H. Alban, 'Abwong District', 20.12.30, NRO Civsec 57/2/8 and SAD 212/14/214; A. H. Alban to governor UNP, 14.12.31, SRO UNP 66.B.11). The Nuer remember him as an honest man who translated correctly and did not take bribes to present cases favourably, as other interpreters used to do.

66. Coriat had originally been very enthusiastic about this experiment, criticising Struvé for his scepticism about its value and praising Willis for pushing it forward.

67. Not found.

Roll of Chiefs' Police.
Annual exp. & Grant Grass clearing & Sanitation.
Grant & Expenditure Landing Grounds.
Medical statistics and receipts.
General cattle account, this includes, cattle from Malakal, Patrol cattle etc. and all cattle other than Tribute, shown in Tribute book.
Chiefs' Courts receipts & Expenditure.
Rifles & Small Arms on charge.
Markets in District.
Traders Tax assessment.
List of Discharged Soldiers & Police in District.
Devolution expenditure.

I have placed notes in the relevant pages in this book relative to the various headings.

Devolution and road estimates will have to go in for 1930. Also grant required from Provincial budget for Local Services.

These notes should be read in conjunction with 'General Information in respect of District' report.

If there is any further information you require or anything not understood, please let me know. I am doing this away from the Station and there may be things I have forgotten.

The general Policy laid down is a Native Administration. I have interpreted this in the following way and have tried to work on these lines.

Peace. That is, because authority is to be maintained in the Chiefs, there can be no reason why there should be innumerable intersection fights and fights have been punished with severe fines.

I do not think a Chief should obtain fine cattle as a result of blood feuds and Shieng fights, and any fines collected either by Government or Chiefs go to Government. They will eventually go to a fund administered by the Chiefs themselves but not to the Chief's pocket.

Devolution of Authority. It is no use giving a Chief authority to do this or that if he has not the means or the will to control his own people and the sections have had to be disciplined and still have to be in some cases. If the Chiefs had the requisite influence it would be different but as yet they have not got authority on their own and without a backing as regards the Nuer is concerned. Given a Chief with determination and provided he is loyal, he should get all the moral and material backing he wants. There are not many Chiefs of this sort and that is why our problems are not those of Mongalla [Province] and Uganda etc.

Tribal Integrity. I do not allow long shirts, i.e. Arab clothes in the District. The

Ngok have now evolved a national dress (a sort of Toga with belt)[68] of their own and there is no reason why the Lau should not do the same. As soon as the odd lad is allowed to put on a jellabia he apes the Jellaba in manners and behaviour. This seems a small matter but I think it counts. Tribal boys are not encouraged to go to Malakal. In the past a fellow had to put on a shirt and talk Arabic before he could get near or curry favour with the 'Turk'. He is now just as proud of being a Nuer or Dinka in the Station as out of it and the people themselves realise that they mean just as much to Government as the Policeman, Peddlar or watercarrier in the Station.

The Foot Police and the escort of Mounted Police have no authority whatever with the Tribes except under your orders.

The Serraf has to show as much respect to the Chiefs as he would to an Arab Patriarch.

No Government Policeman is allowed under any circumstances whatever to leave the Station, either to collect tribute or people or any other reason. The only time Government Police have been outside the Station is when they have accompanied me as my escort. None of the Chiefs' Police are ex-soldiers or Police except Ruot Malwal of the small Rueng settlement at Kofkiot about whom I left you a separate note. Ruot is an ex-U.N.P. Policeman and is a special case.

All employees, watercarriers, herdsmen, sweepers, labourers are Tribal and local.

Authority of Chiefs. In their present stage of development, the more influence a Chief can obtain the better and other than blood feuds or fights as mentioned above, I have been quite prepared to hear a Chief has pocketed a fine off somebody or other for disobedience or truculence.

It is very unlikely to occur but you will soon hear of any abuse of authority on the part of Chiefs. If you do get complaints of this sort, probably the first ones will be from Tribesmen talking Arabic and general hangers on.

Kujurs when they crop up will require to be watched very closely and I think I failed in this, otherwise the 1928 Patrol would not have happened. (Don't down all Kujurs.)

Chiefs' Police [see Plates 9 and 10]. They are really the backbone of the Native administration at this stage. They are more reliable than the Chiefs, do not fear their people, being young bloods themselves and have an amazing esprit de corps. They are produced by the Chiefs and selected by the D.C., because until the Chiefs (I think they do now) realise what we are driving at, they imagine the most suitable fellow is the Arabic speaking hanger on.

Chiefs' Police start and end on 10 pt. per month pay plus a red armlet. They are given a toga of cloth as they are inclined to be shy if in Malakal.

68. A *loua*, the same in Shilluk.

They are responsible to Government as well as to their own Chiefs.

Courts. There are too many Chiefs functioning because I did not want to discourage people at the start and it was difficult to get a few strong Chiefs who were not afraid of giving decisions at the Courts without the moral backing of all the other Chiefs. This need not apply now and both with the Dinka and Nuer, the time has arrived for selection of the more important Chiefs to sit on Courts.

With the Dinkas this can apply to general Administrative purposes but with the Nuers it will have to be tentative.

In conclusion, I think the Nuers are a fine people and believe you will like them as you will the Dinkas in the District. They will seem stupid and probably deceitful at first but not when you know them.

As an instance of how one can get a mistaken impression, you might easily camp by some Luak and ask the owner whose it is. He might reply that it was Chief so and so's hut (naming his Chief) and you would thereupon ask him where the Chief was and he would say he was on a journey somewhere. You would then go away thinking it was the Chief's hut you had visited, to find out later that it was not and would conclude that the fellow was a liar and trying to deceive. All he meant was to please you and as his name conveyed nothing to you and he knew you knew the Chief, he had thought that by telling you that the hut belonged to his Chief you would be pleased and think what a sensible fellow he was.

I do not know whether the above conveys what I am trying to get at but I cannot think of any other way of impressing that they have got to be tackled with patience and that at present one should not deal with the Chief only to the exclusion of the ordinary people. For some time, unless they know you, they probably will not care much who their Chief is. This as far as the Nuer is concerned, but it is through the D.C.'s backing that they will respect and obey their chiefs & ultimately appoint them. There will be a lot of hard work and shidding [Arab., 'moving from one point to another'] in the District before one can sit back and watch the Chief's administration functioning.

The Nuer Settlement was not a punitive patrol against the Lau but an attempt to hasten up organisation and discipline and control by Chiefs and to assist the settlement in Gaweir. That is, a final [end] to the Patrols and marches of past days and which still seem to go on in some Districts where the administration is supposed to be more advanced and peaceable.

Pog Pan	Malakal
Gaing Kan	..
Ngun Munjang	..
Riak Kweth	..
Fathot Chodwey	..
Shwol [Shol] Rut	..
Chang [Can] Kwain	..
Majug [Majog] Wi	..
Dul Kai	..
Giel Lulog	..
Kweth Diu [Diow]	..
Gai Trel [Twil]	..
Kong Garakwoth	..
Shan Wel [Wal]	..
Pod Poal	..
Nyangweg Chai	.. ⎫ Of Shieng Lam
Shan Bidong	.. ⎬ Headman
Rieg Log	.. ⎭ Chamjog Chai

Shieng Tiang. Subshieng Goal. Chief Ngwoth Kuin.

Shwol Rueh [Rueth]	Malakal
Reth Rih	..
Leir Deng	..
Pok Kashwol	..
Turuk Kweka	..
Rom Let	..
Mut Belyu	..
Nyith Gweir[74]	..
Gaing Kyeth	..
Shwol Puh	..
Jik Buth	..

Shieng Matchok. Chiefs Weh Turial & Kol Gai.

Tut Wuth	Malakal
Nangwot [Bangot] Thiang	..
Reng Bul	..
Thod Dup	..
Kweth Jith [Jish]	..
Yuek Dag	..
Bul Thiep	..
Lul Ton [Thow]	..

74. A chiefs' policeman.

Shieng Yuong. Chiefs Nuer Ganur, Lam Thon, Yik Turog, Changath Rueh.
Gai Wanjang   Malakal
Kir Kwangag   ..
Kweth Diu   ..
Nuot Kweylual   ..
Niak Ngwot   ..
Jish Lual   ..
Bitho Kai   ..
Kwol Rueh   ..

Shieng Shish. Chief Gwet Thi.
Dwoth Pod   Malakal
Diu Gut   ..   —Gaweir Nuer
Shwol Diu   ..
Luin Met   ..
Kwoin Fathot   ..
Dag Dwot   ..
Reth Wundeng[75]   ..   —Of Wundeng Deng-
                                 kur family

75. Reath Ngundeng: Ngundeng's eldest legitimate son (his eldest son, Riam, had quarrelled with his father and had gone to live among the Jikany before the turn of this century).

SECTION TWO

Fixing the Boundary

FIXING THE BOUNDARY: INTRODUCTION

ONE of the most contentious issues in the pre-First World War administration of the Nuer was the regulation of the Nuer–Dinka border between the Gaawar, Lou, Nyareweng and Ghol. The main conflict between the Gaawar and Ghol was land: the Gaawar had occupied Ghol land on the Duk ridge since the 1890s, and the Ghol wanted it back. The Ghol generally tried to use the government to restore the land to them, and this was one reason why the Gaawar continued to mistrust the government after Deng Laka died in 1907. A tribal and provincial boundary was fixed between the Gaawar and Ghol in 1909–10, with the hope that this would regulate intertribal movements and prevent intertribal fighting. It was spectacularly unsuccessful in achieving either objective, and government attempts to enforce the border only contributed to the tension and antagonism between the peoples it separated. The inclusion of Duk Fayuil in the Upper Nile Province in 1926 helped to remove the provincial rivalry which had aggravated border disputes in the past. Nevertheless, a tribal boundary between Nuer and Dinka remained government policy well into the 1930s, despite reservations expressed by many district officials (Johnson 1982*a*).

After 1918 there were closer and friendlier relations between the Gaawar and the government, especially after Coriat's appointment to Ayod. It was therefore easier than in the past for the government to appear to be dealing with border problems even-handedly. Thus when a border clash occurred in 1925 it was possible for Coriat, Major Wyld (DC Duk Fayuil) and the Gaawar and Ghol chiefs involved to meet and reach an agreement (doc. 2.1 below).

With the outbreak of hostilities between the Nuer and government in 1928, however, the government adopted a sterner and more punitive attitude towards the Nuer and their Dinka boundary. In 1929 a no man's land was declared between Gaawar, Lou and their Dinka neighbours, ostensibly for the greater control of the Nuer and the protection of the Dinka. At the time this policy was enforced Coriat was no longer involved in the administration of either the Lou or Gaawar, but since no one else seemed to know precisely where the old tribal boundaries ran, his advice was eventually sought (doc. 2.2 below). By that time it was evident that a tribal no man's land was unrealistic and unenforceable. Both the no man's land and the tribal boundary were abandoned five years later.

Document 2.1

SETTLEMENT OF
OL DINKA–GAWEIR NUER
BOUNDARY DISPUTE

Between 1918, when Dual Diu submitted to the government, and 1925 there were many Nuer invasion scares among the Dinka of Bor district, but no invasions. The government attributed these rumours either to Dinka nervousness or Dinka intrigue. In 1925 a fight did occur along the Gaawar–Ghol border, and it appeared as if the Gaawar might invade the Dinka after all, as they had done in 1914 and 1916. Coriat was sent to the border in December 1925 to effect an agreement between the disputing parties.

This is his report of the border meeting which took place at the end of 1925. It is notable for many points which should alter standard interpretations of Nuer–Dinka hostility. First, the Gaawar movement south along the Duk ridge was precipitated by ecological factors (the alteration of water distribution following the 1916–18 floods), not by internal political segmentation. Secondly, the conflict following *the movement came about through the extension of Nuer inter-sectional feuds into Dinka territory, with the Dinka siding with one Gaawar section but not becoming directly involved in any fighting themselves. Thirdly, the Gaawar, through Dual Diu, were prepared to accept mediation and a restriction on their movements. This willingness to negotiate was due in no small part to the personal friendship between Coriat and Dual.*

Settlement of Ol Dinka–Gaweir Nuer Boundary Dispute
By District Commissioners Dinka–Nuer District
MP [Mongalla Province] and Southern District UNP

The District Commissioners Abwong and Duk Faywil[1] met at DUK FADIAT on 17.12.1925.

The D.C. Abwong was accompanied by Chief Dwal Diu (9)[2] and about 200 retainers and other minor Gaweir chiefs.

The D.C. Duk Faywil had with him Chief Mankweir Mahbub [Moinkuer Mabur][3] of the Ol and other Dinkas.

In order to prevent any possible friction it was decided that Chief Dwal's men should return to their homes and the D.Cs. then proceeded to Duk Faywil accompanied by Chiefs Dwal and Mankweir each with a few chiefs and personal retainers. Two days were spent at Duk Faywil in investigating the causes of the dispute and examining both parties separately and a return was made to Duk Fadiat on 21.12.1925.

The Chiefs were instructed to proceed direct to Amiel for the second meeting, while the D.Cs. made a tour along the line of the boundary from a point two miles north of Duk Fadiat westwards through Fachok, thence to Amiel by Wey Borley and Wey Thorley which covered the area in dispute.

Considerable difficulty was experienced in following the boundary line defined by Struvé, Owen and Fox at Wirfoi in 1910, owing to the uncertainty of the west fula of Khor Kabaij and the absence of any record of Captain Fox's exact delimitation.[4]

As arranged Chiefs Dwal and Mankweir met the D.Cs. at Amiel on the morning of 23.12.1925.

It was found that the chief cause of the trouble was the presence on the boundary of a few of the weaker Gaweir Shens, including Shen Kan Boi[5] (referred to later) who was not connected with Dwal or concerned with the original settlement made after Machar Diu's invasion.

The erection of four 'Luaks' at Wey Thorley some few months ago by Dwal Diu led to fighting with Shen Boi and this brought matters to a head with the Dinka for the following reasons: After Shen Boi's expulsion from Gaweir (ref. inter-Shen feuds. Gaweir S.C.R. dated Fasheir)[6] they migrated into Dinka

---

1. Major J. W. G. Wyld.

2. For the numbers in parentheses in this document, see above, Gaawar section lists, in docs. 1.2 and 1.3.

3. See above, doc. 1.3 n. 7.

4. See above, doc. 1.3.

5. Kan Boi was the leader of the small *cieng* Boi (named after his father), until his death in 1922. See above, doc. 1.3 n. 26.

6. The only known surviving documents describing the feud between Dual and Kan Boi are

country south of Duk Fadiat. Later they were given a village at Folo by Mankweir Mahbub's father[7] who took them under his protection. Some years after this and after Machar's death [1914], the country now in dispute having been vacated by both Dinka and Nuer was settled in by Shen Boi with the approval of Mankweir.

With the exception of a small fight between Shen Boi and chief Dwal Diu's (9) section in 1916[8] matters remained peaceable although as it is known Dinka rumours of Gaweir invasion have been persistent.[9] In addition to Shen Boi's settlement, other Gaweir from Fasheir and Dongayo (north of the boundary) filtered in and occupied the country close to Shen Boi without protest from the Dinkas. Turning to more recent events, it is evident that the Duk ridge has lost its attraction for the Gaweir since the flood years 1916–18 and Shens have drifted back to their old country west of the ridge.

Dwal himself, whose first village on the ridge was Buk, gradually moved South in search of better grazing and water for his cattle and possibly with designs upon the more desirable pastures of the Dinkas. In any case the latter was the motive ascribed to Dwal by the Dinkas.[10]

This Chief's present village at Turawo (or Turug [Turu]) is poor in grazing ground and ill supplied with water and separated from the dry season 'Toich' by a large waterless stretch of country. To the west along the northern side of the boundary, the plains are inhabited by sections of Shens Tod (4) and Bedeed (1) of Gaweir although this is the country originally occupied by Dwal's brother Machar during his conquests, which he afterwards vacated. This appears to have been one of the reasons for Dwal's move to Wey Thorley, which lies on open country about one mile south of Wey Borley and Shen Tod (4) and an equal distance north of Nkak [Okak], Shen Boi's village, which is also occupied by some of Mankweir's men.

This move was looked upon by Shen Boi as the preliminary to a further attack on them by Dwal in [an] attempt to reopen the old blood feud and by the Dinkas as a recommencement of the old Gaweir land raids, confirming

---

listed in n. 8 below.

7. See above, doc. 1.3 n. 7.

8. This fight took place in April 1918 (Abdulla Kher el Sid, MT, OC detachment 12th Sudanese, Awoi to OC Upper Nile District, 10.04.18, and inspector Bor District to governor, Mongalla Province, 25.04.18, both in SRO UNP SCR 14; also MPMIR April 1918, NRO Intel 2/48/408). Subsequent to this fight men from *cieng* Boi captured some of Dual's cattle and fled to the Lou (MPMIR October 1918, NRO Intel 2/48/408 and SRO TD SCR 36.H.2).

9. Contemporary reports of these rumours can be found in MPMIR: Dec. 1918, March 1921, June–July–Aug.–Sept. 1922, Sept. and Oct. 1924, NRO Intel 2/48/408 and SRO TD SCR 36.H.2; and governor, Upper Nile Province, to governor, Mongalla Province, 19.12.20, SRO UNP SCR 14.A.5.

10. See above, doc. 1.3. Dual came grazing near Duk Fadiat, complaining of lack of water and bad pastures around his home as early as the dry season of 1920 (Ibrahim Abd el Rahman, mamur Kongor to governor, Mongalla, 09.06.20, SRO UNP 66.B.11).

Dwal's threat to descend on Amiel, the heart of Mankweir's section and a Dinka Kujur centre. Actual hostilities at Wey Thorley were started by Shen Boi, although they were the only sufferers, losing one killed and two wounded. After discussion it was decided that:-

1. Kongleir and Wey Borley were definitely Gaweir.
2. Nkak was definitely Dinka.
3. That all country between these villages should remain unoccupied for the present.
4. This country will only be reoccupied by mutual consent of the Dinkas and Nuers and after reference to Government.
5. Shen Boi and other Gaweir to return to their own country in order to remove all cause of jealousy.

The following day in order to give effect to the above, Shen Boi and section of Shodgwar (13) and Tod (4) of Gaweir were evacuated and all huts burnt.

Chiefs and their followers then accompanied the D.Cs. through Nkak and the neutral territory to Kongleir in Gaweir where the final meeting was held before the parties dispersed to their homes.

The Nuers and Dinkas affirmed complete understanding of all arrangements and the limits of their respective territories. Owing to limited time and lack of requisite instruments it was found impossible to define an exact boundary for record. The D.Cs. agreed to do this as soon as possible and before any further misunderstandings can arise [see Fig. 1, in doc. 2.2 below].

In view of the fact that the Chiefs behaved extremely well and the absence of any friction between the parties, it is hoped that inter tribal feeling will cease to be hostile and in course of time may even become friendly now that the chief cause jealousy has been removed by the evacuation of Shen Boi.

The D.C. Abwong arranged that Shen Boi should return to their original home at Fasheir [Pacier][11] and promised an enquiry into the blood feud between them and the Shen Giel (Chief Dwal.9) with a view to a final settlement.

The D.C. Abwong was favourably impressed by the behaviour of Chief Mankweir Mahbub and whatever his past history this young Chief now shows himself to be possessed of good sense and anxious to maintain his territory in peace.

The constant rumours of Gaweir invasion in the past have undoubtedly been due to one or two of his prejudiced and influential followers.

There is evidence to show that Dwal himself has followers equally prejudiced and anxious to intimidate the Dinkas. Among these may be cited the following:-

---

11. It had been proposed as early as April 1918 to repatriate *cieng*s Boi and Bedid to their old homes (Inspector Bor District to governor, Mongalla Province, 28.04.18, SRO UNP SCR 14).

Gaweir
Biel Diu.[12] A brother of Dwal already known for his aversion to Government and cunning and intriguing character.

Ruob Gyark [Ruop Joak].[13] An ex-U.N.P. policeman of one year's standing with predatory instincts.

Dinka
Kwol Ateir. A cunning and soft spoken sub-Chief extremely prejudiced to Dwal and related by marriage to Shen Boi.

Deng Amon. An aggressive and quick tempered sub-Chief.

The D.Cs. agreed that for some years to come it will be necessary to maintain supervision over affairs on the tribal boundary and the necessity of an efficient post at Ayod or some other position in Southern Gaweir is still apparent.

Kongleir
Christmas Day, 1925

---

12. See above, doc. 1.3 n. 15, and below, doc. 3.3.
13. See above, doc. 1.3 n. 16.

DOCUMENT 2.2

NUER–DINKA RE SETTLEMENT INTERTRIBAL BOUNDARY

In 1927–8 the government fought the Lou prophet Guek Ngundeng because of his refusal to organize road work among his section of the Lou (see Section 3 below). Many Lou fled to the Gaawar, where they were followed by Coriat and a column of troops. The outcome was that Dual Diu broke with the government and raided the Dinka and government outposts at Duk Fadiat and Duk Fayuil in August 1928.[1]

At the end of 1929 the government decided to end the war with a massive forced resettlement, known as the 'Nuer Settlement'. The Lou and Gaawar were ordered into specific concentration areas, while a no man's land between the Nuer and Dinka (employed as a demilitarized zone) further restricted Nuer movements. Coupled with the no man's land was the policy of mass repatriation of Dinka living north of the boundary, to strengthen the southern Dinka by increasing their numbers. The author of this policy was C. A. Willis, governor of Upper Nile from 1927 to 1931. Before retiring from the province in 1931 he reaffirmed his instructions to his DCs 'that Dinka should go to Dinka country and Nuer to Nuer',[2] *as the cornerstone of the new administrative policy regarding the two peoples.*

This order was impossible to enforce. The Rut and Thoi Dinka living with the Gaawar refused to be transferred to the political control of Ghol and Nyareweng Dinka leaders. The Luac Dinka living on the Khor Fulluth were forcibly expelled from their homes and arrived in their new settlements just in time for a rinderpest epidemic, a locust plague, and general flooding. They soon drifted back home to the Khor Fulluth against government orders. The

---

1. See Wedderburn-Maxwell 1928; Wyld 1928; Dual Diu 1930; Gaawar texts 4.8, in Johnson, in preparation.

2. C. A. Willis, governor, Upper Nile Province, to district commissioners, Zeraf Valley & Bor and Duk, 15.03.31, SRO UNP 66.B.11.

Rumjok Lou living next to the Nyareweng Dinka also refused to leave those of their homes designated as part of the no man's land.

The two strongest advocates of both the no man's land and the repatriation policy had been governor Willis and Major Wyld, the DC for Bor and Duk District. Both left the province in 1931. The new governor, A. G. Pawson, was clearly unhappy with the policy he had inherited. He sought Coriat's advice, though he was now the DC for the Western Nuer and was not involved in enforcing the new policy. Coriat, too, had his reservations. The advice he offered in this document was pragmatic, based on an appreciation of recent Nuer–Dinka relations. Both of Coriat's successors, Captain Alban among the Lou and Wedderburn-Maxwell among the Gaawar, gave similar recommendations to those outlined here. Pawson eventually began to reverse Willis's policy in 1933, and the no man's land was abolished in 1936 (Johnson 1982a: 200).

Governor [3]
Upper Nile Province
Malakal

In accordance with your instructions—I have attempted to give an outline of the past history and general sequence of events which led to the resettlement of Nuer and Dinka sections on the east bank of the Zeraf.

I am writing from memory and my statements may not be entirely accurate.

Past History

Until 1910 there was no recognised boundary between LAU and GAWEIR Nuer and the Duk sections of the Dinka. Up to that time the history of the border was a succession of Nuer raids and encroachment of Dinka territory by the Nuer; partly by conquest, partly by a process of absorption. In 1910 the boundary was defined, Nuer were confirmed in possession of land conquered by them and it was agreed that there should be no violation by either side of the line drawn until such time as the Nuer and Dinka could by mutual consent live together.

The delimitation was as follows:-

> West to the Khor KABAIJ east to the Khor FULUS [Fulluth], through MANKWAKA, FATITET, JUAT, FANYOK, WARAWAR, DUK WARAWAR. GAWEIR to the North, Dinka to the South. (Struvé, Owen, and Fox at WIRFWOI).

Raids continued and in 1914 the GAWEIR under MACAR DIU occupied a number of Dinka villages whence they were ejected by the 1914 Patrol but to

---

3. A. G. Pawson: Introduction, n. 56.

which they returned in 1915.[4] Conditions on the border remained unsettled but there were no further conquests by the Nuer.

In 1926[5] there was considerable agitation among the Dinka owing to occupation by the Nuer of land close to or on the border. The Nuer were removed after a meeting by the District Commissioners concerned (Wyld and Coriat) [and] a strip of territory on the west side of the Duk ridge was declared No Man's Land. The line WEY BORLEY to the Zeraf was established as the Southern limit of the Nuer and OKAK to the Zeraf as the Northern limit of the Dinka. Villages between the lines were destroyed. The Gaweir appealed against this but there was no further aggression on their part.

Though the Lau Nuer occasionally assisted their Gaweir brothers in raids against the Dinka, conquered territory went to the Gaweir and relations between the Lau Nuer and Duk Dinka were on the whole friendly. Those sections of the Lau who lived in LANG and adjacent to the Dinka are probably 60% Dinka. In fact so great has been absorption of Dinka by Lau that possibly not more than 60% of the Lau as a whole are pure bred Nuer.[6]

Nuer Settlement

Trouble throughout the Nuer areas led to the Nuer Settlement. One of the objects of the Settlement was to establish a No Man's Land between Dinka and Nuer as an effective bar to Nuer aggression.

Primarily the Gaweir were concerned and at the conclusion of operations, all Nuer villages South of Ayod were ordered to move North or off the Duk ridge.

This decision affected the Rut Dinka living in and near Fangak, the LUANG DENG Dinka of central Gaweir,[7] the Dinka sections living near LAU country East of Duk Fadiat and the sections of Dinka occupying the banks of the Khor Fulus from KAN to the mouth of the Khor. A number of these sections were willing and anxious to move but others, particularly the FULUS people who had for years been friendly with the LAU and who lived close by their brothers, the NGOK Dinka of Abwong, were loath to move.

As an outcome of this policy which in effect was Nuer to Nuer and Dinka to Dinka, and in order that there should be an unoccupied area between the

4. For a history of Macar Diu's raids, see Kulang Majok, text 2.5, in Johnson, in preparation.

5. December 1925 (see above, doc. 2.1).

6. Evans-Pritchard gave an estimate of 50%–75% (1933: 5, 53), while Crazzolara estimated 50% (1953: 36).

7. See above, doc. 1.3.

Lau Nuer and the Dinka, all Nuer sections living South of the old Upper Nile Province Mongalla boundary line were with a few exceptions ordered to evacuate. The whole of the LANG area is South of this line.

Present Position

The Fulus Dinka have moved. They were ejected by force and there may still be backsliders.[8]

The Fulus country is essentially a durra growing one and unfitted for Nuer occupation.

The Nuer in LANG never intended to move and have no intention of moving now. Short of prolonged operations by mounted police with a District Commissioner nothing will induce them to move. It is doubtful whether even this would be successful. The Lang country supplies excellent water and grazing for Nuer cattle. The Lau country as a whole is notably short of dry season camping grounds and their only other outlet, without LANG, is west to the Gaweir 'Toich' or east into Anuak country on the GENI and PIBOR.[9]

Evacuation of LANG is to make the whole country from approximately south of the line FADDOI, MWOT DID to the Mongalla hills a vast uninhabited area. The result of settling Dinka on the Duk ridge in the country immediately south of Ayod has been to abolish any advantages which may have been obtained by the decision to declare a neutral territory between the two tribes. Thus we have, as regards the Dinka and Gaweir, reverted to a boundary between the two tribes, whereas between the Dinka and Lau who were least affected by a No Man's Land, there is a large tract of neutral territory containing some of the best land in their domains. To allow the Nuer grazing in Lang and prevent permanent occupation would mean neither one thing nor the other to the people and would be quite impracticable.

Conclusion

I am not qualified to give an opinion as to whether or not the border policy should be reconsidered but I am convinced that it will be difficult if not impossible to carry out present intentions quite apart from any hardship to the

---

8. Almost all the Luac had returned to the Fulluth by early 1933.

9. For discussions of the excessive seasonal dryness of Lou country, see Evans-Pritchard 1940: 118–19 and Jonglei Investigation Team 1954: 144–5.

people concerned without protracted forcible measures.

It might however be possible without reversing previous decisions to modify the general terms of the policy.

Any Fulus sections who do not wish to live with the Southern Dinka could be allowed to return to their homes.

The Lau might be allowed to occupy the Lang and neutral territory could be restricted to a narrow strip of country running from the Duk ridge east to the eastern edge of the Dinka and thence south.

Roughly this would run as shown in the diagram below:

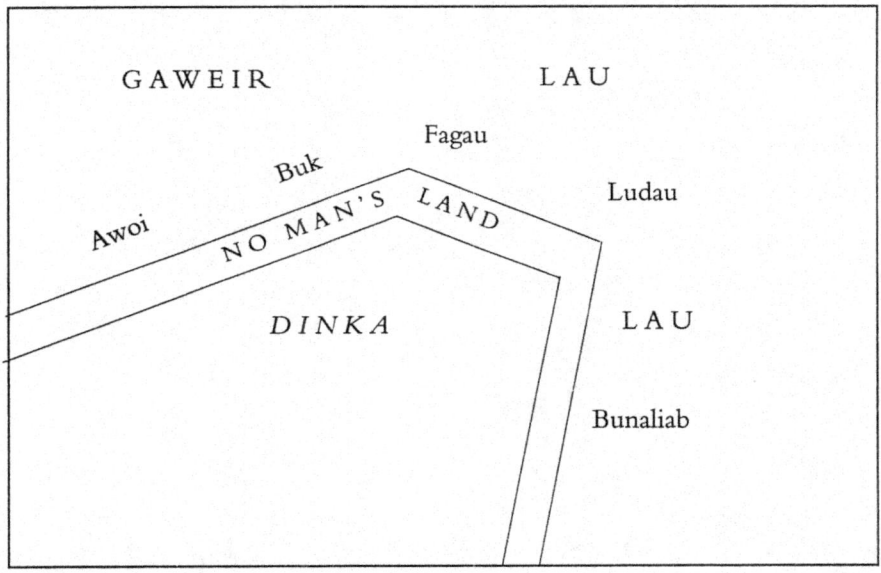

FIG. 1 Nuer–Dinka boundary, 1931

The suggestion is a tentative one and the District Commissioner concerned may produce a better and easier solution.

Malakal
28th November 1931

P.C.
District Commissioner
Western Nuer

SECTION THREE

The Nuer Settlement

THE NUER SETTLEMENT: INTRODUCTION

THE most dramatic series of events during Coriat's term among the Nuer concerned the Lou Nuer prophet Guek Ngundeng in 1927–9. These events were all the more startling, perhaps, because Coriat's relations with Guek from 1923 to 1926 had been unexceptional. Guek had faded into the background as Coriat developed local administration among the Lou and found other leaders willing to conform to government. Guek's rebellion was perhaps as much of a surprise to Guek as it was to Coriat.

The only piece Coriat wrote on the Nuer which has been relatively widely circulated was his article 'Gwek the Witch-doctor and the Pyramid of Dengkur', in *Sudan Notes and Records* in 1939. It was written a full ten years after the events it described, and some eight years after Coriat had left Nuer administration. He apparently did not have all the relevant papers at hand when he wrote this article, and there are some major discrepancies between what he wrote at the time and what was published ten years later.

A fuller account of Guek's rising is given elsewhere (Johnson 1979; Johnson, forthcoming), and the main events are summarized in the documents which follow. It is only by comparing Lou Nuer testimony[1] with contemporary government documents that doubts about the seriousness of Guek's 'rebellion' emerge. The rebellion began during the rains of 1927, when Coriat was not only out of the district, but home on leave. Guek had shown some reluctance to carry out government orders to clear a new motor road before Coriat had left, and there had been attempts by Lou intermediaries to get the two men to discuss the issue more fully. Rumours began to circulate of Guek's preparations for war just as Coriat was about to leave the province. The sources of these rumours were not convincing, coming as they did mainly from Major Wyld and his Dinka chiefs and interpreters, persons who had already demonstrated a credulous hostility to all things Nuer. Khartoum decided to take no final action until Coriat could report back. By the time he returned to his district in November 1927 preparations for hostilities were advanced on both sides.

The four documents in this section are the fullest contemporary record in Coriat's own words of the events surrounding the conflict with Guek. They are a substantial corrective to the account he published in 1939, where he tended to exaggerate or elaborate on some of the incidents recorded more matter-of-factly here.

1. Jackson 1927 and Lou texts 4.2, in Johnson, in preparation.

20. Nov. 1927

Arrived Khartoum. 10 am. Put up with Col. Nosworthy. A.A.G. Reported Civil Secretary 11.30. Handed files and reports from Malakal re. trouble in Lau. Kujur GWEK WUNDENG of DENGKUR pyramid continued agitation after departure of self on leave. Duk Fayent reports great slaughter of bulls at pyramid and threats by GWEK against Nuers not supporting him. Lau said to be eating meat and blood to strengthen them for coming fight. GWEK forbids tribesmen to work on road except for small amount of clearing, near Duk in order to delude Government. Signal for rising to be murder of self and escort when all Nuers will rise against Government. Nasser reports JEKAING Nuers approached by GWEK but refuse assistance owing failure of LAU to support JEKAING against Government during 1920 Patrol. Other reports state Kujur DWAL DIU of GAWEIR had interview with GWEK but has not promised support and other Nuer sub-tribes will sit on fence until result of first rising is known. Nuer plan said to be meeting of self by Chiefs who will accompany me to pyramid when GWEK will give signal for tribesmen to attack. Rifles of Government will fail to function.

First page of Percy Coriat's 'Gwek Diary', November 1927 (reduced by 25%). *Source:* Coriat MSS, Rhodes House, Bodleian Library, University of Oxford, MSS Afr.s.1684. (Reproduced with the kind permission of the Curators of the Bodleian Library.)

Document 3.1

GWEK DIARY

The rumblings and rumours surrounding the Lou had not been sufficiently urgent to recall Coriat prematurely from home leave, but when he returned to Khartoum in early November it suddenly seemed imperative to rush him to Malakal. Arriving in Khartoum on 20 November 1927, he was then flown to Malakal on the 24th in one of the RAF Middle Eastern Command's obsolescent DH9A two-seaters. In Malakal he only had enough time to gather together a few rations and a single servant before being dispatched by steamer to Abwong to begin his intelligence-gathering mission. He had to forgo the DC's standard fare of tinned foods and game, relying on Nuer grain instead. Even this minor inconvenience added to the air of crisis, Willis commenting, 'Mr. Coriat was reduced to eating raw millet boiled in water before he returned—Political Conditions must indeed be serious to justify the stomach-ache that that means.'[1]

This diary of events comes from Coriat's personal papers, now in Rhodes House. It covers the time from his arrival in Khartoum to the beginning of his trek in Lou country. He may not have used it in compiling his report on Patrol S8 (document 3.2), as he sent it to his wife with a shorter letter. It does contain a number of personal observations about the build-up to the campaign which do not appear in his official reports.

---

20 Nov. 1927

Arrived Khartoum 10 a.m. Put up with Col. Nosworthy. A.A.G.[2]

1. Willis to civil secretary, 10.12.27, NRO Civsec 5/2/10.
2. Colonel (later Lt.-General Sir) Francis Poitiers Nosworthy, DSO, MC, chief staff officer and second in command SDF 1926–30, and acting adjutant-general, November 1927.

Reported Civil Secretary[3] 11.30. Handed files and reports from Malakal re trouble in Lau.[4] Kujur Gwek Wundeng [Guek Ngundeng] of Dengkur pyramid continued agitation after departure of self on leave. Duk Fayuil reports great slaughter of bulls at pyramid and threats by Gwek against Nuers not supporting him. Lau said to be eating meat and blood to strengthen them for coming fight. Gwek forbids tribesmen to work on road except for small amount of clearing, near Duk in order to delude Government. Signal for rising to be murder of self and escort when all Nuers will rise against Government.[5] Nasser reports Jekaing Nuers approached by Gwek but refuse assistance owing failure of Lau to support Jekaing against Government during 1920 Patrol.[6]

Other reports state Kujur Dwal Diu of Gaweir had interview with Gwek but has not promised support and other Nuer sub-tribes will sit on fence until result of first rising is known.[7] Nuer plan said to be meeting of self by Chiefs who will accompany me to pyramid when Gwek will give signal for tribesmen to attack. Rifles of Government will fail to function. Nuers all nervous of Gwek and among other yarns state that Gwek ordered several young men to load their rifles and then gave them order to fire when cartridges failed to explode, thus proving his ability to render firearms innocuous. Dinka tribes apprehensive of raids and attacks by Nuers.[8] Reports from Nasser state that Abyssinian invasion of Annuak [Anuak] territory on Sudan border is threatened owing to murder of an Abyssinian party at Itang.[9] Fugitives from Annuak [Anuak] country if driven into Lau would complicate Gwek affair.

Saw memo by Gov. general reference to probable use of troops in Lau. G.G. considered political influence should be used before hostilities and Gwek's attitude and grievances to be determined.[10] Saw MacMichael, CS [Civil Secretary] and explained events prior to departure on leave. Interview with Gov. Gen. arranged for following morning.

3. H. A. MacMichael, CMG, DSO, civil secretary 1926–33, KCMG 1931. Later governor and commander-in-chief Tanganyika 1934-8, high commissioner and commander-in-chief Palestine, high commissioner Trans-Jordan 1938–44.

4. Now in NRO Civsec 5/2/10.

5. Report from a Dinka chief and Duk Fayuil interpreter: J. W. G. Wyld to governor, Upper Nile Province, 18.09.27, NRO Civsec 5/2/10 and UNP 1/5/27. The plot to kill Coriat was subsequently denied by another Dinka agent (J. W. G. Wyld to governor, Upper Nile Province, 02.10.27, ibid.).

6. J. Lee to governor, Malakal, 16.10.27, NRO Civsec 5/2/10 and UNP 1/5/27.

7. The reports in fact claim only that Guek had sent messages to Dual (J. W. G. Wyld to governor, Upper Nile Province, 18.09.27 and 02.10.27, NRO Civsec 5/2/10 and UNP 1/5/27). Dual and Guek never met.

8. J. Lee to governor, Malakal, 16.10.27, and acting governor, Upper Nile Province, to civil secretary, 22.10.27, both in NRO Civsec 5/2/10 and UNP 1/5/27.

9. Itang was a small trading post set up on the Ethiopian border in Gaajok country in 1904.

10. Sir John Maffey, 19.11.27, NRO Civsec 5/2/10 and UNP 1/5/27.

Discussed situation with Nosworthy who was acting Kaid during Gen. Huddleston's[11] absence South. Considered if reports even partly true, trouble to be expected.

Foley[12] & Stevenson from War Office to dinner.

21 Nov.

Went to Palace for interview with Gov. Gen.[13] 11.30 a.m.

G.G. very pleasant and enquired after personal affairs etc. referred to last meeting at Abwong[14] and enquired as to whether I knew GWEK. Explained with deference that I considered he had 'got hold of the wrong end of the stick' and described events previous to my departure from Abwong on leave, GWEK's truculence and his seizure of opportunity to stir up trouble and regain power and prestige lost during past four years by declaiming [*sic*] the benefits of new road, owing to his knowledge of the unpopularity of this among tribesmen. GWEK may also have had considerable success with 'tricks' and reported drought in LAU after his threat to withhold water until tribe attacked Government, a signal piece of luck for him.[15] Gov. Gen. amused and was extremely decent. Stated he had not known situation among LAU and concurred that although it may have been possible to use political influence in the first instance, as I was fully acquainted with GWEK and tribe it was only necessary for me to explain what I wanted done. Informed Gov. Gen. that only one of two things could occur, either GWEK would obtain support of tribesmen and would fight or he would fail to rally tribesmen and would become a fugitive. GWEK himself having gone too far to submit.

Gov. Gen. agreed that this was clear and suggested troops and/or aeroplanes be used immediately. I objected to this as it would be preferable to discover what actual support GWEK had raised and pointed out that I should be allowed to proceed to Abwong and if necessary inland to determine actual situation. Gov. Gen. agreed and sent for Col. Nosworthy to whom discussion was explained. It was then decided that I should meet Kaid, Governor and Wing Commander

---

11. Later Major-General Sir Hubert Huddleston, KCB, DSO, MC, commander-in-chief SDF 1924–30, governor-general of the Sudan 1940–7.

12. Captain (later Major) Guy Francis Foley, CMG, OBE, MC (Royal Artillery), 1896–1970, EA 1920–5, SDF 1925–30, director of stores and ordnance, and later director of economics and trade in Khartoum.

13. Sir John Maffey (1877–1969), later 1st Baron Rugby (1935), Indian Civil Service 1899–1924, governor-general of the Sudan 1926–33.

14. In June 1927; see below, doc. 3.2.

15. In 1921 Guek was credited with destroying Mor Lou crops with heavy rain as a punishment for their continued disobedience to government orders (*SMIR* 326 (Sept. 1921), 4).

Reid of Air Force[16] on 7 Dec. at Abwong and situation would again be discussed. Willis[17] due to arrive at Khartoum 25th could reach Abwong by this date. Nosworthy suggested it would be much more satisfactory if I could by that date know whether it was war or not and offered to send me by air to Malakal if this would enable me to reach Abwong in time to sense atmosphere and give definite information by 7 Dec. Steamer route would take me 7 days and by air 5 hours. Flight plan adopted and interview terminated after Gov. Gen. impressing me with necessity of avoiding putting myself into undue danger or taking unnecessary risk.

Saw Wing Commander Reid at War Office and formed opinion he was definitely against use of Air Force in event of Patrol being required. Motored over to Air Squadron[18] lines with Reid and arranged matter of baggage with Sq. Leader Cox.[19] Arranged to visit lines following morning.

Nosworthy told me at tea time that Reid much against use of planes in Lau particularly without ground force, though he will not admit it or state objection in writing. Policy as regards internal trouble, that Air Force must be used and tried. Success of Air Force in Irak administration compels trial in Sudan in order to determine their use, one way or the other.[20]

22 Nov.

Postponed trip till 24th and to visit Air lines 23rd to watch bombing and gunning practice.

Saw MacMichael in Office and given written instructions not to go into danger zone. Did not ask him how one knew what was or was not a danger zone before going into it!

23 Nov.

Up at 4 a.m. and drive to Air Force lines. Fly with Sq. Leader Cox to practise ground and land and watch bombing and gunning practice, flying back to breakfast 9 a.m.

16. Wing Commander George R. M. Reid, DSO, MC, commander of No. 47 Squadron RAF in Khartoum.

17. Willis, too, had been on leave since August.

18. No. 47 Squadron, RAF.

19. Squadron Leader Claude R. Cox, AFC.

20. The RAF had been used effectively in conjunction with the Arab Legion to combat nomad raids (Cox 1985). No. 47 Squadron was stationed in Khartoum earlier in 1927, partly at the insistence of Winston Churchill in order to expand the use of the RAF and guarantee its survival as an independent force (Killingray 1984).

Cox informed me machines were D.H.9.s but new machines were expected.[21]

Dined at MacMichael's, also Nosworthy, Reid and Davies the D.I.[22] Avoided talking of LAU affair till just before leaving. Returned home with Nosworthy 12 p.m. and bid good bye to him before going to bed. An extraordinarily decent fellow and was most helpful officially as well as being a charming host. Leave cook with heavy baggage to come on with Willis.

24 Nov.

Motored to Air force lines 4 a.m. Breakfast on a bottle of soda and find myself in the air by 6 a.m. with Fl. Lt. Grey driving me. Escorting machine driven by Harrison and accompanied by mechanic Bolton.[23] Smooth going for first three hours and greatly interested in aspect of country. Recognised Kosti and Renk[24] and other stations. Air bumpy owing to rising sun last hour. Landed at Malakal 10.30 a.m. after a good flight. Landing, machine banked somewhat acutely by Shilluk village and Grey admitted later he had not given himself quite enough room. Met by Cann, Morris, Moir and Wileman.[25] Put up with Cann and Mrs.

All well at Malakal. Crouch, Henderson, Tunnicliffe, Inglis-Jones also in Station. Wyld and Mrs. at Bor.[26]

Hear of all developments from Cann. Informed Alban of Mongalla Province[27] at Abwong. Dine with Waller's,[28] also there Canns, Crouch and Moir. Hear that Bay pony has died of 'fly'. A very grievous blow.[29]

---

21. The aircraft were DH9As, a post-war modification of the old DH9. They were replaced by the Fairy IIIa, a two-seater biplane.

22. Reginald Davies, director of intelligence 1927–8.

23. Flying Officer Andrew N. Grey, Flight Lieutenant Anthony C. B. D. Harrison, MC, and mechanical fitter Dolton (not Bolton). An escort plane with mechanic was sent along in case of mechanical failure or a forced landing.

24. Kosti is where the railroad crosses the White Nile on its way to El Obeid. Renk is the northernmost town in Upper Nile Province.

25. Captain G. P. Cann, see above, doc. 1.5 n. 7; Morris, Moir and Wileman are found on neither the civil nor military staff lists of the time.

26. Dr H. A. Crouch, Sudan Medical Service 1923–44; Dr L. H. Henderson, Sudan Medical Service 1926–43; Captain E. C. Tunnicliffe, formerly 12th Sudanese, OC Police UNP 1925–7 and 1934–7, ADC Pibor District 1927–34 (see Plates 18 and 19); Captain John Alfred Inglis-Jones (Grenadier Guards), SDF 1924–9. At this time Major Wyld's wife, Mika (a White Russian emigrée), was the only DC's wife in the province allowed to live outside Malakal.

27. See above, Introduction, n. 5.

28. Standish Waller, inspector Egyptian Irrigation Department, Malakal.

29. The death of Coriat's pony was later attributed by some to Guek's powers.

25 Nov.

Flight returns to Khartoum early morning.

Leave after playing bridge at 'Equat'[30] mess with Inglis-Jones and Crouch and dining with Canns at 10 p.m.

Army & Political side of Malakal, also Morris see me off on steamer! Take troop of Mounted Police with me.

26 Nov.

Horribly monotonous chug chug of 'Shabluka' the slowest steamer on river,[31] continues throughout the day.

27 Nov.

Awake to find myself at Abwong. Dress and meet Alban who I find is busily occupied with 150 Dinkas clearing a landing ground for aeroplanes. Ground nearly completed.

Breakfast with Alban. 'Shabluka' returns after disembarking Police and mules.

Alban informs me a Chief of Lau came in with elephant tusk as offering to Govt. and on being pressed stated GWEK had forbidden them to work on road. Learn later that Chief was DTHO DIENG [Dhiew Dieng], a particularly cheerful and enlightened Chief.[32] Cann considered him to be a spy of GWEK's but personally, think he may have come in both to scout the lie of the land for Nuers and to ingratiate himself with Govt. A difficult situation for one finding himself between the Devil and the Deep Sea as represented by GWEK on the one side and Govt. on the other. Alban has no further information but Police Sgt. full of alarmist reports.

Find second pony and servants well. Kapato, the small boy still with Mrs. Wyld and should return with Gov. on 7 Dec.

---

30. Equatorial Corps, SDF, a non-Muslim battalion raised primarily among the Zande and Moru of what was then Mongalla Province for use in the Southern Sudan, replacing the old Sudanese battalions composed of Muslim ex-slave soldiers.

31. SGS *Shabluka*, a small stern-wheeler built with a boiler and machinery salvaged from Mahdist steamers in 1904; scrapped about 1930 (Hill 1972: 208); nicknamed 'Shabbyloo' by province personnel.

32. Dhiew Dieng reported back to Guek after this visit that the government was planning to attack him. According to the Lou this report was crucial in Guek's decision to fight. See below, doc. 3.2.

29 Nov.

Left for reconnaissance of Lau with 2 troops Mounted Police.

Document 3.2

GENERAL REPORT: PATROL S8
(LAU NUER) 1928

This report summarizes the administration of the Lou from 1923 to 1927, taking up the narrative where the preceding document leaves off. It was written against the background of the suspicion that Coriat could have prevented the rising by a more vigorous handling of Guek during the dry season of 1927. Here Coriat is trying to explain why Guek did not appear to be a serious threat before the rains of 1927. In many ways modern Lou testimony confirms this assessment.[1] In the end the most convincing evidence Coriat could produce which confirmed a long-held grievance on Guek's part rested on the assumption that Guek was trying to regain power lost to the government in its victory over the Lou in 1917. We now know Guek played no leading role in that campaign and did not even become a prophet until after 1917. The charge that Guek was trying to regain influence lost in the earlier campaign is repeated in Coriat 1939, where Guek is also portrayed as more blatantly hostile than he appears here.

Document 3.1 reveals that military plans were well advanced before Coriat returned to his district. Matters of high policy, decided in London and passed on to Khartoum, dictated the experimental use of the RAF on an internal patrol in the Sudan, despite the local wing commander's reservations about the logistical feasibility of such a demonstration. Coriat's orders, too, restricted his options. He argued prior to the campaign for the use of Mounted Police rather than the army and repeats those arguments here, but the impetus of the military imperative was too strong to resist.

Little satisfaction can be taken from military operations which go wrong, but if Coriat's handling of Guek was considered too lenient, he was able to point out that confidence in the RAF's ability to crush the rising was too high. Far from overawing the Lou, it dispersed them before the army could deal an effective blow. The campaign to track down Guek and other

1. Lou texts 4.2, in Johnson, in preparation.

fugitives continued for another year, spilling over into the Gaawar and expanding the Nuer rebellion.

Governor
U.N.P.
Strictly Confidential

Events Leading up to Patrol

The following short note on the Kujur Gwek Wundeng [Guek Ngundeng] and Kujur in general in the Lau country will enable a more clear appreciation of the sequence of events leading to the Patrol.

Gwek Wundeng of Shieng Shish [Cic] of the Gun division of Lau, was born at Keij (Dengkur) in the Lau country some 45 years ago, son of Wundeng Dengkur [Ngundeng Bong] by a Jekaing [Jikany] Nuer woman.[2]

Gwek's father Wundeng Bung acquired the name Dengkur after the spirit by which he is said to have been possessed[3] and was the originator and builder of the Dengkur pyramid recently destroyed. This edifice, which was 60 ft. high and constructed of mud, was the symbol of Wundeng's Kujurial power and as far as can be ascertained was completed about 20 years before the birth of Gwek and on the site of his Grandfather's grave.[4] Tribesmen from all the Nuer countries were summoned for the labour on its erection and for many years previously and in order to ensure sufficient food for the labourers, it was customary for men, women and children visiting or passing the site to take with them a small amount of grain to be deposited in the granaries of Wundeng's village. This custom prevailed until comparatively recently.

There has never, as far as I am aware, been any similar monument among the Nuer and it is uncertain why the Witchdoctor should have chosen this particular method of demonstrating his power to the tribes, though occasionally a small conical mound 4 to 5 ft. high is to be found at the grave of a noted Kujur or Leader.[5] On Wundeng's death, the son Gwek inherited his father's supernatural powers and although he seems to have been anxious to maintain the family

---

2. Guek was in fact probably no more than thirty-one years old when this report was written. See above, doc. 1.5 n. 19.

3. Dengkur was Ngundeng's ox-name; Deng was his divinity. 'Wundeng' is the Dinka pronunciation of Ngundeng (see Deng 1973: 208, song no. 90).

4. The Mound was built in the 1890s and had nothing to do with Ngundeng's father, who lived and died among the Eastern Jikany. Coriat published a more detailed account of the building of the Mound in Coriat 1939: 223–5. See also Alban 1940: 201.

5. Known precedents for the shrine include Puom Aiwel on the Bahr el-Zeraf and Luang Deng in Rut Dinka country. See Howell 1948.

prestige, he was not successful in retaining the hold over Nuer tribes other than the Lau, which his father had. The coming of Government had largely to do with this.[6]

The Lau relate that at some time during Wundeng's lifetime, the 'Turk' (possibly slave raiders), coming from the direction of the Sobat, carried out a raid on the Pyramid and carried off a quantity of ivory with which the base and apex of the mound had been adorned. This is the only record of any outside influence having been felt in central Lau before the present Government.[7]

I have no data regarding the Lau or Gwek's attitude to Government previous to the 1917 Patrol, but the principal cause of this expedition was the attack on and annihilation of a Platoon of the 9th Sudanese under a Native Officer. Gwek with other Kujurs is said to have been the directing hand in this.[8] The Policy of despatching troops for the collection of tribute cannot be held to have been the most successful method of obtaining the confidence of the people and combating anti-Government Kujur influence. The 1917 Patrol was not successful in effecting the capture of Gwek and its results politically have been recorded in past reports.[9]

From 1917 and for some years, the administration of Lau was limited and in 1921 following reports of Gwek's anti-Government activities, a visit was paid to Dengkur by the then Deputy-Governor of the Province [H. C. Jackson] who reported that he had been able to influence Gwek in the right direction and had left the Kujur in an attitude entirely friendly to Government. At the same time the Deputy-Governor appointed a half-brother, Bul Wundeng [Bol Ngundeng] as Government Chief to represent Gwek in matters affecting his own Sub-shieng of Shieng Shish.[10]

In 1922 a report of disturbance in Lau and various rumours of Gwek's activities came to nothing.[11]

6. Ngundeng died in January 1906. Guek was still a boy then. He did not inherit his father's divinity until after 1917.

7. This was the 1902 'Dengkur Patrol' of Governor Blewitt (Johnson 1982*b*). This account differs from Coriat 1939: 225, which claimed that Ngundeng had been raided twice by slavers. In fact, Ngundeng was never raided by the old Egyptian government, the slavers, or the Mahdists, but only by the Anglo-Egyptian government.

8. Guek was not involved in the 1917 fight, at least not as a leader. The Lou fought under Pok Kerjiok (see above, doc. 1.5 n. 45 and below, doc. 3.4). It was only after Guek fled to his maternal relatives among the Eastern Jikany following Pok's defeat that he became seized by the divinity Deng.

9. See particularly SRO UNP SCR 15.10, 'Lau Nuer Patrol 1917'. The company of the 9th Sudanese who were annihilated by Pok Kerjiok in 1916 were not collecting tribute, but had been sent out to intercept a Lou Nuer raiding party who had just captured some Dinka cattle (Johnson 1982*a*: 196).

10. Jackson's accounts of his meetings with Guek can be found in Jackson 1954: 160–8; SAD 465/4; and Jackson 1927.

11. Jackson 1927.

At the latter end of 1923 I was instructed to include the Lau in my District.

A number of existing Shiengs had not then been registered and a proportion of those listed were inaccurate. The majority of so-called Chiefs whom I met had either been appointed by Government in the past or were produced before me by the sections as their Leaders. In most cases they were old and decrepit or of the type of tribesman to be found loitering around a Government Post for what he can pick up. In every section there was, if not an actual Chief, a man with some influence over his particular camp but for some reason these were not forthcoming in dealings with Government.

So far as possible I accepted as Chief any Nuer whether a Kujur or not who had any semblance of control over his section or who appeared to have the makings of a Chief in him.[12] It was some time before the real Leaders, where they existed, were willing to work with Government. As a preliminary step, I visited the Kujur Gwek Wundeng at Dengkur, having previously met Bul Wundeng referred to above. Bul, a youthful tribesman impressed me as being singularly lacking in brains and quite incapable of acquiring any merit as Chief, neither did he appear to have any of the qualities of a Leader either from the point of view of Government or the Nuer.

On my first meeting with Gwek I informed him that as a Sub-Chief I expected him to deal direct with Government and pointed out that there was no further need for Bul as his representative. Gwek demurred in the first instance and pleaded that Kujur precluded his dealing directly with Government, and that he was only able to leave his home at the behest of Kujur, but I assured him that it was the intention of Government to deal directly with the Tribal Leaders and representatives were only required in the case of Chiefs who from age or sickness were unable to carry out their duties, also that where he was dealing with Government his Kujur would obtain absolution from the Spirits.[13]

From thence till 1927 Gwek gave no trouble. At no time during my dealings with the man had I occasion to refer to Kujur except in the instance referred to above, though from time to time I received information as to his activities in that direction.

I had originally intended Gwek to control the whole of Shieng Shish and possibly the Gun Lau, but the more I became acquainted the less did I consider him fitted as a Chieftain and had it not been for his Kujurial power and the necessity of keeping him in a position where he could be watched, I would have been prepared to ignore his influence entirely.

On the formation of Chiefs' Courts and Police in 1927, Gwek was present at the preliminary meeting but appeared to be of so little use that I allowed him to absent himself for the future. His visits to the Merkaz [Abwong] once in

---

12. This was the policy of all administrators among the Nuer in the early 1920s.

13. Modern prophets have used the same argument as Guek to limit their direct contacts with the government. Modern Sudanese administrators (including some Nuer) have countered much as Coriat did.

1925 and once in 1926 seemed a satisfactory proof that he had no ill intentions and he carried out his ordinary section duties and paid tribute. Owing to his inability to combine with other Chiefs in administrative matters I treated him as a minor Chief. My final impression of Gwek was that he was friendly to Government and wished only to be allowed to carry out more or less harmless Kujur. By the end of 1926 I did not consider his influence sufficiently strong to cause any reactionary element to retard the administration even had he wished it.

As regards other Kujur in Lau, mention need only be made of Char Koryom of Duk Fayuil District with whom I had no dealings previous to the Patrol and Pok Keirjok (Kujur name Gar Wi).

Char was said to be harmless and chiefly concerned with rainmaking.[14] Pok of Shieng Nyajakan [Nyajikany] of the Gun Lau was not a hereditary Kujur and is said to have acquired his powers some time previous to the Lau Patrol in 1917.[15] I had numerous dealings with Pok in the past and although an unprepossessing individual and said to have been concerned in the attack made on the 9th Sudanese, I had not considered him worthy of any special concern. His influence could hardly have been widespread as I had occasion to try several cases brought against him by tribesmen. With the exception of one case brought by a Dinka, I have not heard of any claim ever having been made against Gwek, although I had had cases which the tribesmen stated had been heard by Gwek in the past and with whose decision they were not satisfied.[16]

To turn to recent events.

On my return from a tour of South-Eastern Lau in May 1927 a gathering of the Gun division Chiefs was held at Shit [Cith] with the object of discussing the projected Nyerol–Mwot Did road and apportioning sectors to the various groups concerned. The question of roadmaking had been broached to the Lau Chiefs shortly previous to this meeting and though there was no enthusiasm at the prospect of the work entailed and some suspicion as to the objects of a road, it had been agreed that an attempt should be made after a general gathering to discuss ways and means. As the outcome of this Chiefs and followers were convened to a gathering at Shit.

By this time, the Dinka road from Fulus Mouth which was to join the Lau road at Nyerol, was well on its way to completion and was substantive proof to the Lau, not only that a road could be made but that a road was being made.

---

14. Car Koryom, a Rumjok *wut ghok* (man of cattle), was seized by the divinity Deng around 1914. Car gave himself up to the government in 1928 and then escaped, only to turn himself in again in 1931 after the campaign was over. After a brief exile he was allowed to return home and died in about 1948.

15. See above, doc. 1.5 n. 45, and below, doc. 3.4.

16. In 1921 the government insisted on retaining the right to hear appeals against Guek's judgements. Even after the chiefs' courts were set up, Nuer were constantly appealing their local courts' decisions to the DC (Johnson 1986a).

Being anxious to ensure cohesion between the Chiefs and sections as regards the road and to avoid any possible obstructive influence at some later date, I had sent for Gwek Wundeng to be present at the meeting. No portion of the proposed road was to pass through Gwek's own territory, though between Ful Turug [Pul Turuk] and Fanyang it was to pass through the country belonging to two Sub-shiengs of Shieng Shish to which section Gwek and his followers form a group.

Gwek arrived at the meeting after all the other Chiefs had assembled, whether by accident or design I am uncertain. He was accompanied by some twenty followers and minor Kujurs. In my past dealings with him, he had at no time had an escort to equal this neither had [he] ever attempted to effect anything theatrical in my presence and I was surprised at the manner of his arrival as I was later at his demeanour.

Chiefs and followers were seated round me in a semi-circle and room was made for Gwek in the centre of this by the Chiefs and on their own initiative. I discussed other matters with the Chiefs before addressing Gwek and then informed him that I had sent for him in order to let him know that a road was to be cleared through the Gun Lau country and that I should expect his section to give any assistance required by Chief Gwet Thi [Guet Thie][17] of the other Subsection of Shish. He replied that the Lau were unable to make roads and such work should be confined to the Dinkas. I explained that the question of whether a road could or could not be made did not rest with him but with the Government, also that I had already discussed the matter with the leading Chiefs on whom the work devolved. The conversation continued in this strain for some time, until, after informing Gwek that as a lesser Chief I expected him to carry out the orders of the Shieng Leaders, he asked whether there was any further matter I wished to discuss with him and whether he could take his leave, to which I replied that there was not and that he was at liberty to return to his village. He then rose and with his twenty followers made off singing lustily.[18]

I considered it correct to show my disregard of Gwek and to diminish any prestige this local show of truculence may have given him in the eyes of the Nuer by affecting to ignore the result of my discussion with him and the manner of his departure. As later events have proved it was unfortunate that Gwek did not accompany me to Abwong under the care of my Police escort.

The Chiefs made no sign of their having been influenced by Gwek and no reference was made to the interlude; the meeting being terminated after each section had been allotted its sector of road and it being understood that the

---

17. See above, doc. 1.5 n. 17.

18. Coriat later gave a more dramatic and exaggerated account of this meeting, making Guek appear more intransigent and obstructive than he is portrayed here (1939: 231–2; discussed in Johnson, forthcoming).

road would be cleared and ready for use by the beginning of the 1928 dry season.[19]

As I was returning to Abwong in order to be at the Station for H.E. the Governor-General's [Sir John Maffey] visit, a proportion of Chiefs accompanied me and the remainder were, for various reasons, allowed to return to their homes with instructions to be present at Abwong on a date in order that they should be present on H.E.'s arrival. A message was sent to Gwek instructing him to proceed direct to Abwong.

Gwek made no appearance, neither did the Chiefs of Shiengs Nyajakan, Fulkir [Pälker] and Manthep [Manthiep] of the Gun and as transpired later a party of Mor Chiefs on their way in through the Gun country were stopped by Gwek.[20]

It was apparent that Gwek was attempting to foster trouble of some kind and on proceeding by car from Fulus mouth with the object of testing the new road I determined if possible to deal with Gwek at the same time.

Unfortunately, heavy rains prevented my reaching Nyerol and I was compelled to return. As I heard later this was attributed to Gwek's Kujur preventing the car, symbol of the road, entering the Lau country.

On my return to Abwong I left for a tour of the Dinka country on the Sobat and on my return again to the station I found Chief Dtho Dien [Dhiew Dieng] awaiting me (Shieng Manthep). Dtho seemed ill at ease and generally unable to explain satisfactorily the reason for his visit. Before leaving and as an incidental matter, he asked me to discuss the road a second time with Gwek Wundeng before the following dry season and before the sections started clearing. I informed him that I should expect the road to be cleared as arranged and that on my return from leave I should take steps to see that the young men had obeyed their Chiefs' orders, also that I did not see how a minor Chief such as Gwek could influence the sections or run contrary to the orders of Government. I was unable to visit Lau before going on leave and until my departure, was posted to Kodok [Shilluk district headquarters] for duty. While at Kodok reports were received from D.C. Duk Fayuil referring to Gwek's activities. Two Chiefs' Police from Mor came in to see me and corroborated the news that Gwek was attempting to disaffect the tribe. I was told that he had given out a prophecy said to have been foretold by his father that the 'Turk' (Government) would defeat the Lau Nuer and take over their country (i.e. 1917 Patrol), there would then be a period under the 'Turk' and Chiefs and tribesmen would be compelled to meet at Courts regardless of inter-section feuds, young men would be made into 'Turks' (this would appear to allude to Chiefs' Police),

---

19. Guek is remembered by modern Lou as objecting only to the labour involved in the road work (Lou texts 4.2, in Johnson, in preparation). It appears that he was being put forward by the Lou as their spokesman in this matter.

20. Nyajikany and Pälker were part of Rumjok, the southernmost Gun section and the furthest from Abwong. The Manthiep are Dhiew Dieng's section.

finally a road would be started in the direction of the Lau country and on that road reaching a certain point (Gwek obviously meant the Dinka boundary), a small root would be found to have grown at the apex of the Dengkur pyramid. This would be the signal for the Lau to rise and throw off the Turk power and the tribes would then amalgamate and revert to the days of Dinka raiding.[21]

During my absence on leave, further reports were received from the D.Cs. Duk Fayuil and Nasser. Among the various reports and from various sources, the following tales were current on my return from leave: Continual slaughter of bulls at the Pyramid. Threats by Gwek against Nuers not supporting him had already taken effect in two cases. Lau said to be eating meat and blood to strengthen them for coming fight. Gwek forbade tribesmen [to] work on road except for small patches near Duk in order to delude Government. Plan arranged said to be meeting of Chiefs who would accompany D.C. to Nyerol and Dengkur on his return from leave and Gwek would then destroy D.C., this would be preparatory to destroying the Government Stations. Jekaing Nuers reported to have been approached but refused assistance. Gaweir Kujur Dwal Diu had interview with Gwek but did not promise support.[22] Government rifles would not function. In proof of this Gwek ordered several young men to load their rifles and fire them and the cartridges failed to explode, thus proving Gwek's ability to render firearms innocuous. Dinka tribes all said to be apprehensive.

This pointed to an untoward state of affairs in the Lau section of the District and unfortunately, as was proved, beyond a point at which I could deal with them personally.

On receiving instructions vide C.S.5A-131 dated 22.11.27[23] to proceed to Lau in order to gauge the extent of the trouble, I left Khartoum by air and proceeded from Malakal to Abwong accompanied by two troops of Mounted Police, arriving on the 26th December [in fact, November].

The Dinka Chiefs who met me on my arrival, had, as was to be expected alarming tales of a Nuer rising. On the 27th Chiefs Dtho Dien and Kwaiagur Kuin [Kuaigur Kuny][24] accompanied by Gwek's half brother Bul came in. They had with them a small tusk for Government and stated that they had heard that for some reason the Government was angry and they had only been awaiting my return before starting work on the roads.

These Chiefs were instructed to return and await me at Nyerol with any other Lau Chiefs they might meet where I should go into the matter of certain ill reports that I had heard, I also told them I was not satisfied with the conduct

21. Modern interpretations of this prophecy are discussed in Johnson 1985*b*.

22. Dual never met Guek. See above, doc. 3.1 n. 7.

23. 'Memorandum Discussion on Gwek between Coriat and Civil Secretary', 22.11.27, NRO Civsec 5/2/10 and NRO UNP 1/5/27.

24. Kuaigur Kuny died in 1928; see above, doc. 1.5.

of Gwek and some of his followers during the rains and that consequently Bul Wundeng would be detained.[25]

Dtho Dien had already visited the Station before my arrival, when he related the same tale to Capt. Alban, then in charge of arrangements being made for an Air Force Landing Ground.

Chief Bul Kan[26] of a section of Shieng Tiang was then in Abwong having brought in labourers for work on the Landing Ground. From him I learnt that certain sections only were definitely supporting Gwek while others would await results.

On the 28th Chief Pey Ruai [Pec Ruac] with his Police and several followers arrived. This Chief, from the Mor section, said he was prepared to accompany me to Lau, but that he hoped Government would have a strong enough Force to deal with Gwek before he obtained support from some of the Mor sections. Pey stated that as far as he was aware no Mor sections had outwardly rallied to Gwek, though several young men from the sections had joined Gwek's immediate following.[27]

Leaving Abwong on the 29th I arrived at Nyerol by circuitous route on 2nd Dec., returning to Abwong on the 7th. There appeared to be definite resistance to Government confined to Shiengs Fulkir, Nyajakan and Yuong and part of Shieng Shish in addition to Gwek's own followers. I was avoided by the greater number of section Chiefs. Those that I met gave me little information but said the trouble was a personal matter between Gwek and myself.[28] I formed the impression that Lau did not wish to precipitate matters while I was in the vicinity of Nyerol. Gwek was then camped in the neighbourhood of Thul with a large part of his following but owing to the impossibility of securing adequate protection after dark I was unable to attempt a raid. There was also a certain amount of movement between Thul and Ful Maadin and I could not be certain of Gwek's position. I was very greatly assisted by a number of loyal Chiefs' Police I had with me.

I reported the information I had been able to obtain at a Conference held at Abwong on 7th Dec. Vide memo. Patrol S8. 1st. phase. Gen. Staff. S.D.F. 9.12.27.[29]

---

25. Bol's detention is remembered as one reason for Guek's final decision to fight (Lou texts 4.2, in Johnson, in preparation).

26. See above, doc. 1.5 n. 36.

27. The Mor primary section of the Lou were strongly opposed to the Gun, and the two had fought a bitter battle against each other after Ngundeng's death. Both Ngundeng and Guek settled in Gun country, within sight of Mor territory, but encountered considerable opposition from the Mor. Pec Ruac was chief of the Can section of the Mor Lou. See above, doc. 1.5.

28. In the 1940s some Lou still spoke of the conflict as a competition between Guek and Coriat over who was to be the spokesman for the Lou (B. A. Lewis to P. P. Howell, 06.04.43, SAD, P.P. Howell MSS).

29. 'Minutes, S.S. Hafir, Abwong 7.12.27', NRO Civsec 5/2/10.

Since the 1917 Patrol Gwek has lost considerable prestige and consequently his wealth in cattle has diminished in proportion. It now seems probable that for the past year or two he may have been searching for the means whereby he could regain power.[30]

Recent information shows that there was a meeting between Kujurs at Juai in Duk Fayuil District in March 1927 and there can be little doubt that the question of combating Government was the main object.[31]

Where in the past, Gwek was able, through fear of Kujur to wield his influence over the greater part of the tribe and was in the habit of receiving cattle as gifts and offerings, by 1927 his control was hardly felt by the major part of the tribe except in his immediate presence, few young men feared him in the safety of their own camps. Except for an occasional woman, his services as a Kujur [were] not required.[32]

Having shown himself incompetent and unwilling to work with Government Chiefs his position became little better than an ordinary tribesman.

Judging by recent events, it seems that having failed to obtain his ends by enlisting the Chiefs in an attitude of passive resistance, he turned to the young men in order to cause active opposition to Government.

Chiefs' Courts and Chiefs' Police were, as far as he was concerned, the last straw and his difficulty was to obtain the necessary hold over the young men. The proposed road gave him the implement with which he could create disaffection.

It was not difficult to turn a natural evasion to work of any kind into a definite grievance and finally into definite truculence. Given a modicum of fortune and a few judicious conjuring tricks, Gwek had prospects of being at least partly successful and he was fortunate in having had bad rains to help. The issue of free meat to those who wished for it, under the magic shadow of the pyramid did much to further his cause.

Above all Gwek had from May till December 1927 in which to perfect his plans.

The young men were offered freedom from taxation, no work and unlimited Dinka raids.

Sequence of Events during Patrol

The following memos and operation orders contain instructions issued as

30. This cannot be the case, since Guek was not a leader in the 1917 campaign.

31. There was no such meeting of prophets at this time. Guek, Car and Pok met together for the first time only after Guek's Mound had been blown up in 1928.

32. Guek was renowned for curing barrenness.

regards conduct of Patrol and military operations during first stage:

> Note by Kaid El Amm   11 Dec./27   ⎫ re Abwong
> .. .. Wing Commander Reid .. .. .. ⎬ conference
> Memo. Gen. Staff. S.D.F.   9.12.27[33] ⎭

The following events only need be summarised as affecting the Political side of the Patrol.

Nyerol was reached by advance troops on 15th Dec. I was under instructions to remain with troops. No forward action was taken until operations by the Air Force had been concluded and it was agreed to bomb Dengkur on the 18th.

I informed a few Chiefs and men at Nyerol to give out that only cattle camps would be bombed and women and children were therefore to leave camps and remain in villages. I was informed later that this advice was taken by the sections.

At 2.00 hours on the 18th I received information to the effect that bombing would not be carried out and this did not afford me sufficient time to inform the friendlies and others.

The situation deteriorated the same day, a considerable number of friendlies working on the road left. Vide Note of Conference held at Road-head on Dec. 18th 1927 UNP 5-A-1.[34]

On the 19th Dengkur and Ryr [Rier] were bombed. Ryr contained the Jemaish [Jimac] section all of whom were under Gwek. A reconnaissance was carried out towards Thul on the same day. No information was received as to effects until the 23rd when a few Chiefs came in.

On the 27th a cavalry reconnaissance was carried out towards Thul.

Troops remained at Nyerol until 3rd Jan. 1927 [in fact, 1928; the error recurs several times in this document].

Among telegrams despatched during this period the following only need be quoted in part:[35]

Extract from telegram from O.C. Ground Troops Nyerol to *Lewa Khartoum*. GF. 4.23.12.27....Coriat considers it possible operations will develop into series of patrols against guerrilla bands young men scattered over country if air action breaks up concentration and not morale which will occur if young men suffer only few casualties. Mass attack by Nuers still possible....

> From *Political to Governor*. P4. 21.12.27. No further air action required present. Scout missing. No news. Approve my moving south independently after arrival troops in order obtain information.
>
> From *Political to Governor*. P7. 24.12.27. Latest reports casualties negligible morale effect good. Dengkur village reported unburnt but this may be incorrect. Gwek and bands reported area between Khors Thul and Nyanding....

---

33. See NRO Civsec 5/2/10, pp.100, 104, 118–19.
34. Now NRO UNP 1/5/27, also in NRO Civsec 5/2/10.
35. Ibid.

From *Political to Governor*. P12. 1.1.27 .... Consider rapid advance preferable from Political point view and may prevent considerable concentrations Lang.

From *Political to Governor*. P14. 2.1.27. Two alternatives for Patrol slow advance with supply depots by road to Mwot before definite action which would resolve into process of elimination of defiant sections and their destruction when water scarce or other alternative such as now contemplated of base at Fadding and advancing from there with flour only as supply and chasing sections before they are able to disperse. This presuming they do not make combined stand. Unless a stand is made by enemy chances of capturing Gwek are much greater by rapid movement than by awaiting supplies. Ten days from base should suffice and Chidlaw[36] intends doing this .... Believe if Force can knock Gwek and Char many sections should be easily dealt with later by self when not nervous as at present....If later Gwek escapes as an individual it is probable he will make for Jekaing Shen Dorbang at Faweng[37] but he could not do this with following.

From *Political to Governor*. P15. 3.1.27. Chiefs ... have come in. Young men may or may not be controllable but have sent leaders back with instructions to make roads between certain points ... other sections still in Nyin and Lang areas ... above points to lack of stiff resistance and may confine Force to enforcing orders given re roads as sign submission ....

This first phase of the Patrol proved the ability of the Air Force to disperse all concentrations within distance. Although information pointed to an attack by Nuers at Rim near Dengkur, no opposition was met with and leaving Nyerol on 29.12.27 troops returned to Nyerol on 1.1.28 after burning Dengkur which was found intact [see Plate 16].

The total casualties caused to the Nuers by Air Force action was one man killed and several cattle.[38] It was evident later that enemy morale had been destroyed and though not necessarily submissive, the sections had no stomach for a fight.[39]

Gwek at this time was still attempting to hold his following.

Several Chiefs submitted following Air action. From 4.1.28 to 15.1.28 the Force operated in the Kwainjor country with the object of capturing Pok and Gwek and dealing with the sections in this area who had not submitted [see Plate 12].

Char Koryom surrendered on the afternoon of the 11th with 100 young men and 18 rifles, following Air Force operations over his cattle during the morning. A section of Shieng Nyajakan was captured by the Mounted Rifles and some casualties were inflicted. Several camps were found along the waterways and

---

36. Captain John Rhinallt Chidlaw-Roberts, MC (York and Lancs Regt.), King's African Rifles 1917–21, EA 1921–5, SDF 1925–31, OC Equatorial Corps, Torit, 1927.

37. Where his maternal relatives lived (see above, doc. 1.5).

38. Another report gives the figures as two old men and 200 cattle (Willis to MacMichael, 27.01.28, NRO Civsec 5/2/11).

39. Some Lou veterans of the campaign now deny that they were greatly worried by the aeroplanes, since they hid in the grass each time one flew over.

pools and young men were at work on the road. Pok with his section escaped to Gaweir some days previous to the arrival of troops.

No further Air action was taken after this phase and the country from Nyerol along the Fulus to Mwot was considered settled.

The following information re Gwek was contained in telegram despatched as follows:[40]

> *Governor from Political.* P18. 8.1.27 .... Gwek now said to have gone to Tep Jor between Khors Thul and Nyanding as fugitive ....

On the 19th Char Koryom escaped from the Guard by leaping over the Zariba at Fadding. After this man's arrest and as he had surrendered in person, he was allowed to move with the prisoners unmanacled and at the moment of his escape was lying by the prisoners and under the Guard. The group was some three yards from the Zariba which was 4ft. high. Char escaped at midnight.

Information having been received from D.C. Nasser[41] on the 15th that Gwek was at Biel on the Nyanding and attempting to stir up disaffection, the Force was divided into two columns. The infantry operating towards Tok Rial and M.R.[42] south to Faddoi and thence inland towards the Nyanding. A third column of Infantry from Akobo was despatched to work to Faddoi and thence down the Nyanding.

Owing to lack of water the Tokrial column returned from there to Thul. The Akobo column passed several friendly camps south of Fadding and found a number of deserted camps along the Nyanding before joining with the M.R. at Biel. A number of these deserted camps were possibly those of sections who had already submitted through their Chiefs.

The M.R. proceeded by way of Tep Jor where a section of Jemaish was captured, emerged on the Nyanding from whence the two columns returned via Tok Rial.

Tok Rial contained a number of friendly camps.

Gwek was reported in Jekaing and a raid was made on the section with whom he had taken refuge, but no trace could be found of him and he was later reported at Wegin on the Sobat. Recent information shows him to be at Rubdthoal.

The three phases of the Patrol may be summarised as follows:

1st Phase

Concentrations dispersed by Air action. Morale of Nuers broken. Several Chiefs submit. Young men still uncertain.

2nd Phase

All active opposition ended. Operations confined to rounding up fugitives. Gwek

---

40. See NRO UNP 1/6/30 and Civsec 5/2/11.

41. Coriat later complained that John Lee (DC, Nasir) wished only to chase Guek out of his district and refused to co-operate in rounding him up (Coriat to Kathleen 05.05.28, Coriat MSS).

42. Cavalry and Mounted Rifles, normally stationed at Shendi.

still attempting obtain support.

3rd Phase

Gwek a fugitive. Operations confined to attempting capture of Gwek and Jemaish section.

Previous to the return of toops, villages belonging to the Jemaish section were burnt and those on the Kwainjor belonging to the sections who had fled to Gaweir.

The pyramid was destroyed on 8.2.28 in presence of 34 Chiefs.[43]

Results of Patrol

Active resistance to Government ceased, a number of rifles were confiscated and additional work was done on by-roads [see Plate 13] which will assist administration. As regards the objectives of capturing Gwek and destroying Kujur influence, success was not achieved. Though the operations succeeded in proving that the Government was stronger than Kujur, failure to capture the Kujurs may leave at least the Kujurs themselves the heart to try their powers another day. So long as these men are free the tradition of years will still afford them an influence of sorts over the Nuer and fear of Kujur cannot be eradicated as proved by the sections' disinclinations to supply information which would lead to the capture of Gwek.

On the other hand there should be no reason why any further attempts to cause disaffection by the Kujurs, in the event of their not being captured, will result in anything beyond a very local section disturbance and time will continue to enlighten the Nuer as to the evils of Kujur.

It seems possible that a Squadron of Mounted Police would have been sufficient to cope with the trouble and possibly more effectively, without the disturbing element introduced by a Patrol.[44]

The trouble was confined to certain sections and had these been rapidly and effectively punished, there should have been no need to continue operations lengthily.

The Mounted Police being also accustomed to trekking for long distances on local supplies of durra and meat only, the difficult question of supply and Transport for Troops does not arise.

Apart from the capture of individual Kujurs, admittedly a Police matter, there seem to be two alternatives to a Patrol for effective action against the

---

43. Other descriptions of blowing up the Mound can be found in Coriat 1939: 233–4 and MacMeekan 1929.

44. This paragraph is marked by a '??' in the margin, probably by Willis, who forwarded the report to MacMichael.

Nuer, i.e. defeat of determined opposition or chase and punishment of known recalcitrant sections before they have had time to disperse or submit and as an effective punishment for past behaviour.

During the recent Patrol the Air Force were effective in dispersing opposition and resistance and the effect on morale of bombing is extreme. Without the aid of the Air Force it is possible that opposition would have been encountered and it may be that the effects of a defeat in the open field would have more lasting results where the young men were concerned and it is the young men that require punishment when such is needed.

In the case of lack of resistance, a Patrol may resolve into an unwieldy march through the country at the end of which all sections have submitted without the sections responsible for disturbances having had a sufficient object lesson of the consequences of their previous actions.

A small and mobile column would be able to reach sections in the first phase of any disturbance and should be able to effect such action as would preclude any further trouble.

Abwong
20.3.28

Percy Coriat
A.D.C.
Southern District

Document 3.3

NUER SETTLEMENT—GUN LAU (GUNCOL) AREA

With the dispersal of the Lou following the air raid on Guek's Mound, the whole of 1928 was spent chasing Lou fugitives. This brought the police and troops into Jikany and Gaawar as well as Lou territory. The behaviour of the troops and their Dinka auxiliaries in Dual Diu's camp alienated the Gaawar, so that they too attacked government outposts in August that year.[1] Police activities at the beginning of the dry season (November–December) 1928 failed to capture any of the leading prophets.

A meeting was held at Malakal on 5–6 January 1929, with the governor-general of the Sudan, the civil secretary, the kaid al-'amm *(commander-in-chief of the SDF), governor Willis, and the various Upper Nile DCs most directly involved.[2] It was recognized that police and army patrols had failed to have any permanent effect in bringing the Nuer under control, or bolstering the authority of government-appointed chiefs. It was decided that repression without 'constructive administrative policy' would be bound to fail. No patrols were planned for the coming year; rather a 'settlement' backed by 'armed assistance'. The 'Nuer Settlement' consisted of the creation of a no man's land between the Nuer and the Dinka to obstruct raids; the immediate return of Dinka cattle and captives, taken mainly in the Duk raid; the organization of Nuer sections to 'establish proper discipline and control and preclude further disturbance of peace'; the further development of communications; and the undertaking of an economic survey. To achieve this the Gun Lou, the Mor Lou and the Gaawar were ordered*

1. Wedderburn-Maxwell 1928; Wyld 1928; Dual Diu 1930; Gaawar text 4.8; and Dinka text 4.9, in Johnson, in preparation.

2. Sir John Maffey (governor-general), Sir Harold MacMichael (civil secretary), Sir Hubert Huddleston (*kaid al-'amm*), Coriat (political officer), Major Wyld (ADC Bor and Duk District), Captain Alban (ADC Abwong), Captain E. C. Tunnicliffe (ADC Pibor District), and H. G. Wedderburn-Maxwell (ADC Zeraf Valley District).

to concentrate in restricted settlement areas where 'tribal organization could be checked and registered'.[3]

The concentration orders were enforced by three columns of troops, labelled Guncol (Gun Lou), Morcol (Mor Lou) and Barcol (Bar Gaawar) respectively. In none of the three areas was the concentration order fully obeyed: the Mor offered no armed resistance but many stayed out of the column's range or crossed into Ethiopia; only seventy per cent of the Gaawar obeyed the order, and this after several brushes between Dual Diu and government troops; there was more success among the Gun following the defeat and death of Gwek on 8 February 1929.[4]

Coriat was attached to Guncol as political officer. The following document is his report on the Guncol operations: his final official report on the Lou, written within a week of document 1.5. Unlike document 3.2 a copy of this report was found among Coriat's papers. This may explain why his 1939 article faithfully follows the account of Guek's final struggle which is contained here, but diverges from his contemporary report on the earlier Patrol S8.

Governor
U.N.P.

Situation in Lau Previous to Settlement

Following the Patrol of 1928 and after the removal of the troops, conditions rapidly became normal and there was not the setback to the administration that had been a corollary of Patrols in the past. There having been no wholesale burning of villages and confiscation of property, there was little to show of untoward events during the course of the Patrol. The Chiefs, both those who had aided Gwek Wundeng [Guek Ngundeng] in December of 1927 and the January of the following year and those who had adopted an uncertain attitude of neutrality, protested their complete conviction as to the futility of Gwek and the permanence of Government.

After the conclusion of the Patrol and on my return from the Gaweir march,[5] I visited the greater part of the Gun country and the border of Mor. During the tour, a number of Chiefs expressed a wish to visit Khartoum and to become acquainted with the meaning of Government beyond the confines of their own country. This was a satisfactory sign of the change of attitude, particularly as Tribute and remaining rifle fines had been sent in to Abwong by the Gun Chiefs during my absence in Gaweir.

3. Governor-general of the Sudan to high commissioner for Egypt, 09.01.29, and Willis, 'Nuer Settlement', 28.06.29, both in NRO Civsec 1/3/8.

4. Willis, 'Nuer Settlement 1929'; Wedderburn-Maxwell, 'Nuer Settlement—Zeraf Valley District', both in NRO Civsec 1/3/8. E. C. Tunnicliffe, 'Morcol Diary 1929', NRO Civsec 23/5/29.

5. The Gaawar march took place in February–March 1928.

On my return to the Station, having applied for and been granted permission to take a party of Chiefs to Khartoum in August, I arranged for an equal number of Dinka and Nuer Chiefs, 49 in all, to accompany me. I had included the Dinkas in order that there should be no distinction between the Tribes. With the exception of four Elders, the Nuer Chiefs were all of the young warrior class.[6]

During my tour in Lau, Gwek was in the Jekaing [Jikany] country over the border, where he had fled during the Patrol and it was shortly after my return to the Station and while I was arranging the Chiefs' visit to Khartoum, that information was received that he had returned from Jekaing and was building himself two huts near the remains of Dengkur Pyramid. In the first instance reports had it that Gwek had given out his intention of remaining near the Pyramid during the rains and returning to Jekaing in the dry season, when the 'Turk' would be trekking in Lau. While the Chiefs were gathering at Abwong, preparatory to their visit to Khartoum, it was rumoured that Gwek had disclosed his intention of awaiting the 'Turk' and either he or the Government would establish their authority. Chiefs' Police and others came into the Station constantly and reported all that they had seen or heard regarding Gwek. From various sources, it was learnt that he was accompanied by two wives, a brother and a slave and in no case had he been visited by any of the Chiefs, nor had there been any gatherings of young men at the Pyramid. Gwek himself had not left his huts but was occasionally visited by individuals.

The Chiefs who were with me at the time, were of the opinion that Gwek would flee to Jekaing after the rains and would be unable to obtain support in Lau. It is noteworthy however, that they were unanimous, when any suggestion was made to them regarding Gwek's arrest, in stating that while they were convinced the Government could cope with him, they would not and could not effect his arrest without incurring dire results to themselves or their families.[7] In effect, 'Gwek's Kujur cannot harm the Government, but we are Nuers and though we can keep ourselves apart from Gwek, if we were to attempt to cause direct harm to Gwek, his Kujur would destroy us'.

There was little doubt however, that both the Chiefs and the majority of Tribesmen, though they were afraid to incur Gwek's vengeance if directed against them personally, were genuine in their desire to avoid his influence and were anxious for his removal as a menace to their security.

At the time of Gwek's return to Lau, two Lau Chiefs: Tut Lam of the Jemaish [Jimac] section of Mor and Dtho Dien [Dhiew Dieng] of the Manthiep of Gun,[8] gave themselves up at Abwong. These Chiefs had fled with their sections

6. Most of the Lou leaders at this time were of the Luac age-set (Guek's own), marked in *c.* 1908. There were two younger age-sets: Lithgai (1915) and Cayat (1925).

7. Compare this with Kulang Majok's refusal to arrest his maternal uncle (see above, Introduction).

8. For Tut Lam see above, doc. 1.5; for Dhiew Dieng see above, doc. 1.5, doc. 3.1 n. 32, and

during the Patrol, the Jemaish section having been the most prominent among Gwek's supporters and Tut himself being related by marriage to Gwek. The other Chief, Dtho Dien, had been closely connected with Gwek in the past, yet had been one of the more enlightened and progressive of the Chiefs and his disappearance during the Patrol had been unaccountable. Tut Lam had no explanation to offer regarding his behaviour, other than that he had been afraid of Gwek's 'Kujur'. Dtho Dien, on the other hand, claimed that he had no fear of Gwek, but wished to avoid the Government during a time of trouble.

I have given the recent history of these two Chiefs as an instance of the contrast in character that is to be found between two equally strong Nuer Chiefs, and their more recent movements are interesting as a sidelight on the character of the Nuer in general. Defection from Government may not mean recalcitrance but fear or inability to grasp the reasons or intentions of the Government or yet from a suspicion as to the competence of Government, when a Kujur with a rebellious section may withstand efforts made to capture him or destroy his influence.

Tut Lam joined the other Chiefs visiting Khartoum and Dtho Dieng was sent back to his country.

The Jemaish section under Tut Lam and Sub-Chiefs were the first to concentrate at Wegin in the Mor area of the Nuer Settlement, while Dtho again absented himself, leaving it to one of his Headmen and his Chief's Policeman to concentrate the section in the Gun area. Dtho after roaming for a short period in the Mwot Tot forest, fled to the Garjak [Gaajak] border at Tayabur and gave himself up to me at Abwong after the conclusion of the Gun settlement. He gave the same excuse as explanation that he had made in 1928.

In August 1928, I accompanied the Chiefs to Khartoum when they were presented to H.E. the Acting Governor-General and spent five crowded days in seeing the wonders of the world. The great effect the visit produced on the Chiefs, was apparent during the Settlement, when with one exception they were the first to concentrate their sections at the camps allotted them. The exception was Luak Lam of the Lang section of Gun, a weak individual with a difficult section to control and son of the old Chief who is still living and is an ignorant and reactionary type of Elder.[9]

While the Chiefs were still in Khartoum, the Gaweir raid on Duk was reported. On my informing the Chiefs of this, they were unable to explain the attitude of the Gaweir, but were positive in their opinion that no Lau sections would cooperate, though it was agreed that some of the young Lau warriors might be involved.

It will be necessary here to relate the sequence of events that had arisen during the absence of the Chiefs.

At approximately the time the Lau Chiefs left Abwong on their way to

---

doc. 3.2.

9. See above, doc. 1.5 n. 32.

Khartoum, the Kujur Chief Dwal Diu[10] of Gaweir sent messages to the various sections of his tribe and to the Lau, exhorting the Tribesmen to combine in an attack on the Dinkas and asserted that in seven days' time from the day he despatched his messengers, he would lead in person a march on Duk District.

The Lau, on receipt of Dwal's messages, took no action and Gwek, who was at first reported to have joined Dwal in Gaweir, left the Pyramid and went to Thul where the Chief, Luak Lam, to whom reference has been made above, was absent in Khartoum. Gwek did not appear to be successful in enlisting support at Thul and he then made his way to Wunbil to the south and nearer the Duk border, where he was met by Chief Dtho Dieng of whom mention has been made previously. At Wunbil, a number of the Lau collected and it was while Gwek was addressing the gathering, that Ding Twil, one of the younger minor Chiefs of Shieng Fulkir [Pälker], wrested the war spear out of Gwek's hand in an attempt to show the tribesmen the impotence of his Kujur to cause harm. Ding was reported to have said that Gwek had led them by lies in the past and so far as he and his men were concerned, would not again delude them. In spite of the lack of support owing to there being no senior Chiefs present, Ding was successful in preventing a tribal raid and Gwek returned in disgust.[11] He then let it be known that he would not again attempt to lead them, until the tribesmen themselves, by crossing the Dinka border, had shown their worth as men and their superiority to the Dinkas. In the meanwhile however, a number of the young men, realising that whatever the consequences to Gaweir, they would themselves avoid the aftermath by slipping quietly over and assisting the Gaweir as individuals, could not resist the temptation of a genuine old fashioned Dinka raid and parties from the border sections of Nyajakan [Nyajikany], Mathel and Manthiep participated in the loot.[12]

During the Settlement, some sixty names of individual Lau raiders were obtained, but the District Commissioner, Duk District,[13] informs me that there were considerably more. In the case of Shieng Mathel, this section had been ordered to move from their homes on the Dinka Gaweir border, and return to Lau by the end of 1928, their villages being handed over to the Dinkas. This was the cause of particularly bitter feelings against the Dinkas.[14]

On the return of the Chiefs from Khartoum, Chiefs' Police at Abwong reported the position in Lau and before leaving the Station, the Chiefs gave their assurances that there would be no trouble during the rains, either connected with Gwek or Dinka raids. As events proved, they adhered to their promises. A second attempt to raise a following against the Dinka was made by Chief Dtho

10. See above, docs. 1.2, 1.3, 2.1, and below, doc. 3.4. See also above, n. 1.
11. See above, doc. 1.5 n. 22.
12. The Lou raid was organized by Pok Kerjiok and his kinsman Lam Liew Diau.
13. Major J. W. G. Wyld.
14. See above, doc. 1.5.

Dien, but after being unsuccessful, he came into the Station in my absence on leave and informed my Interpreter[15] that his only reason for wishing to raid the Dinkas, was in the hope that he would be able to regain cattle that had been taken from him by a Dinka Chief and wrongly awarded the Dinkas in a case heard in 1923.

On my return from leave in December 1928, punitive action against the Gaweir was decided and as a consequence, with the approval of H.E. the Governor-General, the Nuer Settlement came into being.

Objects of the Nuer Settlement

The numerous Patrols and Marches against the Nuer, that had taken place in the past and had had the effect of disturbing the country without ensuring for the future a peaceable administration, have become still less effective as an administrative or punitive measure, since the Nuer have realised the limitations of troops operating in their country and know that punitive action is taken with the object of punishing an individual section or sections rather than as a show of Force to an unadministered people. A Patrol as carried out in the past, meant that in most cases the offenders would evade punishment, while the cattle of some unfortunate and probably innocent section would be seized and confiscated. To the Nuer, it was difficult to distinguish between these methods and those of the slave-raiding 'Turk' of the old days. Whether the column consisted of Infantry or Mounted Troops, the young men to be punished would slip away either to forest or swamp, or by taking refuge in the camp of an ostensibly amenable section or a section whose Chief was recognised to be loyal. Family ties and the general suspicion as to the intentions of Government, precluded the Chiefs from surrendering, even if they wished to, the harboured evildoers. Sections would take refuge with a neighbouring tribe whose area was beyond the limits of the Patrol and owing to the size and nature of the country, it was impossible to ensure that every forest waterhole which might contain a camp, was visited, nor was it possible to comb through every camp in a 100 square miles of country to arrest wanted men. It was exceptional for the troops to meet organised resistance and the column, moving slowly through the country, would come across camps whose Chiefs had either the intelligence to stand or the fear of the possible consequences of running away and who would be considered loyal though they in all probability contained a considerable sprinkling of warriors whose actions had brought about the Patrol. Villages passed would be occupied by a few old men, women and children, too feeble or sick to run away. Often a fleeing section would be encountered, who as

---

15. Mayan Lam; see above, doc. 1.5 n. 65.

likely as not would be innocent of misdemeanours and were running away to avoid imprisonment and confiscation of cattle, which if caught, was the most probable result.

The Nuer Settlement, intended both as a punitive measure against the Gaweir and other recalcitrants and as an administrative measure for the settlement of Nuer districts, by concentrating the sections within limited areas, ensured against the possibility of loyal sections being encountered by any troops that were required for punitive purposes and lessened the chances of harbouring. Troops operating outside the limited area were not required to distinguish between a peaceful and a rebel section and had a definite objective in that any Nuer found in the operation area was treated as enemy. By concentrating the tribes within areas and restricting movement, it was to their benefit that the objectives of the Settlement should be rapidly attained in order to regain freedom of movement and there was consequently nothing to gain and actual harm in harbouring offenders, while outside the area, it was difficult for the runaway to find food or succour. To ensure that Gaweir did not obtain refuge in Lau, the Settlement was extended to this tribe, though the Jekaing and Western Nuer were excluded.

For the purpose of the Settlement, the Lau and Gaweir were divided into three areas. Within each of these areas, a stretch of country was allotted to the tribes within which they were to concentrate with their cattle and property. After a prescribed time limit all country without the concentration limits was declared hostile and occupants were to be treated as recalcitrant. Within the concentration, each section (Shieng) was allotted a camp and every section received orders to camp in mass under their Head Chief and not to divide into a numerous number of small camps. By this means each Section Chief with his Sub-Chiefs was responsible for his own section who were under his immediate control and not as is generally the case, scattered over the country in small camps, half of whom owed allegiance to no one, except when it suited them or under pressure. As a part of the Settlement, each camp was visited and a census taken of the people. This was made possible by the comparative smallness of the area of concentration. As a further step in the administration, the position of the Chiefs was strengthened by the organisation of the smaller sections under their respective Headmen and concentration of outlying families (Sub-Shiengs) of a Shieng with the parent Section and under the Chief, and also the enrolment of additional Chiefs' Police. Chiefs were instructed to group their villages and dry season camps in the future and to forbid movement of small sections beyond their territory during camping season. At the end of the Settlement, Chiefs were instructed that there need be no restriction of movement provided that the sections remained grouped.

The following is an account of the Settlement as affecting the Gun Lau with which this report is concerned.

Preliminary Measures in Gun Lau (Guncol) Area

On the 8th of January 1929 a number of Chiefs and Chiefs' Police were given their instructions. By the 2nd February 1929 all Lau sections had received their concentration orders.

It was explained that continued trouble in the Nuer country, patrols of 1928 and the recent Gaweir raid on Duk, had necessitated the carrying out of certain operations in order to prevent future trouble and ensure the peace. Chiefs were ordered to concentrate their sections at the camps allotted to them within the prescribed area. The objects of the concentration were explained and it was pointed out that there would be no punitive action except with regard to known recalcitrants and wanted men or people who disobeyed the concentration orders.

The Gun Lau area was twenty-three miles long by some three miles wide and between Shit [Cith] and Ful Tor on the Khor Fulus [Fulluth]. Water and grazing sites were allotted to each camp. No person or cattle were to be allowed to cross to the East of the Khor.

Attached is the plan of the area and names of sections and camps, with their Chiefs [Fig. 2].

A base camp for supplies and prisoners was established at Mwot Dit, consisting of No. 1 Company Equatl: Corps, under the command of Captain T. Kerr, M.C.[16]

Troops for active operations consisted of One Troop of Cavalry and Mounted Rifles and One Troop of Mounted Police. From the 3rd to the 10th of February Guncol Flying Column was under the command of Captain G. R. [in fact, G. A.] Eastwood.[17] From the 11th to the 26th February Guncol Troop of Cavalry was under M. Awal [Mulazim Awal] Mohammed Eff. Osman. From the 27th Feb. to the end of the operations Guncol Flying Column was under the command of Captain N. E. Tyndale-Biscoe.[18] The force had by then been augmented by an additional troop of cavalry. During the period that Captain Eastwood was in command of the troops he was en route for the Mor area and had with him the troops for that column.

Major J. W. G. Wyld D.S.O., M.C. and Captain A. H. A. Alban D.F.C. cooperated with me as Political Officers.[19] Captain E. C. Tunnicliffe,[20] Political Officer Mor Area, assisted from the 3rd to the 10th February while on his way to the

---

16. Captain T. Kerr, MC (Argyll & Sutherland Highlanders), King's African Rifles 1917–23, SDF 1925–33, OC Duk Fadiat, 1929–30. See Plate 19.

17. Later Brigadier G. A. Eastwood, DSO, OBE, served in the Cavalry (Mounted Rifles) and Eastern Arab Corps, SDF 1926–32.

18. Captain Norman Edward Tyndale-Biscoe (Royal Artillery), SDF 1927–34.

19. See above, Introduction, notes 5 and 25. Alban appears in Plate 19, Wyld in Plates 15 and 18.

20. See above, doc. 3.1 n. 26, and see also Plates 18 and 19.

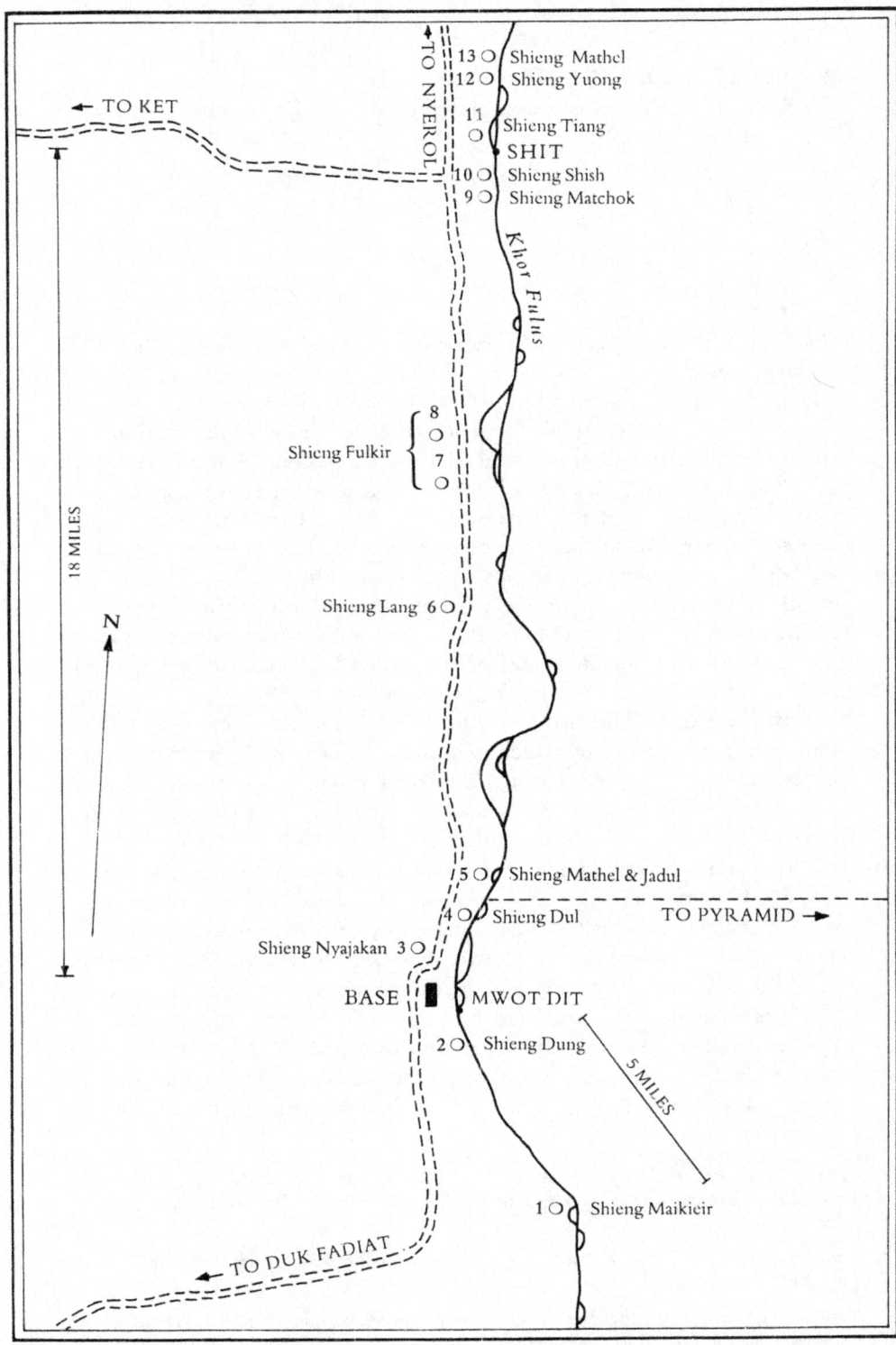

FIG. 2 Gun Lou concentration area, 1929 (not to scale)

Mor area with Captain G. R. Eastwood.[21]

A force of Chiefs' Police was employed both at the Base Camp and with the Flying Column.

Narrative of Operations

The 7th of February was the limit of time given to all sections to concentrate within the area.

Information having been received as to the presence of Gwek Wundeng with a body of Nuer whose attitude was uncertain and who were reported to have gathered at the Pyramid, the combined Morcol and Guncol Mounted Troops left Mwot Dit for the Pyramid on the 6th February. At approximately 06.00 hours on the 8th the Column came within sight of the Pyramid. Parties of Nuer were seen clustered at the base and on the side of the Pyramid and were singing and beating war drums. The troops marched to within 400 yards of the Nuer and halted and dismounted on a selected site, a square being formed. There was no attempt by the Nuer to attack at this stage, though a war dance appeared to be in progress and individuals rushed out brandishing their spears in the front and to right and left of the Pyramid. Two rounds were then fired in an attempt to draw the enemy. This had the desired effect and the Nuer could be seen slaughtering two bulls, after which they drove a bull towards the Government forces and rushed behind it to the attack.[22] Fire was then opened upon the enemy and within 150 to 200 yards of the square they broke and retreated, dividing into two parties, one retiring to the North East and the other to the South East. Troops mounted and pursued, over very rough and broken country, for some three miles. Approximately 800 head of cattle were captured in the pursuit. No casualties were suffered by the Government forces. The enemy killed included the Kujur Gwek Wunding, three other Witch Doctors, Chief Liglig Kuin,[23] who were identified on the spot, and thirteen Nuer, all of whom were identified at a later stage of the Settlement. Information as to other casualties in wounded and killed came to hand later. The Nuer force was approximately 200 strong at the time of the attack, but as transpired later a number who were with Gwek at the time thought better of it after the first

---

21. Spaces for Capt. Eastwood's initials appear between full stops, which may have been filled in on the original, but there is no indication of this in the remaining file copy I used in preparing this document.

22. For a Nuer version of the battle, see Lou texts 4.2, in Johnson, in preparation; also Johnson 1979: 15.

23. Liglig Kuny was the brother of Nguth Kuny (see above, doc. 1.5 n. 35). The other three *dayiemni* ('disciples') killed were Kuankui Nei, Dual Dag and Yor Deng.

round had been fired. Gwek was picked up on the battlefield, armed only with a brass pipe and a thin iron skewer.[24] On the 10th it was corroborated that there would be no further resistance from the Nuer and Morcol continued on its way to Wegin while Guncol returned to its base.

It is necessary here to give an account of Gwek's activities both before and up to the time of the battle. As is known Gwek fled to the Jekaing during the 1928 Patrol (S.8.) and returned to Lau for the rains, when he was unsuccessful in obtaining support for a raid against the Dinka. In 1928 Gwek proclaimed that 'The Great Day' had arrived owing to the appearance of a small root at the apex of the Pyramid (vide report Patrol S8).[25] This year, when the concentration orders were received, Gwek gave out that his failure last year had been owing to the fact that he had obtained no support and that there was little doubt that 'The Great Day' had only now arrived. On the day that he and the assembled Nuer were attacked within the shadow of the Pyramid, the mystic brass pipe about which all had heard would be in evidence and would effect the destruction of the government troops. Gwek himself must have realized that he could not continue to obtain the support of even individual young men unless he could show some measure of success in actual combat. The concentration orders having been received with a natural suspicion by some of the Nuer, who feared the intentions of the Government, they decided to place their faith in Gwek. This was Gwek's opportunity to retrieve his name with a sporting chance. There is a song known to the Lau Nuer as 'Chang Rol' (The Day of the Turkish [red] Bull)—which runs much in this fashion:-

> Oh the day when he cometh, the Bull 'Rol' (Turk)
> Oh the day when we await the Bull 'Rol'
> Then by the shade of the Mound of Wundeng
> Then shall his 'Riek' (flag) be steeped in his blood.[26]

---

24. This skewer is a barbless fishing-spear (*rib*), of symbolic importance in association with Aiwel Longar, the first Dinka master of the fishing-spear whom Ngundeng consciously imitated.

25. See above, doc. 3.2.

26. Coriat did not give the complete song or the Nuer original. Terese Svoboda has brought to my attention a song she recorded in 1976 which is similar to this. In the Nuer version (which she has shown me) the phrase *cang rol* ('day of the foreigner') does not appear, nor does the word *riek* ('shrine stick'), which Coriat translates as 'flag'. Instead the phrases *biim rol* ('ambush of the foreigner') and *ber* ('flag') are used. Some association between the battle at the Mound in 1929 and the phrase *biim rol* does exist. Jackson (1954: 170) gave a description of the battle, based on Major Wyld's account, in which the name of Guek's ox is given as 'bimerol', though this is not a cattle colour. If the following song is in fact the same that Coriat heard, then it is clear from internal evidence that it dates from the 1902 patrol which attacked Ngundeng's village. Svoboda's translation is (1985: 93): 'When he ambushed you in Lit Nhial's camp, he showed no mercy, this man who ambushed you. / That foreigner who ambushed you was waylaid later and we held no parley. / Boong's son, my chief, took the flag. / He will not surrender like Yoor. / He will not surrender like Yoor. / I will keep the Cai from Ret's barn. / I will lay in wait for the foreigners in Ngundeng's barn. / God's thunder will boom from beneath the Bie [Mound]. / So much blood will stream from the barn to avenge the village that it will cover the flag.'

This is a favourite lay sung in promise of the day when the Nuer would conquer the foreigner in his country. One of the many prophecies made by Gwek and his satellites foretold that in the year when the Turk (Government) would be defeated then also would die the family of his chief songster and one Lam Tuthiang (father of the interpreter at Abwong) who had struck Gwek's father, Wundeng, when they were both young men. Whether Gwek intended quietly to do away with these unfortunates on the auspicious day will remain unknown, but it is coincidence that on the day of the battle at the Pyramid, Gwek's songster, Deng Pet, and his brother, Kweth, were killed in the action and the father Pet Nyakur died shortly afterwards. Lam Tuthiang is still alive.[27] The brass pipe, which had been seen by few, and which was housed in a separate hut when not accompanying Gwek in his travels, was reported to have been made for Wundeng Dengkur by an Annuak [Anuak].[28] Gwek claimed that by shaking the pipe at the oncoming Turk they would be incapable of firing their rifles and would be powerless to move, he would then draw first blood with his skewer and the rest would be finished off by the warriors. It was learnt sometime after the battle that Gwek, on hearing of the approach of the troops, stated that the Turk had gone to Gaweir and would return to Lau on some later day and that the force marching on the Pyramid were merely scouts who could be polished off with ease. Gwek's scouts informed him of the approaching column some time in the evening of the day previous to the battle and the night was spent in song and dance and eating of meat. A small calf was slaughtered and tied to pegs in the middle of the path by which the troops were expected to arrive. As this calf when killed fell with its head towards the troops it was taken as a good omen. Unfortunately for Gwek the troops marched on the Pyramid across country. However, as both the bulls which were slaughtered immediately prior to the Nuer attack fell with their heads towards the troops and the bull which led the attack came on with great elan, Gwek's warriors may have been confident of success.

There was little doubt that the results achieved by the death of Gwek and the dispersal of his forces, contributed greatly to the success of the Settlement. At

---

27. Lam was a magician and refused to surrender his magic to be buried in the Mound. He did bring a sick relative to Ngundeng to be cured, but when the man died Lam denounced Ngundeng as a fraud and struck him. Ngundeng then uttered what is considered either a prophecy or a curse, predicting that Lam's family would be swallowed up by the 'Turuk'. Lam died in 1931. His mortuary ceremony is described by Evans-Pritchard (1949: 58–63): it is noted that the hymn to Dengkur, normally sung at Nuer mortuary ceremonies, was not sung at Lam's. The family of Pet Nyakur was linked by several marriages to Ngundeng's family. The brothers Deng and Yang Pet were two of Guek's bards (see below, n. 45).

28. The brass pipe was made for Ngundeng by an Anuak blacksmith, Wor Jogol. See Coriat 1939: 225–6 and Alban 1940: 200. After Guek's death it was kept in the DC's office at Akobo, until the office burned down and the stem and mouthpiece of the pipe were destroyed. The brass bowl and few remaining rings were then transferred to the museum in Khartoum. It was returned to the Lou by presidential order at a ceremony at the remains of the Mound on 26 December 1979. See Plates 17 and 18.

the time, the Kujur Char Koryom was reported to be on his way to assist Gwek with a body of Nuer from the Mor country but these no doubt dispersed on hearing of the result of the engagement.[29]

On the return of Guncol to the base, it was found that a great number of the Gun Lau had concentrated. There were still a few sections and many individuals who had not obeyed the orders.

On the 18th Feb. the mounted force left for a march to the South East by the Mor country. Acting on the information received as to the whereabouts of a recalcitrant Mor Shieng & when within striking distance the force made a march of 45 miles and encountered Shieng Belyu [Bilieu] of the Mor on the night of the 20th. These people were rounded up and the chief was instructed to move with his section to the Mor area at Wegin. Three men were killed and two wounded during the capture of this Shieng. On the 25th the camp belonging to young men of a Gun section was captured. The force reached the base on the 27th. On the 5th March the column under Captain N. E. Tyndale-Biscoe[30] accompanied by Captain A. H. A. Alban D.F.C. marched on Mwot Tot and succeeded in capturing a number of Nuer who had not concentrated. On the 7th March a Lau Chiefs' Policeman surrendered a number of cattle belonging to a Gaweir who had fled from that area.

By this time, the greater number of the Gun had concentrated and Guncol force was required to cooperate with the troops in Gaweir and from the 9th to the 20th March the force was operating in that area. During these operations a Sub Chief of Dwal Diu and nine men were killed and prisoners and cattle were captured. After effecting a meeting with Mr Wedderburn-Maxwell, Political Officer Gaweir,[31] the force returned to Mwot Dit. On the 22nd to the 31st the force was operating in the Lang country of Gun in the south, and from the 1st to the 6th April in the northern part of the Lang. This last march was made in an attempt to catch the Kujur Char Koryom, but owing to an error on the part of a guide the Kujur escaped, though his womenfolk and some young men were captured.

During the course of these operations a census had been taken of the Gun by the Political Officer remaining at the base. Other than Chief Dtho Dieng and individuals, the whole of the Gun had concentrated by the 1st April. Sections had been organized under their Chiefs as stated in the first part of this report. On the 12th April, after being addressed by the Governor [C. A. Willis], Chiefs and their sections returned to their villages. Some 95 wanted men and 45 hostages had been surrendered by the Chiefs when called upon to

---

29. According to one account Car had been with Guek at the Mound the previous day but had refused to take part in the impending battle and left that night, taking half the Rumjok contingent with him.

30. In the original, spaces were left blank between the full stops where Captain Tyndale-Biscoe's initials were to be written in later.

31. H. G. Wedderburn-Maxwell; see above, Introduction, n. 5.

do so and were sent to Malakal as political prisoners. It was explained to the Chiefs that these men would be released when the Government was satisfied as to the future behaviour of the tribe. Fines were extracted from Dinka raiders and other offenders and the remainder of the captured cattle were returned to their owners. The fines totalling to some 1400 head of cattle in all were handed over to the District Commissioner of Duk-Bor District [Major Wyld] for Dinka reparations. The three Lau sections under Duk District were given orders to move into Lau proper early in 1930 and the Jureir Dinka[32] of Abwong District were given similar orders to move to Duk District. It had been intended to move these people at the end of the Settlement but owing to the famine in southern Lau and the shortage of grain seed they were allowed to remain at their villages for the rains.

The effect of this move will concentrate the Nuer and Dinka within separate districts and an uninhabited tract of country will form a 'No Man's Land' between them.[33]

Future Administration in Lau

It will be necessary to follow up the work accomplished during the Settlement if the results are to be permanent. Though it is the intention that the Chiefs should maintain the administration in their own hands, it will be a considerable time before the district can do without the continuous supervision of the District Commissioner. The absence of a District Commissioner even for a period of four months during leave or for some other reason is sufficient to undo several years' work.

Abwong, the headquarters of the district, is some 50 miles from the border of the Lau and with roads now existing in the district it should be possible for the District Commissioner to have his headquarters in some suitable place in Lau.[34] This headquarters should be entirely tribal and other than the District Commissioner's personal escort there should be no Government Police or Junior Officials as in Northern Merakiz.[35] With the Chiefs acquiring greater control the District Commissioner's duty will be to advise and to coordinate.

Before concluding this report, I should like to take the opportunity of acknowledging the great assistance rendered by Captain T. Kerr M.C., to whom

32. See above, doc. 1.5 notes 8 and 9.

33. For a sketch of the no man's land see above, doc. 2.2.

34. No station was built in Lou territory until 1946, when Waat was made into a sub-district headquarters.

35. The intention here was to avoid introducing northern Sudanese (Muslim) police and *ma'murs* into Nuer rural administration.

in large measure was due, the confidence established among the sections in the Gun Concentration Area. Chiefs and Tribesmen came to and fro freely between their camps and the base and it was only owing to the personal contact with Capt. Kerr and the excellent behaviour of the troops under his command that this was possible.

Capt. Tyndale-Biscoe, who commanded the mounted troops, gave every possible assistance and it was due to the mobility and efficiency of the Mounted Troops that success was attained during operations.

The Medical arrangements were in charge of Capt. Davidson[36] in the early stages of the Settlement, who was succeeded later by Capt. Dalziell.[37] The medical work proved invaluable and each section was medically inspected in turn.

The Settlement in Gun area would not have been concluded as rapidly had I not have had the support of Major Wyld and Capt. Alban.

SGS *Kerreri*
24.5.29

P.C.
Political Officer
Guncol Area

Copies to—O.C. Equatorial Coy
           O.C. Guncol Mounted column
           D.C. Abwong
           D.C. Bor-Duk
           File

APPENDIX A: GUNCOL DIARY

Jan. 5th & 6th
Conference at Malakal.

Jan. 8th
Concentration orders issued at Abwong to Shiengs Tshan [Can], Matchok [Macok], Lang, Tiang, Fulkir, Yuong, Shish [Cic] and Manthiep.[38]

Jan. 17th
Arrived Bor a.m. Left Bor with Major J. W. G. Wyld D.S.O., M.C. at 20.30 hrs

36. Later Brigadier T. Davidson (Royal Army Medical Corps), SDF 1924–31.

37. Captain Ewen G. Dalziell, MC, MB (RAMC), SDF 1927–31.

38. Macok, Cic, Yuong and Manthiep are all sections of the Nyarkuac-Gaadbal-Gun Lou; Thiang is a tertiary section of Gaadbal. Lang and Pälker are tertiary sections of Rumjok.

by lorry.
Arrived Kwoinatem [in Twic Dinka country] 24.00 hrs.

Jan. 18th
Left 08.00 hrs arrived Kongor 10.45 hrs. No. 1 Coy. Equatorial Corps under command Capt. T. Kerr M.C. at Kongor. Left with Coy. 16.30 hrs arrived Faiyom 17.00 hrs. Road impassable for wheeled traffic beyond Faiyom.

Jan. 19th
Left 05.00 hrs marched through water for about 8 miles, arrived Wulang 08.00 hrs. Left 10.15 hrs arrived Duk Fayuil 13.00.

Jan. 20th
Left 05.15 hrs arrived 07.45 hrs at Koich. Left 12.00 hrs arrived Duk Fadiat 14.30 hrs. Troop Mounted Police in Duk.

Jan. 21st
Major Wyld and self with 1 section M.P. rode out towards Mwot to survey road. About 10 miles road near Duk unhished [i.e. uncleared]. Information received re arrival Hamla at Mwot Did from Abwong via Khor Fulus.

Jan. 22nd
Major Wyld and self with M.P. escort left for Mwot 15.00 hrs. Arrived Duk Boi Chai 17.30 hrs.

Jan. 23rd
Left 05.45 hrs arrived Faliu 09.45 hrs. Lau Chief Chag Gaing [Cak Gany][39] met on road. Sent back to confirm concentration orders. Reports from Dinkas re impracticability Nyerol road. Runners sent to Fulus mouth with instructions inform Jureir Chiefs collect labour gangs for work with Sapper [army engineers] section. Left 15.00 hrs arrived Warawar 17.30 hrs.

Jan. 24th
Left 05.30 hrs arrived Mwot Did 09.30 hrs. Chiefs Rial Mai, Pur Tiop, Warwel [Warweng] Tudel, Goy Thuin and Thain Pin Dul come in. State sections are preparing concentrate. No sign camps. Chief Chokwel Dthoar[40] fugitive in 1928 Patrol comes in and arrested. Several Jureir Dinka Chiefs from North in. Instructed re roads and given authority arrest all fugitive Lau or Gaweir fugitives in their country.

39. See above, doc. 1.5 n. 24.

40. For Rial Mai (or Mac), see above, doc. 1.5 n. 23; for Warweng Tudel, Pur Tiop, Goy Tony Begh, Thain Pin Dul, and Cokuel Dhoar, doc. 1.5.

DOCUMENT 3.3

Jan. 25th

Rode out with Major Wyld and 1 section M.P. to edge of Beir forest. Chief Maikieir [Maiker] Thijok[41] who was arrested in 1928 comes in. Appears uncertain of his people and unable to account for his own movements. Sent off to collect his people. Chiefs' Police report that Gwek married Chief Maikier's sister[42] few days previously and Maikier visited Gwek at Pyramid before our arrival. Reports confirm Gwek at Pyramid with a few people. Chiefs of Shieng Nyajakan [Nyajikany] bring in 5 men implicated in Dinka raid. Left 14.15 hrs arrive Warawar 18.15 hrs. After leaving instructions with Chiefs prepare Landing Ground at Fathai, prepare shelters for troops.

Jan. 26th

Left 05.30 hrs arrived Wulang 08.30 hrs. Left 13.30 hrs arrived Duk Boi Chai 17.00 hrs.

Jan. 27th

Two hours march into Duk Fadiat.

Jan. 28th–29th

Duk Fadiat.

Jan. 30th

To Dongayo on Gaweir boundary with Major Wyld and 2 sections M.P. Village found deserted and return Duk. Capt. N. Macleod[43] arrived 17.00 hrs from Duk Fayuil. Reports received re presence of Dwal Diu of Gaweir on Duk ridge near Ayod and meeting of Gwek Wundeng, Pok Keirjok and Char Koryom at Pyramid with Chief Kwil Rueh of Mor and others.[44] Mor said to be collecting at Faddoi but intentions uncertain. Jekaing Nuers reported to have refused harbour to several Mor sections.

Jan. 31st

Road through from Fayuil and lorries arrive. 2 sections M.P. leave for Mwot to act as escort on arrival.

Feb. 1st

Equatorial Coy. with Capt. Kerr leave for Mwot 06.00 hrs. Capt. Macleod, Major Wyld and self left by lorry for Mwot 08.00. Passed Coy. at Wulang and arrived

41. See above, doc. 1.5.

42. Nyariek Thijoak Dul was Guek's third wife (governor, Upper Nile Province to civil secretary, 19.03.29, Nasir ENRC [Eastern Nuer Rural Council] 66.A.1).

43. Captain N. Macleod (King's Own Scottish Borderers), EA 1923–5, SDF 1925–33, OC Equatorial Corps, Upper Nile Province, 1928.

44. For Kwil Rueh, see above, doc. 1.5 n. 39.

Faliu 12.15 hrs. Left 15.00 hrs overtook M.P. sections and arrived Warawar 17.00 hrs. Met by several Lau Chiefs and Chiefs' Police. Report sections concentrating. Runner in from Capt. E. C. Tunnicliffe, arrived Mwot from Akobo.

Feb. 2nd
Two hours into Mwot. Capt. Tunnicliffe with 2 sections M.P. in. Various Mor Chiefs and Chiefs' Police in and report concentration orders not clear. Instructed go back Mor and sections given further 20 days concentrate without affecting orders given to Gun sections. Gun Chiefs in, including Maikier Thijok who was arrested. Equat. Coy. arrived 09.00 hrs. Surveyed road as far as Fathai Khor.

Feb. 3rd
Shiengs Nyajakan and Dul in position. Reports re arrival other sections at concentration camps. Gwek reported at Pyramid with individuals from various sections and several minor Witchdoctors. Chiefs' Police state Gwek intends fight.

Feb. 4th
Capt. G. R. Eastwood with 2 Troops cavalry arrived afternoon of 3rd accompanied by Capt. A. H. A. Alban D.F.C. and 1 section M.P. Capt. Macleod and Major Wyld left for Kongor by Lorry. New site at Mwot selected for Landing Ground. Road and ramping work carried out.

Feb. 5th
Gun Chiefs in and given instructions re movements during concentration. Following Shiengs in except for individual backsliders: Fulkir. Nyajakan. Dul. Mathel. Maikier. Dung. Shieng Lang and Chief Dtho Dieng of Yuong, Chief Liglig Kuin of Tiang reported at Jur south east of Pyramid and awaiting developments. Attitude uncertain. Reports confirm presence of Gwek at Pyramid with concentration of warriors from various sections.

Feb. 6th
Combined Guncol and Morcol forces leave for Pyramid. 14.00. Capt. Macleod and Major Wyld returned from Kongor. Major Wyld and self with 1 section M.P. overtake flying column at Ful Shwol 21.00 hrs. Scouts in report number of Nuers at Pyramid. Scouts sent on for further information.

Feb. 7th
Limit of period given to Gun sections to concentrate. Left 14.00 hrs and ran into Shieng Matchok division from Mor on way into Gun concentration. Women and cattle allowed proceed. Young men arrested. Scouts return, report large concentration at Pyramid. Mwot Tot 19.00 hrs.

Feb. 8th
Left 02.00 hrs without transport arrived Budwot within sight of Pyramid 06.00 hrs. Nuers seen near Pyramid. Scouts report Nuers in war array and beating drums. Large numbers Nuers seen on approach beating drums and singing. Dismount and form square within 400 yards of Pyramid. Nuers perform antics but do not attack. Two shots put in by Marksmen and Nuers slaughter two bulls and advance to attack behind a white bull driven in front of them. Open fire and Warriors break within 150 to 200 yards of square. Mount and pursue. Nuers break into two columns and retreat to n.east and s.east. Cattle overtaken but main body of Nuer get away. Return to Pyramid. Gwek Wundeng and Chief Liglig Kuin found dead among other killed. Chief Songster[45] of Gwek brought in wounded by Chiefs' Policemen. Information obtained from him as to Gwek's intentions and movement of sections. Large numbers of Nuer reported to have bolted after first shots fired and about 200 advanced to attack. Cattle driven off before battle. Numbers of warriors said to have been expected at noon. Scouts sent to Faddoi.

Feb. 9th
Left 06.00 hrs arrived Mwot Tot 08.00 hrs. Scouts in report no Nuers Faddoi and many seen going towards concentration area.

Feb. 10th
Capt. Eastwood and Capt. Tunnicliffe with 1 Troop cavalry and 1 Troop M.P. (Morcol) proceeded to Wegin. Guncol with 1 Troop cavalry under Mul. Awal Mohammed Eff. Osman left for and arrived Mwot Did 17.00 hrs.

Feb. 11th
Census taken of Shieng Nyajakan.

Feb. 12th
Col. Nosworthy[46] D.S.O., M.C. arrived from Bor. Wireless Unit arrived.

Feb. 13th
Col. Nosworthy, Capt. Alban and self to Khor Kwainjor by lorry and return same day. Arrangements made for concentrated sections to ramp Khor and improve roads. Information received Shieng Lang on way in. Chief Dtho Dieng fugitive.

---

45. Yang Pet (*guk* Gambiel), died of his wounds (governor UNP to civil secretary, 19.02.29, Nasir ENRC [Eastern Nuer Rural Council] 66.A.1).

46. See above, doc. 3.1 n. 2.

Feb. 14th
Governor and Wing Commander Reid D.S.O.[47] arrrive 07.45 hrs by air and fly over camp to Duk, arriving by car 16.00 hrs.

Feb. 15th
Governor, Col. Nosworthy and Wing Comm. Reid leave 15.00 hrs.

Feb. 16th
To Shit for census of Shieng Yuong. Shieng Tiang of Chief Liglig Kuin in. Shieng Lang reported on way in. Information collected re killed and wounded at Pyramid. Chiefs Red Ruathdel and Diu Muk of Mor[48] in and state people still at villages. Given orders go Wegin. Dr. Davidson and Dr. Crouch[49] arrive Mwot.

Feb. 17th
Dr. Crouch leaves for Bor. Arrange work on ramp. Shieng Lang in. Interrogate wounded and others. Information received re individuals camped near Mor country towards Geni.

Feb. 18th
Capt. Alban to Shit for work on census. Major Wyld and self with force leave 15.00 hrs arrive Fayai 17.30 hrs. Small section of Shieng Maikier met on way in and allowed go in after arresting young men.

Feb. 19th
March 5 hours to Toi arriving Noon. Leave 24.00 hrs and march all night.

Feb. 20th
Arrive Fanyim 0.600 hrs. Few old men and women found and told to go into concentration area. News received re Char Koryom said to be near Thep and suffering from poisoned foot. March to 10.00 hrs. No Nuers met. Halt for 6 hours and then proceed to Ful Burra, leave transport and march on Yoynyang. One Nuer captured reports Char left for Faddoi, two days previously. Concentration of Nuers reported on pool to east. March for 6 hours and at 22.00 hrs find two camps. Camps surrounded and cattle captured. 5 Nuer casualties. Camp of Shieng Belyu of Mor.

Feb. 21st
Chief and several men of Shieng Belyu come in to camp. Given flag and ordered

---

47. See above, doc. 3.1 n. 16.
48. For Reth Ruathdel and Diu Muk, see above, doc. 1.5.
49. For Crouch, see above, doc. 3.1 n. 26.

to go Wegin. No information concerning Char. Pok Keirjok reported to have been wounded slightly at battle of Pyramid and fled to Gila river.

Feb. 22nd
Leave 04.00 hrs arrive Ful Nyuka after 5 hrs march. Several young men captured.

Feb. 23rd
March 2 hours to Nuerthon village found deserted. Chiefs' Police sent to Nuerthon southern end to burn village of Kujur Maiyong Kwey [Mayom Kuei].[50] 2 sections of M.P. sent to Mwot with cattle and prisoners.

Feb. 24th
Return to Ful Nyuka.

Feb. 25th
March 5 hours to Kogmandet. Two men captured with rifles and one killed. March two hours to Ful Buok on return to Mwot. Cattle tracks discovered at 18.00 hrs. Follow and surprise party of Shieng Maikier. Young men get away. Cattle captured.

Feb. 26th
Marched to Mankwauka.

Feb. 27th
Arrived Mwot 12.00 hrs Capt. N. E. Tyndale-Biscoe and 1 Troop Cavalry in. To reinforce column.

Feb. 28th
Fulus road through. See Chiefs.

March 1st
Census work. Reported concentration of Gaweir near border.

March 2nd
Camel Corps Coy. and Sapper section arrive. Work on census.

March 3rd
To Fathai to arrange for labour on bridges. Governor [Willis], Col. Nosworthy arrive. Medical Inspection of sections. Information re camp near Mwot Tot

---

50. Mayom Kuei later gave himself up to the DC at Duk Fayuil (Discom to governor, Malakal, 30.06.29, SRO UNP 5.A.3.42). Not to be confused with the Gaawar earth-priest, Mayom Kuai; see above, doc. 1.2 n. 31.

belonging Dtho Dien.

March 4th
Left with Governor and Col. Nosworthy for Malakal after arranging for column with Capt. Tyndale-Biscoe and Capt. Alban to march to Mwot Tot.

March 5th–6th
Malakal.

March 7th
Lorry breaks down at night near Fathai and run into small party Gaweir. Cattle and two women captured.

March 8th
Mwot Dit. Further arrests of Gaweir made by Chiefs' Police. Visited cattle camps with Major Ellison.[51] Flying column in with captured cattle and prisoners.

March 9th
Capt. Tyndale-Biscoe, Major Wyld and self with flying column leave for Gaweir to cooperate with Barcol.

March 10th
March 6 hours. Run into Gaweir scouts. 2 killed and 2 captured. Captured found to be half-brothers of Dwal Diu. March 2 hours to Liur.

March 11th
March to within hour's march of Juetjuet where scouts reported Gaweir concentration and camp for night in forest.

March 12th
March to Ful Juetjuet and find deserted camp. Follow tracks for hour and run into Gaweir camp. 9 men killed, 4 captured and 100 cattle taken. Killed include Chief Riek Yor[52] sub-Chief of Dwal Diu's. Camp by pool.

March 13th
March 5 hours to Ful Gweir and surprise individual fishing. Found to be Sub-Chief Wol Dup[53] of Gaweir. Bolting camp reported by him and chase for 1 hour, capturing 11 men and 150 head cattle. 1 man killed. Return to Ful Gweir

---

51. Major John Reynolds Ellison (Royal Army Veterinary Corps), EA 1918–25, SDF 1925–8, Veterinary Dept., 1929.

52. For Riek Yor, see above, docs. 1.2, 1.3.

53. Wol Dup is possibly the same as 'Fol Twop' above, docs. 1.2, 1.3.

14.00 hrs and camp.

March 14th
March 3 hours to pool in Majak forest. Cattle tracks found going south. Cavalry scouts fired at by party 10 men who escape in thick bush. Mule tracks found and scout sent off get in touch Barcol. Mr. Wedderburn-Maxwell arrives at pool with scouts mid-day. Reports having captured Dwal Diu cattle and several prisoners. Dwal escaped.

March 15th
Marched to Mr. Wedderburn-Maxwell's camp. Joined Mr. Bacon[54] and Barcol M.P. troops. Stopped half hour and proceeded direction Khandak through forest. Tracks found near pool in forest. Scouts sent out who report odd parties of Nuers, no cattle. Camped for night by pool in Khandak. Second pool close by picketed. Scouts sent out at dusk and return 23.00 hrs report no sign Nuers. Camp fired at 23.30 hrs. Put up Verey lights but saw nothing. Fire returned in direction flashes and enemy retire.

March 16th
Mr. Maxwell considered no further use pursuing Dwal and unnecessary continue with Barcol. Guncol returns for Mwot 06.00 hrs. Cavalry scouts run into party Nuers who fire at them 08.00 hrs. Pursue through thick bush but no men captured. Woman and five children found and discovered to be Dwal's wife and children. State Dwal and young men were at Khandak during night and were expected at rendezvous in forest that morning. Sent Transport and others on and Major Wyld, Capt. Tyndale-Biscoe and self remained with 16 men hidden in dry pool for 2 hrs but nothing further seen. March to Ful Gweir arriving 14.00 hrs. Left 17.00 hrs arrived Pool in forest 20.00 hrs. Gaweir prisoners handed Barcol. Cattle taken by us for Mwot.

March 17th
Police Troops with cattle sent direct Mwot. Remainder march via Farial. Marched for 4 hrs during afternoon and ran into party Nuers who escaped into bush.

March 18th
Marched 2 hrs to pool in morning. Afternoon marched to Khor Kwainjor 2 [and a] half hours.

March 19th
5 hour march to Fayoi. Kwainjor crossed at Lokchak.

---

54. F. J. H. Bacon, ADC Zeraf Valley District 1928–31.

March 20th
7 hour march to Fathai arriving 12.45 hrs. Capt. Kerr and Capt. Foley[55] arrive by lorry. Arrive Mwot base afternoon.

March 21st
All prisoners other than Chief Maikieir [Maiker] Thijok and raiders released. Chiefs given lists of wanted men and raiders required as hostages.

March 22nd
Capt. Tyndale-Biscoe and Capt. Alban with column leave for Piojak, southern end of Lang country where Char Koryom reported.

March 23rd
All wanted men brought in by Chiefs without trouble. Dr. Crouch & Dr. Atkey[56] arrive from Fulus mouth.

March 24th
Left for Kan with Major Wyld to see Dinka Chiefs re transfer to Duk District.

March 25th
To Malakal by lorry from Kan. Stop 2 hours and return Kan.

March 26th
All Dinka (Jureir) Chiefs seen.

March 27th
Return to Mwot Did.

March 28th
Leave for Bor.

March 29th & 30th & 31st
Bor.

April 1st [57]
Arrive Duk Fayuil from Bor 16.00 hrs. Flying column back from South. No Nuers seen by them. Information received re presence Char Koryom at Ful Char. Cavalry leave for Mwot.

55. See above, doc. 3.1 n. 12.
56. Dr O. H. T. Atkey, director Sudan Medical Service 1922–33.
57. In the original, January was written instead of April throughout the rest of the diary.

April 2nd
To Duk Fadiat with Major Wyld.

April 3rd
To Mwot and back to Fanyok. Camp at Fanyok. Information corroborated re Char.

April 4th
Cavalry arrive with Capt. Tyndale-Biscoe 06.00 hrs. Left for Ful Char 16.00 hrs. March all night. Lost way and delayed 3 hrs.

April 5th
Arrive Char's camp 09.00 hours and find it deserted. Cattle tracks found all directions but impossible follow in scrub. Camp apparently deserted half hour previous to arrival. Some women and men caught in bush confirm Char's escape just before arrival. One of women caught, wife of Char. Man wounded trying to escape through bush. Camped for 2 hrs at Pool and left 12.30 hrs. Marched all night till [01.00 hrs.].

April 6th
01.00 hrs arrive at Mwot Base. Chiefs instructed allow sections return to homes.

April 7th
Left by lorry for Wegin (Morcol base).

April 8th to 10th
Duty. Morcol.

April 11th
Arrived with Governor at Mwot.

April 12th
Governor saw all Chiefs and informed them Gun Lau had carried out task required of them. Governor left 15.00 hrs.

April 13th
Majority of cattle returned to owners. Remainder handed to Major Wyld for Dinka reparations.

April 15th
Left for Bor.

April 16th
Capt. Kerr with Equatorial Coy. evacuated Mwot for Duk Fadiat.

Appendix B: Return of Prisoners and Casualties Guncol

Casualties—Government Forces
Killed—Nil. Wounded—1 O.R. [other ranks] near Mwot Tot 6 March.

Casualties—Nuer

Killed—	(By Camel Corps near Nyerol?	in February?	4?)
	At Dengkur Pyramid	Feb. 8th	20
	Camp near Yoynyang	Feb. 20th	3
	Thep Shwor (Kogmandet)	.. 25th	1
	Near Mwot Tot	March 6th	11
	(Operations in Gaweir)		
	Fayoi	March 10th	2
	near Juetjuet	.. 12th	9
	near Ful Weir	.. 13th	1
			51

Wounded—	Dengkur Pyramid	Feb. 8th	4
	Camp near Yoynyang	Feb. 20th	3
	(Operations in Gaweir)		
	Nuer Juetjuet	March 12th	3
	(Guncol)		
	near Ful Char	April 5th	1
			11

Prisoners

Captured during Operations 60. Released 54. To Prison 6.
Handed over by Chiefs Abwong District   117
 .. .. Duk ..   50 ?
               157 [*sic*]

Appendix C: Return of Cattle captured Guncol Operation[58]

Approx. 300 head of cattle were capt. [captured]. All cattle were ret. [returned] except where owners were known to have been inv. [involved] in Dinka raids or were with Gwek at Pyramid on Feb. 8. Of these a fine was levied on each owner varying from 40% to 7% of his cattle.

 The total number rec. [received] in fines 1321 but were handed over for Dinka reparations.

58. Handwritten copy.

Document 3.4

NOTES ON POLITICAL PRISONERS IN MALAKAL

When Dual was captured in January 1930 and gave his reasons for rebelling, Coriat supported some of his complaints.[1] It was the opinion of many later DCs among the Gaawar that Dual had been badly treated by the government during the Gaawar march. He and three other Nuer prophets (Pok Kerjiok, Car Koryom, Kerbiel Wal) were subsequently exiled from their home areas. Car Koryom was soon released, but the others remained in prison.

The men most in favour of exiling the prophets for life in exile had been governor Willis and Major Wyld, DC Bor-Duk District. Both left the province in 1931. It was then that Coriat wrote this letter to the new governor of the province, A. G. Pawson, and while not openly criticising either Wyld (who was a friend) or Willis (who was not), he urged leniency for Dual and Kerbiel. He was able to make a stronger case in favour of Dual than he had been able to make when Willis was governor.

Both Pok and Kerbiel died in exile in Wau. Dual Diu was kept in Malakal until the late 1930s, when he was sent to Adok in Western Nuer District. He spent some twenty-three years in exile because the Nyareweng Dinka chiefs and succeeding DCs refused to consider his release. He finally returned home at his own initiative in 1953 and was allowed to stay by the departing British administration. He was rearrested by the new Sudanese province authorities in 1955 but was allowed to return home again in 1957. This time he married the daughter of Moinkuer Mabur, his old Dinka adversary, and remained in peace until his death in 1968.

---

1. See above, Introduction.

Governor[2]
Upper Nile Province
Malakal

There are 3 Nuer Political prisoners now in Malakal. No one of these men has been tried and as regards their political misdemeanours I do not think any one is less guilty than the other.

Having personal knowledge of them and their respective histories the following notes may be used in determining the policy to be adopted as regards their future.

1. DWAL DIU. Arrested towards the latter half of 1929.[3] Was a fugitive at the time and suffering from small pox.

Dwal is the second son of DIU (DENG LIKER) [Deng Laka][4] the first Gaweir Kujur of repute. The first DIU assumed the hereditary Land Chiefship of Gaweir after defeating the Arabs under Elias Kabsun [Ilyas Kapsun] at Kodni on the Zeraf river during the time of the slave raiders.[5] He became known to the present Government when Matthews & Struvé first visited Gaweir on the survey of the telegraph line.[6] He was well disposed on the whole but the Gaweir were never administered during his lifetime. On his death his elder son MACAR became Chief and was accepted as having inherited DIU's KUJUR powers.[7] MACAR DIU gave trouble from the word go and the 1914 patrol was due to his persistent and repeated attacks on the Dinka for whose protection we were responsible. MACAR avoided capture and the patrol concluded as have other patrols since by marching through the country. In 1915 MACAR led a successful and destructive raid against the DINKA and was killed during the fighting.[8]

His brother DWAL took over the Chiefship.

It may be mentioned that in 1910 the Nuer were confirmed in their rights to land conquered from the DUK FADIAT DINKA.[9] This was I think faute de mieux on our part. DWAL was suspicious of Government and Govt. was suspicious of DWAL. Minor Dinka raids continued and in 1921 when a post was opened in

---

2. A. G. Pawson, Introduction, n. 56.

3. 24 January 1930.

4. Dual was in fact one of Deng Laka's younger sons.

5. See above, doc. 1.2.

6. He first met Bimbashi H. H. Wilson (senior inspector Upper Nile Province) on 7 February 1905, and Governor G. E. Matthews and K. C. P. Struvé on 11 February 1907 (see Wilson 1905 and Matthews 1907).

7. Macar Diu never claimed, nor was he believed to have inherited, the divinity Diu.

8. Macar was killed in 1914 (see above, doc. 1.2 n. 21).

9. See Struvé 1909.

Gaweir (AYOD) DWAL was believed to be preparing to attack on a large scale. The attack never came off and from then on until the year 1928 the history of DWAL and the GAWEIR became a long succession of rumours of impending attacks always originating from the Dinka.[10]

DWAL donned a Government Chief's robe in 1923 and visited Malakal.[11] Apart from our fears regarding his designs on the Dinka, he proved himself a capable & trusty Chief. DWAL was young and hot headed as are most Nuer young men but his frankness, energy and sense of humour ensured him a friendly reception at the hands of District Commissioners who knew the Gaweir.

In 1928 the Witch Doctors GWEK, CAR[12] and KEIRBIEL were in revolt against the Government and at large.

At the conclusion of the Gaweir march in 1928,[13] DWAL was visited at his camp in the 'TOICH' and stood fast. As he himself put it he was the 'one so-called KWOTH to sit.' [See Plate 14.]

Owing to his harbouring a number of LAU refugees and the uncertainty as to the stability of those of his young men who had rifles his camp was surprised and searched shortly after; in fact the morning after the first friendly visit. Few rifles were found. During the operation a number of Dinka followers of the Government forces mutilated some of his cattle. His favourite Dance Bull, it is said, was found with its ears cut off.[14]

The sequel was an attack by DWAL on the Dinka of DUK FAIWEL MERKAZ during the rains of that year. I do not consider his behaviour was surprising.

DWAL has given a promise to settle quietly should he be allowed to go to Western Nuer & I believe that he will not break his word.

2. POK KEIRJOK—A minor Witchdoctor who surrendered in May 1931.[15]

Pok is crafty, ill disposed to Government and thoroughly untrustworthy. He sided with GWEK during the Nuer Settlement and his past history had always been bad. He is probably partly insane.

3. KEIRBIEL. An epileptic and generally not responsible for his actions. In 1928 gave himself out as being under the influence of a 'Spirit' and divinely appointed to lead raids against the Dinka. He controlled a large body of unruly Nuer when Maxwell and Romilly marched in to Gaweir during the early stages of the troubles there and they were compelled to return as best they could from

---

10. See above, doc. 2.1 n. 9.

11. *SMIR* 348 (July 1923), 5.

12. See above, doc. 3.2 n. 14 and doc. 3.3 n. 29.

13. See Wedderburn-Maxwell 1928; Wyld 1928; Dual Diu 1930; Gaawar texts 4.8, in Johnson, in preparation.

14. See above, Introduction.

15. See above, doc. 1.5 n. 45 and doc. 3.2.

an ugly situation.[16]

Numerous surprise marches failed to effect the capture of this elusive individual though his wife and family were not with him. He eventually gave himself up March 1930.[17]

I would suggest that provided the District Commissioner Gaweir agrees, DWAL should be allowed to take his wives, a small number of cattle and any one brother excepting BIEL[18] who agrees to accompany him and be allowed to settle at YOYNYANG or other suitable place in Western Nuer until such time as the Government consider he can be allowed to return to GAWEIR without causing a panic among the Dinka.

The District Commissioner Bor-Duk[19] concurs with this proposal.

It should be possible to allow POK & KEIRBIEL to settle at WAU where they would not attempt to escape and where any foibles or hallucinations they may suffer from would not affect their neighbours. Their wives and families would accompany them.

Malakal
27.11.31

Percy Coriat
District Commissioner
Western Nuer

16. Captain Romilly's entry in his diary for 21 February 1928 reads: 'Visit KURBIEL early but with 10 men, but all seen off by 200 Nuers, K decamps during day. An unpleasant show altogether.' Other unsuccessful attempts were made to surprise him on 24 February and 3 March (Romilly diaries, SAD G/S 833).

17. Kerbiel gave himself up in June 1931 (governor, Malakal, to civil secretary, 23.06.31, NRO Dakhlia I 1/2/6).

18. For Coriat's suspicion of Biel Diu see above, docs. 1.3 and 2.1.

19. R. T. Johnston, ADC Bor-Duk District 1931–4, Major Wyld's successor.

SECTION FOUR

Western Nuer

WESTERN NUER: INTRODUCTION

THE early nineteenth-century homeland of the Nuer lay in the area west of the Bahr el-Jebel and northwest of the Bahr el-Ghazal. Though more accessible by river than other parts of Nuerland, it is bounded on all sides by permanent or seasonal swamps, and is therefore more impenetrable than the broad plains to the east. Administrative contact with the Western Nuer was intermittent until the 1920s. Living in the centre of the Southern Sudan, they yet remained outside government control. Those living in the very north of the territory came temporarily under the jurisdiction of the Nuba Mountains Province (later incorporated into Kordofan Province). A proposal in 1913 that Upper Nile Province should take over the entire area came to nothing. Finally, in 1921, Bahr el-Ghazal Province incorporated the district into its own territory in order to control Nuer–Dinka inter-tribal raiding. The DC from the neighbouring Dinka district of Rumbek, Captain V. H. Fergusson,[1] was sent to make contact with Nuer living in the interior. The Dok and Jagei Nuer had recently suffered serious losses at the hands of the Agar Dinka of Rumbek, and Fergusson found that Western Nuer leaders welcomed government intervention as a way of controlling the Dinka.

Fergusson's relations with the Western Nuer were mixed. Some of the Nuer chiefs became close allies, and he let them run their own affairs with very little supervision or interference. Yet Fergusson never established a permanent headquarters in the district, administering it first from Rumbek and then visiting it by steamer. He never learned to speak Nuer, he had a Dinka wife (by whom he had at least two children),[2] and when trekking through the district he always travelled with a large entourage of Dinka and Azande porters and followers. This perpetual distance between himself and the Nuer had its effect on the course of administration. Fergusson had to resort to troops in 1924 and 1925 to impose his way, and in 1927 he was murdered in a conspiracy instigated by outwardly loyal Nyuong Nuer chiefs.

The division of the Nuer between three provinces was considered inefficient, and in the mid-1920s various attempts were made to bring about administrative uniformity. Fergusson's own proposal to create a large Nuer sub-province with himself in charge was never considered seriously (Fergusson 1930: 160, 167–8). The Nuer of Nuba Mountains Province were placed under his authority, but

1. Captain V. H. Fergusson: see above, Introduction, n. 4.
2. 'Diario stazione Yoynyang dal Nov. 1923 al Nov. 1935', AMC A/145/14.

it was decided to bring all the Nuer together under Upper Nile Province. The transfer of the Western Nuer was scheduled for 1928. Fergusson's death in December 1927 coincided with (but was unrelated to) Upper Nile Province's own problems with Guek. The transfer of the district was delayed while Bahr el-Ghazal Province completed punitive action against the Nyuong Nuer.

Fergusson's death left his district without an experienced administrator. Coriat was the only official in the Sudan with sufficient experience among the Nuer to ensure administrative continuity. He was therefore appointed district commissioner of the Western Nuer, formally taking over the district immediately on the conclusion of the Nuer Settlement early in 1929. He inherited a hierarchy of government-appointed chiefs who were used to working independently of the DC in judicial matters. There was also a government-sponsored cotton-growing programme, unique in Nuer administration. This existing administrative structure was different from that created for the Lou and Gaawar in many ways, and Coriat found himself introducing some measures, such as taxation, which had been part of the normal running of his old districts but absent among the Western Nuer before his appointment. In this respect Coriat continued the work he had done among the Gaawar and Lou, creating the first regular system of local administration in the district. By the time he left in 1931 he had done much to bring it into line with the other Nuer districts of the province.

DOCUMENT 4.1

WESTERN NUER DISTRICT

After Coriat had spent over a year and a half as DC for Western Nuer District, he was ordered by the outgoing governor, C. A. Willis, to compile a district report to be included in a projected, but never completed, province handbook. Coriat's report on the Western Nuer doubled as his handing-over report to Captain H. A. Romilly, his ADC and eventual successor.[1] The report contains nearly as much advice about administrative procedure as information on the Western Nuer. Romilly had come to the district (his first administrative appointment) only in November 1930.

Coriat found many differences between the Western Nuer and the Lou and Gaawar. The district is geographically more compact than the eastern districts; the Western Nuer themselves are also politically and territorially more compact. To Coriat they seemed to possess a 'tribal' organization which was absent among the more dispersed and migrant Nuer of the east. He attributed this to the absence of slave-raiding in the west. We know, however, from nineteenth-century sources that the Western Nuer along the river banks suffered continuously from casual raiding by passing boats.[2] What Coriat noted was a difference created by Nuer expansion. The Nuer to the east had developed a different political organization in the process of their expansion, conquest and settlement.

This appears to be the only comprehensive report on the Western Nuer which Coriat wrote.[3] Very few records of the district were kept during this period, and even fewer have

---

1. Captain H. A. Romilly: see above, Introduction, n. 5.

2. See Pedemonte 1974: 58; Lejean 1865: 89; Baker 1867: i.60; Petherick 1869: i.111, 138–9; Schweinfurth 1874: i.117–18; Gessi 1892: 400; Johnson 1981a: 509–11.

3. There was a report attributed to Coriat in the 'Nuer General Historical' file in Nasir (END 66.A.1) entitled 'Report on Eastern District (Nuers) Bahr el Ghazal Province' which I listed among Coriat's known writings in Johnson 1981b: 206. The report was in fact written by Fergusson in 1927 and can be found under the same title in NRO Civsec 57/1/5.

survived. Its value is thus enhanced by its rarity. Governor *Willis* made marginal comments to this report, and his insertions are set off by square brackets in the text and attributed.

WESTERN NUER[4]

1. Boundaries
2. (a) Distribution of Population
   (b) History & General Organisation
3. Revenue
4. Roads & Communications
5. Economic Development & Possibilities
6. Buildings
7. Forestry
8. Sundry
9. Notes on District Officials & Employees
10. Military & Intelligence
11. Medical
12. Office Organisation
13. Personalities (numbered sheets)[5]
    Appendixes 1 Budget
             2 Area Map [missing]

SGS *Kerreri*[6]
1.2.1931

WESTERN NUER DISTRICT

1. Boundaries

The District may be divided into two separate geographical areas divided by a natural boundary, each with distinct features as regards the physical nature of the country [see Map 3].

The Jebel Island area to the south, inhabited by the Nuong [Nyuong], Dok, Jagey, and Jekaing [Jikany] clans, consists for the most part of a low lying black cotton soil plain interspersed by Khors, with here and there a patch or ridge of

---

4. The contents page included page numbers referring to pagination of the original ms.
5. Not included in this copy.
6. SGS *Kerreri*: see above, Introduction, n. 31.

high sandy ground on which palm trees and scrub grow.

As one approaches the Ghazal river to the north, the high ground becomes more frequent and occasional belts of Palm and Talh [*Acacia seyal*] increase in density. South, in the Nuong country, where the ironstone belt reaches its northernmost extremity, the cotton soil gives way to a hard reddish coloured terrain and sand and the scrub is replaced by well afforested land on which the Ameit (Anogeissus Leocarpus) predominates.

Bounded on two sides of the triangle formed by the confluence of the two rivers, by a papyrus swamp of varying width, the country appears to be a vast swamp when seen from the river. Yet the Western Nuer compares favourably with other Nuer Districts and to the Nuer is more favoured than either Lau or Gaweir. The high ground affords good sites for villages during the rains, while the numerous Khors give ample water and grazing to the herds in the dry season at no great distance from their winter quarters. To the west bank of the Ghazal river in the area occupied by the Leik and Bul Nuer and the Ruweng Dinka, a maze of Khors running both parallel to the river and at right angles to it cover the first five to ten miles inland. Interior of this an open treeless plain of hard soil extends to the Southern Kordofan border.

The Bul country on the lower reaches of the Bahr El Arab is for the greater part under water during the rainy season but ridges of sand and forest land occur on its northern and western limits.

North
From the junction of the Khors Loll[7] and Bau north between the Ruweng Alor and Ngork [Ngok] Dinka, thence in a semi-circle towards the north of Milleim El Deleibi to the southern edge of Lake Abiad and thence south of Jebel Kurondi. From Kurondi due south to Lake No. From the junctions of the Khors on the west the line follows the Province boundary as far east as Jebel Kurondi but the limits given above have not yet been ratified.

Along this northern border the neighbouring tribes are Arab.[8]

East
From Jebel Kurondi, south to and including Lake No, thence the Jebel river forms the District boundary to approximately Kilo Pole 400.[9]

The Shilluk adjoin to the east of Lake No. From thence south is bordered by the Lak and Tiang [Thiang] and the Gaweir 'toiches' of the Zeraf Island and beyond by the Twi [Twic] Dinka 'toich'.

7. Called Lol by the Dinka, Ngol by the Nuer.

8. The northern neighbours are Nuba. It is only during the dry season that the Hawazma and Homr (known collectively to the Nuer as *keregni*) come from the interior of Kordofan to the Bahr el-Arab to graze.

9. Reference poles along the river marked the distance from Lake No. This may be a typographical error, as Adok is reference pole 42.

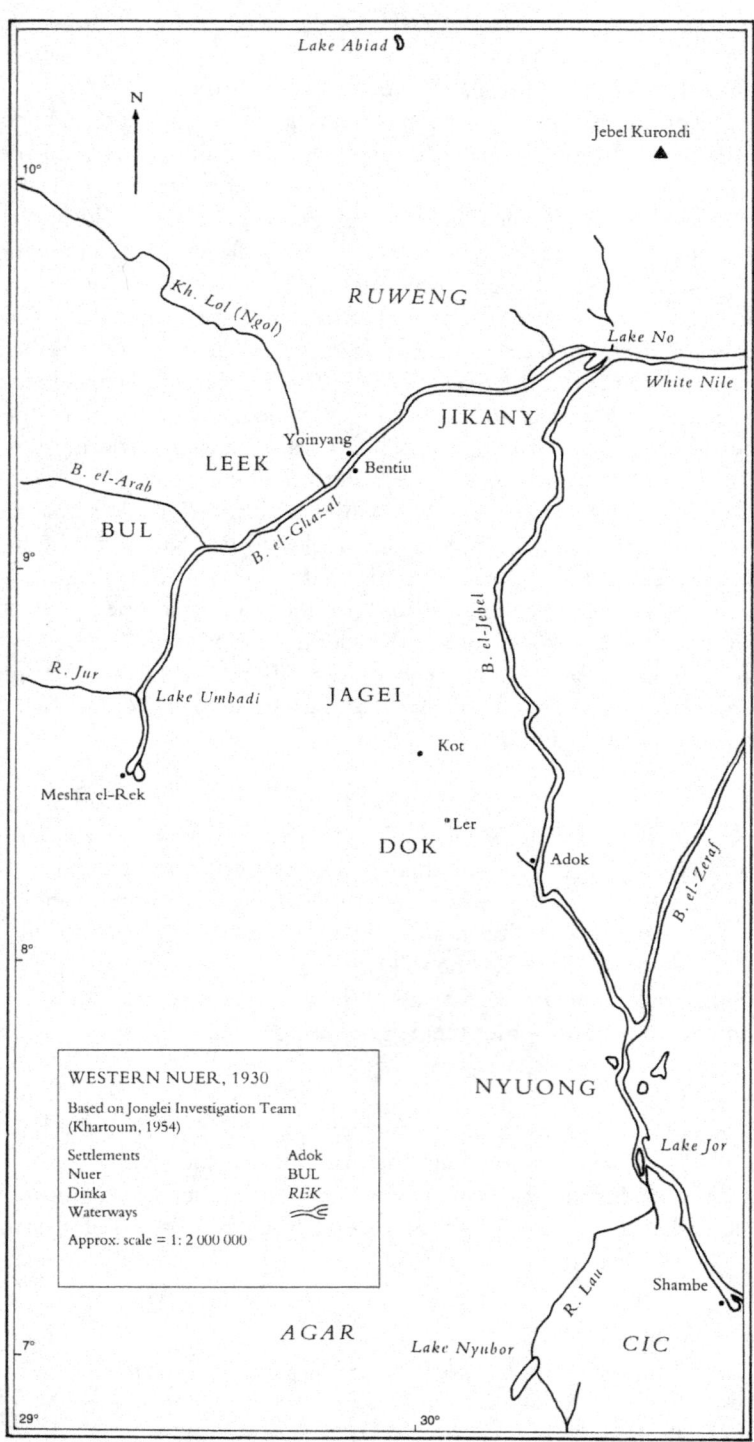

MAP 3 Western Nuer, 1930

South

From approximately Kilo Pole 400 on the Jebel river, southeast to point N. lat. 7° E. long. 30° 30′ and due west to long. 30° [00]′.

Shish [Cic] Dinka are neighbours to the south.

West

From point N. lat. 7° E. long. 30° due north to point N. lat. 7° 47′, thence west to point E. long. 29° 45′ and north west to south of Lake Umbadi.

From Lake Umbadi to Lil (N. lat. 9°2′. E. long. 29°45′) and west to the southern junction of the Khors Lol and Manding and following the line of the Khor Manding to its northern junction with the Lol. Thence along the Lol to its junction with the Khor Bau.

The Agar Dinka inhabit the country on the western border to its south. Northwards the Meshra Dinka tribes and the Mareig of Tonj adjoin.[10]

The Dok, Jagey and Nuong clans have much intercourse with the Gaweir of the Zeraf Island with whom they are friendly. The few rifles that find their way into the District are brought over by Gaweir.[11]

The Agar and Shish Dinka are hereditary enemies of the Jebel clans.[12]

The Jekaing are of the same sub-tribe as the Jekaing of Nasser District and have the same divisions, i.e. Gatjo [Gaajok], Gatjak [Gaajak] and Gatwang [Gaaguong].[13]

2(a) Distribution of Population

GEBEL [JEBEL] RIVER CLANS

Area & Tribes	Chief	River Post	Population
C. Dok	Buom Diu	Adok	11063 (1927)
D. Jagey	Thiey Poich [Thiei Poic]	Tarjath & Ryer	5195 (..)
B. Nuong (Northern Gatliath)	Galwak Nyag [Gaaluak Nyagh]	Nuong	3305 (..)
A. Nuong	Won Kwoth [Wuon Kuoth]	Belek	4116 (1929)

10. The Rek Dinka gave their name to Meshra al-Rek, the Ngok Dinka live along the border of Kordofan and Bahr el-Ghazal Province, and the Twij Dinka were contained within Tonj District, Bahr el-Ghazal Province.

11. See doc. 1.2 above.

12. See Fergusson 1921*b* for an account of warfare between the Western Nuer and the Agar and Cic Dinka.

13. The Thiang section of the Western Jikany are the equivalent of the Gaajak in the east.

Distribution of Population (continued)

Area & Tribes	Chief	River Post	Population
	GHAZAL RIVER CLANS		
E. Jekaing	Badeng Bur (s/chief of Twil Ran of H.)	Yodni	4021 (1927)
F. Jekaing & Kilwal	Gatkek Dwoich [Luop] of Jekaing & Ruai Wur of Kilwal. Both s/chiefs of Twil Ran of H.	Bentiu	2953 (1927)
H. Leik [Leek] & 2 Sections Jekaing	Twil Ran[a]	Yoynyang	3120 (1930)
J. Leik	Nuel Juel	Wathjak	8353 (..)
K. Bul		Wagkal	10924 (..)
G. Ruweng Dinka	Bilkwey Duot		9000 (1926)
			62060[b]

1930 Paramount Chief of Bul not yet appointed
Ruweng Dinka transferred to Western Nuer

a. Now limited to part of Leik only [note by C.A. Willis].
b. The population figures were of registered male taxpayers only, based on a survey undertaken by Fergusson before his death in 1927. Even as an estimate of the adult male population the figures are low and cannot be accepted as an accurarate or complete census.

2(b) History & General Tribal Organisation

Nuer mythology traces a common ancestry for the sub-tribes the origin of which was a miraculous descent from Heaven at Kot (a Tamarind [*Tamarindus indicus*] tree) in the Jagey country of Western Nuer, some 300 to 350 years ago.

There are some local variations of the legend concerning the person and manner of origin of the semi-divine ancestor or ancestress but in neither of the tribes does memory appear to go back more than 400 years.[14]

Western Nuer regard their habitat as the home of the founder of the tribe and it is reputed from here that the various Sub-Tribes migrated.

14. Versions of the tree myth are found in Fergusson 1921*b*: 148–50; Jackson 1923: 70–1; Crazzolara 1953: 8–9, 66–8; and Evans-Pritchard 1956: 6, 10.

Whatever their origin, it is probable that the Nuer at one time in their history came from farther to the west[15] and it is credible that when Western Nuer was first inhabited by them, it was as one Tribe, which expansion caused to break up into separate clans who turned to the east in search for new homes.

The Dinka are their hereditary enemy and conquest of new land meant conquest of the Dinka. Those Tribesmen who elected to remain or were unable to leave the Western Nuer, contented themselves with raids and counter-raids against the Dinka. From 1870 onwards, the sport of Dinka baiting was varied by the advent of the slave raider and in their clashes with the 'Turk' it was not always the Nuer who suffered defeat. As with other tribes of the Nuer they have to their credit one decisive victory when in 1883 the Tribesmen attacked the Turkish Post and Arab allies at Rumbek and succeeded in massacring the garrison and killing the Arab leader Morgan Ali.[16]

Though the slave-bands never penetrated far into Western Nuer and hardly at all into the Jebel Areas, as a consequence of which their Tribal Organisation was not broken up as in Lau and Gaweir, nevertheless their influence was felt sufficiently to engender a feeling of mistrust of all foreigners. Seemingly it is due to the slave-raider that attempts to attain friendly relations with the Nuer have been difficult and their administration has not progressed smoothly and yet it is not easy to conceive that but for the slave-raider they would otherwise have been docile. Although Casati writes of them in 1880 as 'once a peaceful amiable nation, but to-day jealous, timid and hostile,'[17] the primitive and warlike character of the Nuer could not have been acquired in a few generations. Notwithstanding this it is certain that had it not been for the Turkish era, their administration would have been less unsure.

After the occupation the tribes were a constant source of embarrassment to the Government owing to their propensity for raiding their more peaceful Dinka neighbours, but the country was unknown nor was any attempt made to penetrate it. The first record of a visit by an official was in 1913 when a Mr. R. A. Williams of the Egyptian Irrigation Dept. carried out a survey from Adok (Hillet El Nuer) to Bentiu (Ardeiba). The Nuer reported as not actively hostile but suspicious and unfriendly.

In 1914, the Nuong led an attack against the C.M.S. station at Lau and El

---

15. Seligman (1932: 207) reports a story that the Nuer claim to have come from a waterless country to the west of present-day Bul Nuer country.

16. Slave-raiding against the Western Nuer began well before 1870. Murgan Ali was one of Emin Pasha's agents, appointed to Rumbek in 1880. Rumbek was overwhelmed by a combined Dinka–Nuer assault in July 1883 (See 'The History of the Eastern District, Bahr el Ghazal', 13 May 1911, NRO Intel 2/26/208; Junker 1892: 285; Emin Pasha 1922: 490–1).

17. Casati's text (1891: i.38) reads: '... the Nuer, once a peaceful and amiable nation, but today jealous, timid, and hostile. The frequent raids made on them by the slave dealers of Khartoum have changed their feelings to hatred and animosity.' This passage was also cited by Jackson (1923: 88). It refers specifically to the Western Nuer.

Bimb. Bally[18] was sent to Adok for the purpose of reporting on a suitable site for a Government Post but the project was dropped and no further action was taken until 1922 when Capt. Fergusson was instructed to march through the Nuer country and to get in touch with the tribes with the object of initiating some form of administration.[19]

In spite of tribal raids against the Dinka and many setbacks, he succeeded before his death at the hands of the Dur Nuong in 1927 in establishing a definite system of administration and reorganising the clans under either their own leaders or Chiefs appointed by himself.

During this period 1922–1927, there were three punitive patrols, two in 1925 against the Dok and Nuong and one in the Jagey area; all of which were the result of disaffection promoted by Witchdoctors and raids against the Dinka.[20]

In December 1927, Fergusson was murdered by Tribesmen in Dur Nuong. A patrol was despatched and active operations were undertaken against the two Nuong areas. There were few casualties to the Nuer but heavy losses in cattle were reported caused by Aircraft bombing fugitive camps located in the swamps.[21]

Galwak Nyag, a young warrior Chief of the Northern or Gatliath Nuong who had previously given trouble concerning the return of Dinka cattle raided by his Tribe, gave himself up shortly after operations began. Presumably on further evidence he was suspected of having instigated the murder and was arrested and confined.

In 1929, one of the actual murderers [Cuol Weng] gave himself up and after trial was executed in the District. In 1930 an agent effected the arrest of the other Tribesman [Gatkek Jiek] concerned in the attack on Fergusson. Evidence obtained at his trial led to conviction of a Sub-Chief for complicity and a Headman [Gaaluak Buth] was remanded. Both these men were from the Dur section of the Nuong and Cag Riang, Chief of the Tribe was deposed. The Sub-Chief (Dang Dungjiek) died in hospital shortly after being sentenced and the murderer was executed in the area. Galwak Nyag proved innocent, released and reinstated.

In effect the murder of Fergusson by two tribesmen was the outcome of a plot conspired by a group of Dur Chiefs with ambitious ideas and ignorant of

---

18. The Lau post mentioned here was on the Lau river in Rumbek district and has no connection with the Lou (Lau) Nuer of Upper Nile Province. Bimbashi E. D. Bally: second inspector Bahr el-Ghazal Province 1913–16, second inspector Upper Nile Province 1916.

19. See Fergusson 1921a: 11; Fergusson, 'Visit to the Nuong Nuers', 06.03.21, NRO Civsec 1/2/5; and Fergusson 1930: 113–39.

20. There were patrols in March 1923 and January and December 1925. See 'Patrol S.1, Intelligence Reports 1–4', NRO Intel 2/27/217; Fergusson 1930: 182–5, 212–27; *SMIR* 344 (March 1923), 4; 377 (Dec. 1925), 6; 380 (March 1926), 5; and Collins 1983: 40.

21. See Collins 1983: 133–4; Killingray 1984: 437–9.

Government intentions.[22]

During 1928–9 four areas, Bul, Leik, Jekaing and the Ruweng Dinka were visited by a District Commissioner with an escort of troops.[23] The Tribes were said to have been disturbed and disobedient to their Chiefs. In the Bul, which had only twice been visited by Capt. Fergusson and was the most backward area, the intention was to concentrate the clans within an accessible site on the Bahr El Arab. The Bul failed to respond to this suggestion, which appears to have been premature and after a second visit by a District Commissioner early in 1930,[24] it was abandoned.

The Ruweng Dinka originally under Kordofan were transferred to Western Nuer in 1926 but were again placed under the Kordofan administration in 1928. In 1929 they were retransferred to Western Nuer.

Capt. Kidd[25] followed Capt. Fergusson as District Commissioner in 1927 and handed over to me on his transfer in 1929. Capt. Masterman[26] was appointed a second Assistant District Commissioner in May 1929 and was transferred in August 1929 when he was succeeded by Capt. Romilly in November 1930.

The present Tribal Organisation is as follows:-

Area A. Dur or Southern Nuong

Won Kwoth.[27] A hereditary 'Kwar Mon' [*kuaar muon*] (Leopard-skin) and Chief of the tribe until deposed for malpractices in 1924. Prior to the present administration Won was a warrior leader noted for his successes against the Dinka. After his deposal, Galwak Nyag of the Gatliath Nuong was appointed Chief of both his own and the Dur Areas.

Early in 1927 the Dur were removed from Galwak's control and placed under Cag Riang[28] who was neither a hereditary Chief nor a Fighting Leader and his

---

22. The investigations into the murder and transcripts of the trial of the murderers can be found in NRO Civsec 5/4/14–15.

23. See SRO UNP 5.A.3/31, and *SMR* 2 (Feb.–March 1929), 4–5.

24. *SMR* 5 (May–June 1929), 3; Masterman, 'Notes on Bul Nuer 1930', Nasir END 66.A.1.

25. Captain H. F. Kidd: see above, Introduction, n. 56.

26. Captain J. Masterman: ibid.

27. Wuon Kuoth was seized by the divinity Diu (Crazzolara 1953: 162) and was one of the first Dur leaders to make peace with the government in January 1923. He co-operated in Fergusson's cotton growing schemes but was deposed for unfairness in hearing cases in August 1925 *(SMIR* 373 (Aug. 1925), 6). He helped to capture Gatkek Jiek, his own relative, who killed Fergusson, and though reappointed chief of the Dur after Cak Riang was deposed, he was confirmed only as a headman under Gaaluak Nyagh when the latter was reinstated. Wuon Kuoth was one of those accused of causing Gaaluak's death by magic in 1938. By 1941 he was promoted to head chief of the Dur and was known to have good relations with the Dinka and to deal in magic roots ('Upper Nile Province Personality Report no. 49', NRO UNP 1/3/276).

28. Cak Riang (sometimes spelled Tchak Riah) was present when Fergusson was murdered and was the one who first implicated Gaaluak Nyagh as the instigator of the murder. It was only

rule does not appear to have been successful. He was deposed and succeeded by Won Kwoth in December 1930 after having been tried and found not guilty, owing to insufficient evidence, of complicity in the murder of Capt. Fergusson.

Owing to the trouble of 1927 and consequent changes in the Chiefship, the Dur are in more backward state than the neighbouring Dok and Jagey Clans but the Tribal Organisation exists and given an era of peace it should not be long before their administration becomes as little dependent on Government resources as the former Clans.

Won Kwoth is reputed to dabble in witchdoctory but this should not affect his qualities as a leader if he remains loyal. He is slow in action, peculiarly unexcitable, ambitious and appears now to realise something of the meaning of Government. Provided that due allowances are made and a high standard of efficiency is not expected and that Won can maintain a balance among his heterogeneous collection of Sub-Chiefs, he should succeed.

There are 30 individual Shiengs under their respective Headmen, including two sections of Angai Dinka[29] living in the country. These are divided into five main groups under Sub-Chiefs.

Area B. Gatliath or Northern Nuong

Chief Galwak Nyag.[30] A hereditary 'Ut Ok' [*wut ghok*] (Cattle Chief) and Fighting Leader. Paramount of both sections of the Nuong from 1924 to the end of 1926, when he was believed to be exceeding his authority and made trouble over the return of cattle raided from the Dinka and his Chiefship was confined to the Gatliath while the Dur were placed under Cag Riang. In 1927 he was arrested on suspicion of having instigated the outbreak in December of that

---

later that it was learned that Cak himself had helped plot Fergusson's death, but he was acquitted in 1930 on a technicality (NRO Civsec 5/4/15). The governor of Bahr el-Ghazal Province had earlier recommended him for the British Empire Medal for so tirelessly trying to track down Fergusson's murderers, and he is mentioned with favour in Fergusson's biography (Fergusson 1930: 328).

29. The Angai (or Angac) seem to have been an independent group until the middle of the nineteenth century, when many of them crossed the Nile to settle with the Ric Dinka in the east (Poncet 1937: 49). They then seem to have merged with the Agar Dinka but intermarried with the Nyuong.

30. Gaaluak Nyagh is presented as the villain in Fergusson's biography (Fergusson 1930). He was from an impoverished Nyuong *wut ghok* (man of cattle) family. He was seized by the divinity Dapir in about 1919 and organized a number of successful raids against the Dinka. He refused to agree on peace terms with Fergusson and allied with Kulang Ket in resisting the government in 1923–5. After Gaaluak's surrender Fergusson took a liking to him and made him a chief. In November 1927 Fergusson discovered Gaaluak had been hiding guns and hoarding cattle collected in fines. In punishment he was demoted and half his section assigned to Cak Riang, a personal rival. Gaaluak immediately surrendered to the government on receiving news of Fergusson's murder, but because of Cak Riang's accusation he was kept in detention in Malakal for over two years. On being proved innocent he was reinstated as chief of his section in 1930 and appointed head chief of the Dur and Nyuong Nuer in 1935. Having learned Arabic while in prison in Malakal, he was considered a highly satisfactory chief up to his death in 1938.

year and was imprisoned. After his removal the area was placed temporarily under Cag Riang who was then also controlling the Dur. In June 1929, Caath Bang[31] a Dok Chieftain who had been deported to the Agar country in 1924 for oppressive acts, was appointed to the Gatliath. Caath was killed elephant hunting in August 1930 after he proved himself remarkably able.

After capture of the 1927 murderers, Galwak Nyag was proved innocent and was reinstated in December 1930.

The Gatliath comprise 18 Shiengs under Headmen and 4 Sub-Chiefs.

Galwak is young and has complete and unquestioned authority over the Clan. Three years imprisonment may have done much to curb an impetuous nature but it may also have embittered him and it is probable he will require some years of restraint before he can be given a freer rein.

Area C. Dok

Chief Buom Diu.[32] A Witchdoctor and Fighting Leader who led the Dok before Government control. The Dok have in the past had a Tribal Organisation which is practically that of the present day and the Clan has been less affected by changing conditions than any other of the Nuer Tribes.

Buom wields a paramount influence over a populous Tribe and administers the Area with a minimum of help from Government. He is harsh, possibly oppressive at times and little liked but that he realises in greater measure than other Nuer Chiefs the meaning of Government and the inevitable consequences of misrule, there can be little doubt. His autocratic methods seem best suitable to the people he has to rule and I believe his apparent harshness to be not inconsonant with a sense of fairness.

Buom has under him 42 sections under their respective Headmen and 6 Sub-Chiefs.

---

31. Caath Bang (or Caath Obang) was a staunch government ally in the patrol against Kulang Ket and Gaaluak Nyagh in 1924–5. He was taken to visit Khartoum, where he was photographed wearing Fergusson's kilt (Fergusson 1930: picture opposite p. 126). Caath was deposed along with Wuon Kuoth for unfairness in hearing cases in 1925 (not 1924). There was a feud between Caath and Kulang, and Kulang was given into Caath's care upon his surrender in 1925. It is now widely believed that Caath killed Kulang by burying him alive. Kulang is said to have prophesied to Caath that the next time they would meet, Kulang would be an elephant. This came to pass when Caath was killed by an elephant he was hunting in 1930. Collins (1983: 40) mistakenly identifies Caath as a 'Dok Dinka chief'.

32. Buom Diu was seized by the divinity Teny in about 1921. He was known as a very brave warrior, but stubborn and hot-headed. He was arrested in 1923 to prevent him from joining Gaaluak and was deported to Yirrol in early 1925. On his return he became one of Fergusson's most reliable chiefs (Fergusson 1930: 243, 276, 318; 'Nuer Chiefs and Persons of Note. Bahr el Ghazal Province (1927)', NRO Dakhlia I 112/13/87). He protected government property during the aftermath of Fergusson's murder and was well thought of by Coriat. He was deposed by Romilly for extortion and being an 'unconstitutional autocrat' and was exiled first to Akobo and then to Yirrol. He was allowed to return home in 1948. Buom was the only prophet Evans-Pritchard met and is mentioned in Evans-Pritchard 1935: 56, 1940: 186, and 1956: 307.

Area D. Jagey

Chief Thiey Poich.[33] Hereditary 'Kwar Mon'. Appointed on the death of Mani Kolong[34] the witchdoctor in 1926.

The country occupied by the Rangyan [Rengyan] group of this area is reputed the ancestral home of the Nuer and Witchdoctors have become a perennial growth in Jagey, possibly because of this. Thiey has the qualities of a Chief but lacks the fighting character needed to make his position entirely secure from the machinations of the wizards. His Chiefship is not an easy one but he has done well and has little more need of assistance than Buom Diu of the Dok.

Although a smaller tribe than the Dok, the sections and Headmen number 51 with 7 Sub-Chiefs.

Area E. Jekaing

This Area includes 15 Jekaing Headmen with their sections under 4 Sub-Chiefs, the Senior of whom, Badeng Bur,[35] is responsible to Chief Twil Ran of Area H. [Note by C. A. Willis: Twil has now been removed and 4 subchiefs appointed to run Jekaing.]

The Jekaing on the Ghazal river border have been more harried by slave raiders and more influenced by the Arab than the neighbouring Jebel clans and their organisation is less secure. The petty jealousies of Twil Ran and Sub-Chiefs has rendered a closer administration necessary, which it has not been

---

33. Thiei Poic (b. *c.*1895) was sub-chief of the Padang-Rengyan but was appointed head chief of the Jagei when his brother Jeic was deposed by Fergusson. The government often expected him to deal firmly with 'anti-government witchdoctors' (*SMR* 23 (Nov.–Dec. 1930), 6), but in the 1940s he proposed that he hand over the chiefship to Nyaruac Kulang, the daughter of Kulang Ket and then prophetess of Maani. This proposal was not taken up ('Upper Nile Province Personality Report no. 15', NRO UNP 1/34/276).

34. Kulang Ket, the prophet of Maani. Kulang was seized by Maani sometime after the appearance of two other prophets of Deng and Teny among the Western Nuer. He visited Khartoum (or perhaps Omdurman) on his own at the turn of the century (possibly before the end of the Mahdiyya), and on his return to his own country succeeded in becoming the most influential prophet among the Western Nuer. He was probably in his eighties by the time the government made contact with the Jagei in 1921, and he agreed to try to curtail raids against the Dinka. In this he lost the support of many young men, including his own son Majok. Majok died leading a raid against the Cic Dinka in 1922, and Kulang was gradually forced by public opinion among the Jagei to ally with Gaaluak and take up arms against the government. The Jagei were defeated in battle in January 1925 and Kulang surrendered in March. He was detained at Adok where he died (or was murdered) on 24 June 1925 (*SMIR* 372 (July 1925), 5). His daughter, Nyaruac, a divorced woman, tended him during his captivity, and was subsequently seized by Maani after her father's death. She eventually acheived the same spiritual eminence as her father and died, greatly respected, in 1973. See Fergusson 1923: 5; Fergusson, 'Report on visit to Madi', NRO Civsec 1/2/5; 'Summary of Events Leading up to the Trouble in the Nuer Country Bahr el Ghazal Province in December 1924', NRO Intel 2/27/217 and Civsec 1/2/5; Crazzolara 1953: 167–8.

35. Badeng Bur remained loyal to the government after Fergusson was killed. He and Gatkek Luop shared authority over the Jikany after Twil Ran was deposed in 1931. He was murdered in 1932 ('Upper Nile Province Personality Report no. 13', NRO UNP 1/34/276).

possible to give.[36]

I am uncertain whether Badeng Bur the Sub-Chief of this Area is incapable of controlling his Headmen or is unwilling to assert himself in the face of cross-currents of opposition to his Chief Twil and Twil's apparent untrustworthy method of dealing with his own supporters.

Area F. Jekaing & Kilwal

Gatkek Luop[37] a Sub-Chief responsible to Twil Ran of H has under him 7 sections and Headmen and is assisted by one Sub-Chief.

The Kilwal, a branch of the Leik Tribe are controlled by Sub-Chief Ruai Wur also responsible to Twil Ran. Kilwal sections are under 6 Headmen.

Gatkek is young, able and has the confidence of his sections but is ambitious and independent and has antagonised Twil possibly from over assumption of his authority.

With the Chief and Sub-Chiefs at cross purposes, the Headmen have been able to run loose and the Jekaing of both Areas E and F are unsettled.

Ruai Wur with the Kilwal has managed to steer clear of Jekaing intrigues and is competent subordinate leader.

Area H. Jekaing & Leik

Chief Twil Ran.[38] Hereditary 'Kwar Mon' and a Leik by birth. Until appointed Chief in 1924, Twil was unknown to his people either as a Chief or Leopard-skin and spent most of his youth piloting and escorting Arab traders and hunting parties around the country. On his appointment he was given control of the Jekaing of Areas E and F in addition to the two Jekaing sections in Area H and also the Kilwal of F and the Shwak [Cuak] division of Leik of Area H. Being a Shwak Leik himself he elected to live in this Area. The Shwak are grouped into 11 sections under their Headmen and 2 Sub-Chiefs.

Twil has a liking for power and is energetic but completely unscrupulous and hardly less untrustworthy. He is sufficiently intelligent to be loyal to Government, yet without restraint it is certain that he would abuse any position he

---

36. It was more than petty jealousy. The Jikany chiefs resented being subordinated to a Leek chief.

37. Gatkek Luop (b. c.1895), was appointed a sub-chief by Fergusson in c.1925. He shared authority with Badeng Bur after Twil Ran was deposed as head chief of the Jikany, and he became head chief himself after Badeng was murdered in 1932. Government reports noted that he was popular with the people because he saw to their complaints quickly, but unpopular with his sub-chiefs, who felt unduly restricted. As a *tut wec* ('bull of the cattle camp') without any spiritual claims, he often came into conflict with the *kuar muon* ('earth-masters'). He was still head chief of the Jikany when the Sudan became independent in 1956 (Upper Nile Province 'Who's Who', Malakal, UNP SCR 66.D.4).

38. By 1927 Twil Ran was already noted to be too strict with his people, but he remained loyal to the government after Fergusson's death (see 'Nuer Chiefs', cited in n. 32; 'Political Report Patrol S.9', NRO Civsec 5/4/14).

held by misrule.

It is probable that the Jekaing will be removed from his Chiefship and his authority confined to the Leik.

Area J. Leik

Chief Nuel Juel.[39] Was appointed a Chief by Fergusson when the Leik were still little known. Nuel was removed and imprisoned at Malakal for some months during 1928 as he was alleged to have been truculent during the 1927 trouble but was later reinstated. He is crafty and unpleasing and only partially controls the Leik who are in too close proximity to the Bul to be amenable to proper control. Not being a Chief by heredity and lacking the instincts of a Leader, it is doubtful whether Nuel will last.

Feuds are still prevalent in the Area and there is enmity between the Leik in Area H and the Leik divisions under Nuel who form 37 Shiengs with Headmen and 5 Sub-Chiefs.

Area K. Bul

A paramount Chief has not been appointed and is unlikely to be for some years.

The Bul were twice visited by Fergusson but other than the two marches of Troops into the Area in 1928–9 were left to their own devices until 1930. They have much intercourse with the Arabs from the North and have intermarried with them. The country is difficult of access the greater part of the year but if they can be got at their administration should not be difficult.

In 1930 Bul Belyu [Biliu], Teg Jiek [Tegjiek Dualdoang] and Pey Poar were appointed Sub-Chiefs of the Myindeng, Dijul [Dieng] and Gok Areas respectively.[40] Bul Belyu is half Arab and by far the most intelligent of the trio.

Pey Poar had for some time been treated as Head Chief but lacked any kind of control and is old and utterly incompetent.

Area G. Ruweng Dinka

The Ruweng Ajiba and Ruweng Alor were in 1930 transferred from Kordofan Province. They were originally within the Western Nuer and placed under Kordofan in 1928 as it was considered unfeasible to administer them from

---

39. Nuel Juel was a *wut ghok* (man of cattle) and was made chief of the Leik by Fergusson in 1925. He was deposed in 1926 and exiled to Yirrol but later reinstated. In the aftermath of Fergusson's death he was considered to be anti-government and was once again arrested and sent to Malakal in 1928. By the end of that year he was reinstated as chief of the Leik and was considered 'satisfactory', but by 1934 he had become very unpopular (see 'Nuer Chiefs', cited in n. 32; A. D. Home for governor, Upper Nile Province to civil secretary, 08.12.1928, NRO Civsec 36/2/4; Romilly Diary 1934, SAD G/S 833).

40. Bul Bilieu was from the Gek–Gaak–Kuac section of the Bul Nuer. Pei Poar died in 1931 and Tegjiek Dualdoang, an earth-master of the Dieng section, was appointed head chief of the Bul Nuer on Pei's death (Masterman, 'Notes on Bul Nuer 1930', Nasir END 66.A.1; 'Upper Nile Province Personality Report no. 22', NRO UNP 1/34/276).

the Upper Nile. For obvious reasons they cannot be administered satisfactorily from the Headquarters of an Arab Province.

The Ruweng Ajiba, the Chief of whom is Mai Belkwey [Bilkuei], have more intercourse with the Nuer than the Alor. Mai's father Belkway Dwot, an old man, is alive and much feared by the Jekaing as a dabbler in the more virulent forms of magic.[41]

For the past four years the Ruweng have been more or less dependent on their own resources. They are quiet amenable people though tiresome when they afford refuge to recalcitrant Nuer. Occasionally there are clashes with the Jekaing and Leik arising out of disputes over some wretched waterhole on the border.

General Notes on Organisation & Judicial System
The administration initiated by Fergusson was developed on Tribal lines and has the foundation for an essentially native structure.

The Chiefs with a few exceptions were Tribal leaders in the past and it is noteworthy that it is with the exceptions that there have been failures and greater progress has been evident in Areas where the Chief was a Leader before the present administration set in; that is if progress is to be measured in terms of lessening contact by a District Commissioner and dealing direct with the people.

The problem here has been not so much to organise and centralise as with the Lau and Gaweir but to consolidate and secure. The organisation and the Chiefs exist, which they did not in the Eastern Nuer and the District Commissioner is not impelled to make such contact with the people nor to discipline the young warriors; rather it is his work to check and guide the Chiefs and to ensure that the structure remains balanced and is improved where is needful. A closer approach to the work of the District Commissioner Adviser of the future. [Note by C. A. Willis: I do not agree—I think the chiefs are too powerful and need to be reduced if the system is to stand.]

Headmen throughout the Areas were and are appointed by the Chief without reference, the only rule being that they should be Tribesmen selected direct from the section they are to control.

Sub-Chiefs are elected by the group of Headmen subordinate to them and approved by the Chief and District Commissioner.

---

41. Bilkuei Duot was taken captive during the Mahdiyya and spent some time in Shilluk country. He returned to the Ruweng at the end of the nineteenth century, bringing with him a mirror and matches by which he demonstrated his strength as a magician, in addition to possessing *ring*, 'priestly power'. Makuei de Bilkuei, a younger son, inherited *ring*, plus another of his father's divinities, Minyel ('smallpox'). Makuei became famous for curing people through his divinity during the smallpox epidemic of 1933, by which time his father was dead. Mai de Bilkuei, the eldest of Bilkuei's sons, was made chief of the Kuil Ruweng in 1933, but was deposed in 1934 for unwillingness to collect fines (Chatterton, 'Ruweng Dinka' (1934) SRO UNP 66.E.4). Makuei de Bilkuei was interviewed, as a very old man, by Francis Deng and appears in Deng 1980: 68–89.

Except where the individual holds a dual position as a Government Chief or Headman and also a Tribal Functionary, the Chiefs, Sub-Chiefs and Headmen are purely administrative, though not precluded from hearing or giving decisions in the settlement of Tribal cases. It is only in blood-feuds or in matters concerning Tribal rights as also in Rites and Functions that the hereditary Leader is absolute in his authority. Though he is not part of the Government machine as such, his duties are distinct and definable and without him there would be a collapse of the Tribal system. It rests with the Chief to ensure that the 'Kwar Mon' or 'Ut Ok' does not run contra to Government authority and it is here that the snag lies as the mantle of a witchdoctor falls more easily on the Spiritual Guide.

Tribal Courts in so far as a Bench of Chiefs is implied do not exist in Western Nuer. Headmen hear their own people's cases and trivial cases brought against them by outsiders. In more important disputes or where there is question of offence and in cases raised from other Tribes the Chief adjudicates; sometimes with Sub-Chiefs or 'Kwar Mon' as assessors, more often alone. [Note by C. A. Willis: This is to be altered—The courts are an important check on the chiefs.]

That the system works is proved by Areas such as the Dok and Jagey where there is remarkably little litigation, the people are contented, the few appeals there are do come to light and in the presence of the Chief and seldom is there dissatisfaction in cases brought by Tribesmen from other Areas and Districts. More remarkable is this where the Dinka is concerned.

Chiefs' Police[42] (1 to 190 population) are enlisted proportionately from the different Shiengs and are responsible to their respective Headmen within their own sections but are used as a Tribal body under the orders of the Area Chief for the maintenance of Law and Order generally.

There is an establishment of one Clerk to each Area Chief. This has been in being only 8 months and decisions only are recorded on the hearing of cases. Most of the boys are inefficient and until competent Clerks are available it will not be possible to record the full hearing. The Clerks are also responsible for keeping a roster of fines.

3. Revenue

The Tribes in Western Nuer were not taxed until 1929. During Fergusson's administration they were encouraged to sell their surplus bullocks and cotton growing was made compulsory in order that when the time came for a tax the people would have sufficient money to enable them to pay a poll tax and would avoid the uneconomic and unequable [inequitable] Tribute in cattle. A

---

42. For Chiefs' Police, see above, doc. 1.5.

tax of 5 pt. per adult head of population was levied in 1929 and was collected by Headmen and made payable as Tribute. In 1930 this was revised to 10 pt. per adult male.

		Tax Paid 1929	Tax Paid 1930
A.	Southern Nuong	Nil	£E. 141.400 m/ms
B.	Northern Nuong	..	88.500 m/ms
C.	Dok	£E. 221.820 m/ms	254.400 m/ms
D.	Jagey	108.150 m/ms	162.300 m/ms
E.	Jekaing	⎰ 120.955 m/ms	152.400 m/ms
H.	Leik	⎱	42.700 m/ms
J.	Leik	43.685 m/ms	183.300 m/ms
K.	Bul	39.900 m/ms	Remitted cattle tribute
G.	Ruweng Dinka	To Kordofan	Kordofan
TOTAL		£E. 534.510 m/ms	£E. 1025.000 m/ms

Fines, mostly in cattle are levied by Area Chiefs and credited to item Chiefs Courts in the devolution Budget. There is no fee for the hearing of cases. Cattle are sold locally, those from one Area being sold in another.

Revenue in Fines

1929	1930
£E. 565.575 m/ms	£E. 662.900 m/ms

4. Roads & Communications

There are ten river ports in nine of the Areas as shown in 'Distribution of population' and a port will possibly be opened at Lake No for the Ruweng Dinka. Each of these is accessible from the mainland and in addition to a Landing stage there are a merchant's shop on each, Rest Houses for Chiefs and quarters for a Guard and Agricultural Dept. employee.

Belek the Southern Dur meshra on the mainland side of a Lake [Jor] is at times inaccessible from the river owing to sudd blocks at the mouth of the passage into the Lake, and Nuong is 4 hours upstream of a side-channel some 3 hours steaming south of Adok. Both these areas are now more approachable from inland via the new road and their only use is for export of cotton and trade goods.

Started in 1929 and completed by the end of 1930 a road now runs throughout the length of the Jebel river Areas. Southern roadhead is at Ameij on the Southern Nuong–Shish Dinka border, from whence it runs northwards to Bentiu on the Ghazal river. A subsidiary road from Adok provides an outlet on the Jebel river. It is proposed to maintain a Ferry at Bentiu and to continue the road north through the Jekaing and Ruweng to join with the Tonga–Talodi road. With the provision of funds it would also be possible to connect Ameij with Rumbek and Yirrol Districts by clearing to Akot (C.M.S. Station) or to a point on the Rumbek–Fakam District road.

A G.R.F. [Grant for Roads and Ferries] grant, originally submitted in 1928 as an estimate for upkeep and erection of river ports, has been used for road work as the amount was in excess of that required for Meshras.

WESTERN NUER ROAD

	Interim dist.	Total (miles)
Adok (Jebel river post)		
Kh. Wathlual (ramp)	3.6	3.6
Kh. But (ramp)	5.4	9.0
Kh. Woat (ramp–Rest House)	1.5	10.5
Junction.		
To Nuong		
Kh. Woat		
Kaati (water at Chir 2 m.)	32.9	32.9
Nyandong (wells–Rest House)	24.5	57.4
Ful Shun (water)	12.7	70.1
Kwil (water)	20.3	90.4
Ameij (Roadhead–Dinka border)	9.5	99.9
To Ghazal River		
Kh. Woat		
Kui (wells) Resthouse proposed		52.4
Dwar (water) ramp.		
Kh. Rial (water ramp.)		
Tharlil (water) possible sites for new Hqs. Post.		87.4

A District Headquarters will be built during 1931, possibly at Tharlil.[43]

5. *Economic Development & Possibilities*

The output of cotton could be greatly increased if the crop were of sufficient economic value to withstand the cost of transport.[44] Hibiscus [*Hibiscus sabda-*

---

43. A district headquarters was opened at Bentiu in January 1946.
44. Compulsory cotton-growing ceased in 1931.

riffa] grows wild inland and it would possibly be feasible to cultivate flax inland. Bananas, sugar cane and sisal grow well by banks of Khors and at the edge of the sudd. Sisal should flourish in the waterless areas.

The Nuer is entirely pastoral and cultivation does not appeal to him and it is doubtful whether there will be any inducement to encourage him to farming on a large scale. Cattle are the beginning and end of all things and an improvement in the quality of their herds will eventually tend to better conditions of life in the Nuer country.

Rinderpest is scarce but Pleuropneumonia and Trypanosomiasis are rife particularly in the swampy areas in Nuong.

The amount of trade carried on by the merchants at the shops on the river stages is small and of little value.

The following shows exports for 1929:-

Hides	*Ivory*	*Cattle*
1779 pkgs	3138 rtls	349 head

In 1930 there was a decrease in hides and ivory and a slight increase in cattle.

EXPORTS OF COTTON

	1926/7 KANTARS	1927/8 KANTARS	1928/9 KANTARS	1929/30 KANTARS
Area A.	–	–	243	237
Area B.	–	–	2	208
Area C.	113.66	356.66	1335.24	1200
Area D.	109.23	345.58	816	973
Area E.	–	632.77	386.49	563
Area F.	–	–	294.31	476
Area G.	–	61.38	48.46	–
Area K.	–	–	50	221
Area H.	–	386.05	350.32	824
Area J.	–	356.48	385.66	973
TOTAL	222.89	2138.92	3910.48	5674

6. Buildings

Area A. Resthouses and quarters for employees at Belek.
Area B. Resthouses and quarters at Nuong. Namlia rest house at Nyandong.
Area C. Resthouses & quarters at Adok. Namlia resthouse and Chiefs' Court house at Kh. Woat. 2 Cattle huts.
Area D. Resthouse & quarters at Jagey. Cattle hut 8 miles inland. Employees quarters at Ryer.
Area E. Resthouses & quarters at Yodni. Galvanised iron cotton store shed.

Area F. Resthouses & quarters & 2 cattle huts at Bentiu.
Area H. Resthouses & quarters & 1 cattle hut at Yoynyang.
Area J. Resthouses & quarters at Wathjak.
Area K. Resthouses & quarters & brick petrol store on R.A.F. Landing ground.

Resthouses at river meshras are native huts for Chiefs only and are built under their own arrangements. Quarters are for one Meshra Guard and Agricultural Dept. employees.

7. Forestry

In the Nuong the country is well afforested and palm belts are frequent in Jagey.

The Ameit (Anogeissus Leocarpus) is the most valuable timber in the southern areas and grows prolifically. The erect white ant-proof branches are excellent for building. The Ghazal river banks are well wooded chiefly with Talh.[45]

There is a Woodstation at Tunglual east of Wathjak.

8. Sundry

There are vegetable gardens at Adok and Bentiu and several young fruit trees have been planted at both these posts. There is also a large garden in the R.C. Mission compound at Yoynyang.

There is ample water in the Khor Rial for a Garden if the new Headquarters post is built at Tharlil.

As there is at present no District Headquarters other than the 'Kerreri' it has been impracticable to keep a Merkaz herd of cattle. All cattle are kept by the various Area Chiefs except at Adok and Dur Nuong where there are Government Herdsmen. Cattle are continually being transferred to and from the various Areas for sale as cattle fines are sold outside the Area from which they are obtained.

A sounder of 13 pigs until recently kept at Tharjath has been handed to the R.C. Mission at Yoynyang. These are from an original herd of 2, now numbering some 40 strong, started at Abwong in 1927. They are destructive and indestructible.[46]

Poultry are kept with the merchants at the various meshras and there are

---

45. There has been much deforestation in Western Nuer following the sustained high floods of 1961–4.

46. For the Abwong pig herd, see above, doc. 1.5.

turkeys at Tharjath and geese and turkeys at Adok.

Not more than two merchants are permitted at each meshra and a shop with a red zinc roof is compulsory. Merchants are encouraged to stock a small quantity of provisions in addition to ordinary trade goods.

Chiefs are being given an issue of clothing for 1931 after which they will be required to purchase their own. A distinguishing red band is part of the issue. Chiefs' Police do not wear clothes within the District.[47]

An R.C. Mission was opened at Yoynyang in 1924. The normal establishment is a Father Superior, two fathers and two lay Brothers.[48]

It is proposed to open a C.M.S. station at Leira on the Adok-Bentiu road during 1931. The site is 17 miles inland from Adok.[49]

There are some 40 boys at School in Yoynyang Mission and 4 boys from the District at the C.M.S. Station at Malek.[50]

A Memorial Cairn erected to the memory of the late Capt. Fergusson stands on the site where he was murdered at Belek.[51]

9. Note on District Officials & Employees

Interpreters

Ator Boi	An Afak Dinka[52] served from first entry into the District in 1922. Reliable, honest, hard working and generally an exemplary character. His Arabic is poor and he is rather stupid. Pay raised to £E.2 p.m. in 1930.

---

47. See above, doc. 1.5, for Coriat's clothes policy among the Lou.

48. In 1930 the station contained fathers Mlakic (Father Superior), Crazzolara and Tonelli, and brothers Tosi, Guadgnini and Placido ('Diario stazione Yoynyang dal Nov. 1923 al Nov. 1935', AMC A/145/15).

49. The CMS school was opened at Ler in 1931 (Sanderson 1981: 187).

50. The CMS school twelve miles south of Bor, opened in 1907 (Sanderson 1981: 52–3). Many of the pupils then at Yoynyang had been brought in personally by Coriat, including some Gaawar from Fangak district (see 'Diario stazione Yoynyang', cited in n. 48). Before that, the mission had some difficulty keeping its students. Fr. Mlakic complained to Coriat's predecessor in 1928, 'Since the death of Mr. Fergusson only 2 boys of Twil [Ran]'s district entered our school. One, brought by Twil, escaped after a week; the other, the son of subchief Bwoth, is still here. With this boy of subchief Bwoth there are now 7 boys of Twil's district in our school; 6 of them are the remainder of the 22 boys of Twil's district, who were in our school before the death of Mr. Fergusson. These boys continually come and run away and so render any schoolwork useless' (Fr. Stephen Mlakic to Mr. Kidd, DC Nuer District, 11.10.28, AMC A/169/3).

51. Fergusson's body is now buried in the War Cemetery in Khartoum.

52. The Apak section of the Atuot.

Lam Yuong	2nd Interpreter. Stupid and unreliable, pay at 75 pt. p.m.

Dressers

Ahmed Eff. Bilal	A.M.O. on 'Kerreri.' Posted from and paid by Medical Dept. Talks Nuer. Is efficient and reliable.
Weir Galwak	A Bul Nuer acting as dresser at R.C. Mission at Yoynyang. Learnt to read and write at Yoynyang and trained at Malakal Hospital. Qualified to give injections. Pay £E.1.200 p.m.

Tribal Dressers are under other arrangements and are dealt with under para. 11 Medical.

Clerks

Constantine Libra	From Wau. English speaking Clerk on 'Kerreri'. To be replaced in February. Pay £E.1.000 p.m.
Majui Mabur	Dinka from Malek Mission. Inefficient. Clerk to Chief Buom Diu. Pay 75 pt. p.m.
Elicha Matok	Dinka from Bur [Bor]. Very poor standard. Clerk to Chief Thiey Poich. Pay 50 pt. p.m.
Philip Manyang	Dinka from Malek. A little more competent than Elicha. Clerk to Chief Nuel Juel. Pay 50 pt. p.m.
Gaing Twil	Jekaing Nuer trained at Yonyang. Comparatively good. Clerk to Chief Galwak Nyag. Pay 50 pt. p.m.
Dwar Caath	Son of Caath Bang, late Chief of Gatliath Nuong. Trained at Yoynyang. Not up to requisite standard. Clerk to Chief Won Kwoth. Pay 50 pt. p.m.
Paul Gai Nein	Mixed breed trained at Yoynyang. Ability very good. Has unpleasant habits. Lately Clerk in Bul. To be transferred to Jagey. Pay 40 pt. p.m.

Guards

Dthuol Nuonke	Agar Dinka. Guard at Yoynyang. Lazy & corrupt. Pay 75 pt. p.m.
Tob Ret	Dok Nuer. Guard at Tharjath. Quiet and hardworking. Pay 75 pt. p.m.
Yo Dagweir	Jagey Nuer. Guard at Ryer. Hardworking and intelligent. Pay 75 pt. p.m.
Bain Athwel	Shish Dinka. Appears to keep Meshra clean. Guard at Wathjak. Pay 60 pt. p.m.
Riak Mabur	Agar Dinka. Unreliable. Guard at Wangkai. Pay 60 pt. p.m.

Gai Reith	Dinka. Guard at Yodni. Pay 50 pt. p.m. Newly employed.
Deng Kur	Jekaing Nuer. Guard and Gardener at Bentiu. Hard-working and reliable. Knows nothing about gardening. Pay 75 pt. p.m.
Dud Sabahi	Nuer. Ex-Onbashi and E.A. Pensioner. In charge of landing ground and store Wangkai. Pay £E.1.000 m/ms p.m.
Mo Maluk	Guard at Adok. Works very well. Pay £E.1.000 m/ms p.m.

Herdsmen

Shwet Manyang	Shish Dinka. Chief Herdsman. Generally at Adok. Thoroughly reliable. Pay £E.1.000 m/ms p.m.
Deng Adwot	2nd Herdsman. Pay 60 pt. p.m.
Kwerey Alueng	3rd Herdsman. Pay 50 pt. p.m.
Gatweng Bidthal	Local boy. Tends herds i/c Chief Dur Nuong. Pay 30 pt. p.m.

Gardeners

Ateir Gwogo	Gardener Adok. Works well but knows very little. Pay 60 pt. p.m.
Bakheit Guma	Gardener Adok. Knows a fair amount about gardening but extremely idle and unreliable. Pay 60 pt. p.m.

10. Military & Intelligence

With the exception of the Bul and possibly the Leik Areas, there are no rifles in the District.

It is unlikely that the Clans would combine, nor is it likely that there would be opposition which could not be dealt with by Mounted Police action though the more powerful Area Chiefs could raise comparatively strong forces.

Night attacks and ambush in long grass are the tactics they have and after a first encounter opposition generally resolves into a guerrilla warfare. The Nuer is becoming more addicted to stabbing than throwing a spear.[53]

Punitive Patrols as in the past are unlikely to be effective and the only

---

53. Spears were 'recycled' in intersectional and intertribal fights because each side picked up and used those spears thrown at them as well as their own; thus spears were rarely lost. As government forces were armed with rifles, spears thrown at them were never returned. The Nuer change in tactic appears to have been an attempt to conserve spears.

successful method of dealing with recalcitrant Nuer is on the lines of the Nuer Settlement of 1929/30 in Lau and Gaweir.[54]

The swamps on the eastern border of Nuong afford a refuge which is almost inaccessible but no Nuer will remain long in the swamps with his cattle and women, and forests and inland waterholes are the most likely haunts for fugitives. Knowledge of the country and mobile troops should ensure a speedy and effective end to any punitive expedition.

A Landing Ground at Wangkai is available and other Landing Grounds could be cleared at Nuong, Dok and Jekaing.

The Bul would be the most difficult Area to operate in.

Approximate numbers of fighting men in Areas:-

A.	1200
B.	800
C.	2500
D.	1800
E.	1800
H.	500
J.	2000
K.	3000
G.	2400
	16000

Without a knowledge of the language intelligence is difficult to obtain and uncertain. There are always odd Dinka to be found in the country with a ready story but they invariably have an axe to grind and are mostly untrustworthy. A reliable Interpreter provides a useful source of information.

The demeanour of the people is a good sign of the stability of an Area but is not infallible when a Witchdoctor is up to some trickery. Chiefs are sometimes ignorant themselves and are not always willing to tell all they know.

I have personally found it necessary to employ 'agents', young men whom one knows, not always of the better kind and who are willing to give information in return for a 'Pourboir'. The 'Pourboir' is not always given when the information is received and they are in effect on irregular pay roll but in any case action should seldom be taken on the report of one agent and in the subject of the report.[55] It would be fatal to antagonise a Chief by showing mistrust in him.

---

54. See above, Section 3.

55. The meaning of this is unclear as written.

11. Medical

A great part of Fergusson's work up to the time of his death was to better the health of the people and the fact that he was able and found time to do medical work himself must have done much to establish the confidence of the Tribes.[56]

Yaws was prevalent particularly in the southern Areas and in 1926 the Medical Inspector concentrated on the Nuong sections where several thousands received injections of N.A.B. [Neoarsphenamine].[57]

In order to build up a tribal Medical Service, young boys were selected from the various sections and were given a course of training in simple first aid work, they were then issued boxes and sent back to their villages. By 1930 the Tribal Dressers had increased to 120 in number and grant was received for payment of all Dressers. It has however been found impracticable to ensure that the work is being carried out efficiently and training is not possible with the large number of boys, consequently Dressers are being reduced and the selected few will be properly trained and paid higher rates. It is intended that suitable boys will be trained on the new 'Lady Baker'[58] for more advanced medical work and will eventually become Tribal A.M.Os.

12. Office Organisation

Treasury Chest Book. A copy of this is made out at the end of the month and sent to Malakal together with R.Os. [Received Orders] & O.Ps. [Orders for Payment]. Against each entry of receipt or expenditure is shown the item in the Budget to which it is to be credited or debited. At the end of every month totals of the various items are recorded.

Tribute Book. Payments of Tax as received are entered with number & date of R.O.

Shieng Book. Contains a list of all Headmen, Police, Dressers and sections and showing the villages of each.

Census Books. Of all Areas. Should be revised every 3 to 4 years.

Pay Books. Nominal roll & monthly payments of Chiefs, Chiefs' Police and Employees. Payments to Chiefs and C.P. are made irregularly.

Medical & Dressers Book. Nominal roll of Tribal Dressers and Dressers returns. Payments made to Dressers and medical statistics.

56. Fergusson's medical work is described in Fergusson 1930: 243–60.

57. A trivalent arsenical, formerly used extensively against a variety of diseases, including syphilis, yaws, relapsing fever, trypanosomiasis and malaria.

58. Commissioned in 1929 for medical work to replace the *Lady Baker I*, a hospital ship used by the Sudan Medical Service since 1922. Later renamed the *Wad el Nugomi* (Hill 1970: 143).

Appeals Register. Record of appeals in Tribal cases.
Prisoners Register. Record of Tribal and other prisoners.
Stores Ledger.
Magistrate's Case Book. Record of non-Tribal convictions only.
General Book. Ivory sales, register of merchants and trade, nominal roll of boys at Mission Schools, Cash fines.
Cattle Book. Record of cattle received and disposal.
Grain Account Book. Durra receipts and issues.

Monthly reports provide a resume of events but the general history of the District is to be found chiefly in Tribal file 66/B.[59]

In & Out letter Books. File registration numbers as Mudiria.[60] Card index is not kept and numbers are not subdivided.

Returns

Annual	*Monthly*	*Quarterly*
Firearms Licences	Ivory Sales	Police returns
Traders ..	Cattle Account	as shown in standing
Traders Permits	Grain ..	orders (Rendered June,
Agent ..	Treasury ..	March, November and
Ground rent—Mission		December)
(Rendered January)		

59. Each district was required to forward to the province headquarters a monthly report, written to a set format. The province monthly diaries were compiled from these district reports and sent to Khartoum, where they were used in the writing of the *Sudan Monthly Record*. Tribal File 66/B was the heading for 'Intertribal Questions' (see also following note).

60. The civil secretary's office under Sir Harold MacMichael established a file registration system that was adopted by all provinces and districts of the Sudan. Numbers were assigned to various headings, and letters assigned to standard sub-headings. Thus: (1) Administration, (2) Agriculture, (5) Army, (57) Reports, (66) Tribal, etc. 1.A was 'Administration, general rulings', 1.B was 'Administration, general correspondence', and so on. In theory, the headings used in district and province offices were supposed to correspond exactly. In practice, district filing systems were rather more relaxed than the standard set by the civil secretary's office.

Appendix 1: Western Nuer Budget 1929–1930

1929–	Receipts & Expenditure from District Funds	
	Expenditure £E. 192.920 m/ms	

1930 (exp.)	1930 (estimate)	1931 (estimate)

Devolution

Receipts. Court & Chiefs' fines

1930 (exp.)	1930 (estimate)	1931 (estimate)
£E. 657.750	£E. 550	£E. 550

Expenditure

1930 (exp.)	1930 (estimate)		1931 (estimate)
109.900[a]	114	Pay of Chiefs	135
111.[a]	216	Chiefs' Police	336
31.250[a]	54	Clerks	54
43.600[a]	171	Dressers	120
23.960	25	Training Tribesmen	25
6.990	35	Rations	25
22.126	25	Clothing	25
29.140	30	Rewards	50
		Reserve	

General Budget

Receipts. Tribute

1930 (exp.)	1930 (estimate)	1931 (estimate)
£E. 1025	£E. 500	£E. 1000

Expenditure

1930 (exp.)	1930 (estimate)		1931 (estimate)
30.300	68	Interpreters	76
26.250[a]	54	Herdsmen	39
83.200[a]	81	Guards & Gardeners	81
6.700	10	Grass cutting	10
7.360	106	Mud Buildings	200
		for new post include shed.	
	10	Landing Grounds. Grant	35

G.R.F. Grant for Roads & Resthouses

£E. 1500. Expended 1930—£E. 816.150 m/ms

a. Further payments to be made [Coriat's own annotation].

DOCUMENT 4.2

ADMINISTRATION—WESTERN NUER

Before leaving the district Coriat addressed himself to the problem of economic development, which he saw as linked to the question of tribal integrity. His assessment of the situation among the Western Nuer and his proposals for the protection of the 'tribal' character of society and administration are given in this report.

As a postscript to his proposals, it should be noted that between 1932 and 1934 chiefs were brought under stricter control than Coriat advocated. Opportunities for graft were closed while at the same time pay was not increased (Coriat had suggested that an increase in salary would remove the temptation to extort cattle and fines from the people). In 1931 compulsory cotton cultivation was abandoned.[1] *Though the government did not adopt Coriat's specific proposals on raising chiefs' salaries, it was in basic agreement with him on running an administration which limited the Nuer's access to the wider nation.*

Governor [2]
U.N.P.

The Western Nuer were unadministered until 1922 and on Fergusson's first visit,[3] ignorance of the people and the state of the country precluded any question of a definite policy being formulated even had it been considered desirable.

1. Romilly, 'Report Western Nuer 1929–1934', Nasir END 66.A.1.
2. C. A. Willis, who was in his last month as governor.
3. Fergusson first began visiting Western Nuer villages in February–April 1921. See *SMIR* 321 (April 1921), 6; Fergusson 1930: 118–29.

Fergusson's efforts at the outset were confined to acquiring what knowledge he could of the habits and customs of the people and it was not until this had been accomplished that it was possible to turn to the problem of administration of the Clans.

As has been enumerated in 'General Information Report',[4] the Western Nuer, possibly owing to physical barriers, were not harried by the Slave raiders to the extent that were the Eastern Nuer clans and as a consequence the Tribal organisation exists. Not only in that there are Tribal Functionaries who continue to be an essential part of native life but the people themselves, not having been scattered and broken up into innumerable small sections owing allegiance to none, are disciplined and recognise the authority of their Leaders. Trouble when it comes is brought about not so much by the predatory instincts of young warriors as by the machinations of Witchdoctors and Chiefs.

Throughout the Western Nuer, it is the Bul Area alone that is different in this respect.[5]

The existence of a Tribal Organisation and Tribal Leaders and also that there was no attempt to levy a Tribute or Tax until the Administration had developed, were primary factors in making the task at all possible without the aid of military intervention in the first instance.

Reference to a report written by Fergusson in 1923[6] shows that his intention then was to build up a Native Reserve in which the administration was to be entirely in the hands of the Chiefs unaffected by outside influence in the form of Traders or a large staff of Officials. Writing in 1927[7] he says:

> Looking into the future it is hoped that once having established a firm system of control we shall be able to develop gradually a craving for trade and luxuries of civilisation.

Referring to the training of boys at the Mission school and as Clerks and Dressers:

> If we can do this we shall have done much to preserve Tribal unity and control until the people have been sufficiently educated to fight or we should say absorb the many undesirable traits and ideas which civilisation must eventually press upon them to the detriment of local customs and authority. . . . As soon as there is sufficient money to allow of more merchants making fair profit, they will be increased.

---

4. See above, doc. 4.1, sub-section 2(b).

5. See above, doc. 4.1.

6. I have been unable to find a copy of this report, but he clearly expressed this intention in 1921 when he wrote, 'If I get this place, it is to be closed to everyone except myself—not even a native merchant or clerk to be allowed in' (Fergusson 1930: 119). See also the extracts from an early report of Fergusson's cited in 'Dok and Aaak Nuer', 01.01.45, SAD P.P. Howell MSS, file 66.B.

7. Fergusson, 'Report on Eastern District (Nuers), Bahr el Ghazal Province', June 1927, NRO Civsec 57/1/5.

From the above one can infer that a Tribal Administration and development of the economic resources of the country was the keynote of the policy to be adopted.

It is here that one is uncertain, even were there a latent wealth in the Nuer country,[8] whether economic development can be made to fit into an entirely Tribal system of control.

In my opinion economic progress in the Nuer country can only be attained in one way; by creating a demand for some luxury which will eventually become a necessity as they develop a civilisation in our meaning of the word and by compelling the Nuer to supply a commodity required by civilisation and in return for which they will be given the wherewithal enabling them to obtain that for which we have inculcated a demand. In reality barter in which money becomes the medium and which on the one side is unwanted and unnecessary.

To do this the country must be opened to Traders and the corollary is penetration of foreign and anti-Tribal influences.

In the Western Nuer we gave the people cotton seed to grow in order that they should supply that which we required and to enable them to purchase something we could supply.

Cotton was valuable when first introduced and the more they could supply the better were we pleased. By encouraging the people, and encouragement is sometimes compatible with compulsion, an output of 250 kantars in 1925/6 was increased to 6000 kantars for 1929/30. False prices were paid to a cultivator who knew nothing of fluctuation of values and who did not in fact even know what to do with the money given him. Other than payment of taxes, the penalty of administration, no regard was paid to whether the Nuer had learnt to want something which his surplus cash would enable him to acquire.

In exchange for the cotton thrust on him we have attempted to create a demand in the Western Nuer for cloth, sugar, tea, iron, beads and other trade goods but in 8 years the amount purchased in proportion to the population is infinitesimal. The one want which is a vital and essential part of Tribal life, the supply of cattle, we have been unable to offer in sufficient quantities to keep pace with the amount of money put in to the country for cotton and there is probably hundreds of pounds worth of silver lying hoarded in holes under Nuer homes.

Even were economic development considered essential in the administration of a backward people such as the Nuer and presuming their country can be made a source of wealth to them, it would seem a surer and safer method of attaining this would be by allowing normal and voluntary development consistent with cultural progress under an enlightened Native Administration.

Personally I feel that economic development by a system of forcing can but lead to tribal disintegration.

---

8. Oil in exploitable quantities was first discovered in the Sudan in Western Nuer District in the 1970s.

There may be Tribes similar to the Nuer where material development has not affected their Tribal outlook or organisation but without wishing to plead that the Nuer is of a different character it is hard to believe that in such Tribes the Chiefs, unless there have been years of peaceful administration behind them, are Leaders in practice and not merely in name.

There would appear to be two alternatives, a Tribal Administration from which all outside influences are excluded and Government assistance is confined to improving the moral welfare of the people, betterment of health conditions and sanitation and gradual improvement of the quality of livestock and food crops; any desire for material progress would come from within. The other alternative is an Administration permitting the intrusion of foreign ideas and influences in the desire to foster trade and material development of the country. The people would be forced to cultivate whatever crops were deemed of value in order that money and other benefits of civilisation could circulate freely. The result would I believe be a collapse of Tribal custom and though it might be possible to point to clothed and wealthy Chiefs and a semblance of Tribal life, this could not exist. There would be new modes of living and new codes.

If the first alternative is to be the choice, it seems to me that two things are essential, firstly that the authority of Chiefs within their own areas should be paramount, secondly that Tribal Chiefs should be given sufficient incentive not only to rule their people loyally and with the aid of Government but to rule their people loyally and for the Government; the difference between the Tribal Leader whose strength is the Government at his back and the Leader whose strength lies in his own ability.

The first to some extent exists but whether it will continue seems uncertain. If administrative progress is to mean imposition of Ordinances and the conferring of Magistrates' powers on Chiefs,[9] the Tribal Code will become obscured. Although it may be necessary to grant powers to Chiefs enabling them to cope with anti-Tribal offences, the greater latitude allowed in this respect the better. In their present stage the people cannot understand hard and fast rules for the exercise of Chiefship. If a Tribal Leader is able to do this and unable to do that where his individual authority is concerned, he must to some extent lose prestige.

As regards the second essential, it will be sufficient to cite an example in this District. Buom Diu, the Chief of Area A,[10] received £E.1.500 m/ms per month in pay from the Government. He was a Tribal Chief of the Dok in the early days when he amassed many cattle and wives by witchdoctory and raids against the Dinka. During 1930, Buom paid in £E.254 in Tribute based on a Poll Tax of 10 pt. per adult male & cattle received as Court fees and fines to

---

9. Then being discussed in proposals concerning the Chiefs' Courts Ordinance; see Collins 1983: 158–65.

10. See above, doc. 4.1 n. 32. The Dok were known as area C.

the value of £E.400. He also collected several hundred head of cattle raided from the Dinka in 1927 by the Nuong [Nyuong] clans[11] and distributed among friends in Buom's territory. Numbers of cases heard by him, both recorded and unrecorded were settled and decisions were carried out. There were two appeals against his decisions. 1335 kantars of cotton were grown by his people in the rains of 1929/30 and brought in to Adok for sale. In addition 40 miles of new road were cleared. This was done without the aid of a single Government Policeman and except for calling at Adok, I only twice passed through his country, both times en route for some other Area. It is impossible to expect that Buom is doing this for £E.1.500 m/ms a month. If one is not to ignore a tendency to be dishonest on the part of an efficient Chief, there should be greater reward from the Government. In Buom's case I believe that £E.200 per year would be a more suitable pay.

It may be said that greater emolument from the Government will not detract a Chief who wishes to be dishonest, but the fact that a Chief receives sufficient reward should give one a greater pull in combating dishonesty.

The only effective check on a powerful and efficient Chief is by the contentment or not of his people, which should be obvious, the number of would be migrants and emigrants and the manner of life of the people generally. This should be an adequate test in spite of the fact that 'ramps' [i.e. 'swindles'] of a petty kind must be inevitable in a Native Authority, yet if cognizance is to be taken of more flagrant offences of this nature and unless Chiefs are properly compensated for their services, we shall be faced with a long series of dismissals and appointments to the ruin of any Native Administration.

In order therefore that my successor shall have a clear line to follow, I should be grateful for your views as to future Nuer Administration and the possibility of substantially increasing the pay of deserving Tribal Leaders.[12]

SGS *Kerreri*
5.2.31

P.C.
District Commissioner
Western Nuer

11. Administered separately from the Dok; see above, doc. 4.1.

12. Willis's answers to these proposals can be inferred from the marginal notes in doc. 4.1 above. The chiefs were to be given no further rewards, and their powers were to be restricted.

SECTION FIVE

The Administrator and Anthropology

THE ADMINISTRATOR AND ANTHROPOLOGY
INTRODUCTION

THE campaign against Guek, the murder of Fergusson, and the rebellion of Dual Diu combined to convince the government in Khartoum that it knew too little about the Nuer to be confident of future peaceful administration. 'I believe the fact of the matter is', Sir Harold MacMichael minuted to the governor-general,

> that to obtain an understanding of the recesses of the savage mind one must either be a savage or a very highly trained anthropologist of wide technical knowledge on the one hand and of a broad human sympathy on the other. At present we fall between the two stools. (MacMichael, quoted in Johnson 1985a: 144–5)

It was for this reason that the government decided to commission an anthropological study of the Nuer, and pressure was brought to bear on E. E. Evans-Pritchard, then studying the Azande, to undertake it.

Coriat had been DC in Western Nuer District for under a year when Evans-Pritchard arrived in the province to begin his work. The two men agreed that Evans-Pritchard should go first to Coriat's district, and they arrived together by steamer at the mission station of Yoynyang on 19 January 1930. Evans-Pritchard's early fieldwork among the Nuer was fraught with difficulties, many created by governor Willis, and he left the Western Nuer on 15 February 1930 to begin work in Lou country.[1] Two months later, when he left Nuerland to return to the Azande, Evans-Pritchard briefly visited Adok. 'The Poet (Evans-Pritchard) came here while I was away and has left for Zande again', Coriat recorded. 'He writes that the Nuer are harder to know than ever. He can get nothing out of them.'[2]

Evans-Pritchard's second period of fieldwork in 1931 went little better, aggravated as it was by malaria and by Willis, who retired as governor that year. A projected trip to Yoynyang had to be cancelled when Evans-Pritchard returned to Malakal from the Sobat ill with fever in June (Johnson 1982c: 239). He had

---

1. 'Diario stazione Yoynyang dal Nov. 1923 al Nov. 1935', AMC A/145/15. For Evans-Pritchard's first year of fieldwork among the Nuer, see Johnson 1982c: 234–6.

2. Coriat to Kathleen, 18.04.30, 'En route Adok', Coriat MSS. Collins (1983) assumes that Evans-Pritchard was generally known among members of the Sudan administration as 'the Poet', when in fact this was a private joke between Coriat and his wife and appears in this letter only.

to abandon further fieldwork among the Nuer until 1935, by which time Coriat had left the province and was working in Kordofan. It is possible that the two men met again during the Second World War, when both were serving in Libya, but the period of their collaboration on the Nuer was confined to short periods in 1930 and 1931. When Evans-Pritchard finally began to write his own ethnography he disagreed with Coriat over a number of matters of interpretation, but the two men respected each other, and Evans-Pritchard acknowledged Coriat, not just out of courtesy, as 'a man who knows far more about the Nuer than myself' (Evans-Pritchard 1934: 45).

Evans-Pritchard's publications on the Nuer, beginning in 1933, transformed the administrative perception and description of Nuer society. For the first time abstract principles of Nuer actions and social organization were proposed. A later generation of more scholarly minded officials working among the Nuer often disagreed with his ethnography on specific details and interpretations. Yet frequently they found themselves more in agreement with Evans-Pritchard than with Coriat. This raises a final question about Coriat's writings. How many of his conclusions were based on partial evidence and generalization from only a few cases, and how much of what he described represents an earlier period of Nuer society, before it was affected by more comprehensive administration? This question can be answered only through extended fieldwork and the thorough study of oral history in the districts where Coriat once served, which can then be brought to bear on continued source criticism of contemporary records.

DOCUMENT 5.1

NOTES ON A PAPER ON THE NUER READ BY MR. E. EVANS-PRITCHARD AT A MEETING OF THE BRITISH ASSOCIATION FOR THE ADVANCEMENT OF SCIENCE, SEPTEMBER, 1931

When Evans-Pritchard left the Sudan in 1931 he was uncertain whether his research on the Nuer could continue. In the middle of that year he presented a preliminary paper on the Nuer to the British Association for the Advancement of Science. While convalescing in Malakal he consulted with Coriat before writing this paper.[1] The paper was copied and distributed to various government offices in the Sudan. In its revised and expanded form it was published in three parts as 'The Nuer: Tribe and Clan', in SNR, *1933–5.*

Coriat's comments on the paper were also copied and distributed (with Evans-Pritchard's initial, as D, instead of E for Edward, incorrectly given in each copy). They were forwarded to Evans-Pritchard who cited some of them in the final version of his paper.[2] As this is one of the few ways in which Coriat's observations have been introduced to a wider audience, it is appropriate to reprint the entire text here as Coriat's final contribution to Nuer ethnography. Some differences in ethnographic observation which follow can be explained by the fact that Evans-Pritchard's experience was confined mainly to the Mor Lou, the Eastern Jikany and the Leek Nuer, while Coriat's lay more with the Gaawar, Gun Lou and those Western Nuer south of the Bahr el-Ghazal.

---

1. Coriat to Kathleen, 02.07.31, 'Kerreri', Coriat MSS.
2. See Evans-Pritchard 1933: 10–12; 1934: 44–5; 1935: 56, 66–7.

I have read with interest the paper on the Nuer by Mr. E. Evans-Pritchard.

Further study of the Nuer by Mr. Evans-Pritchard should be of great help in the future to officials working in their country and the following few notes may be of use to him in his researches. They are necessarily limited in scope but may provide information on one or two points which Mr. Evans-Pritchard appears to have overlooked.

Para 1. Mr. Evans-Pritchard states that natural conditions have to a great extent made the Nuer inaccessible to foreign influences.

If we are to believe the testimony of early observers it is because of foreign influences that these people have lost much of their ancient culture and social organisation.

Casati, writing of them in 1898 [in fact, 1891], said they were a timid and shy people who became savage and warlike after the incursion by the Arab.[3]

To foreign influence, intrusion would be a better term, must be attributed their change of outlook and their mistrust and resentment of the foreigners.

There can be little doubt that the slave era was primarily the cause of our difficulties in dealing with Nuer tribes. Arab raiders broke up the clans and sections to such an extent that the tribesmen became predatory and uncontrollable and lost respect for their leaders. It is because of this that the clans became disintegrated and that we were faced with innumerable internecine feuds which impeded a peaceful administration. Particularly has this been so in Lau and Gaweir.[4]

Administration of the Nuer has been disturbed and hazardous, but the killing of Captain Fergusson in 1927 and the rebellion of Gwek Wundeng [Guek Ngundeng] in that year,[5] were only incidents in a long succession of killings and minor revolts. En passant, it may be mentioned that there was no connection between the outbreaks in 1927.

Para 2. It is unfortunate that except for Jackson,[6] the officials who have worked in the Nuer country have lacked either the ability or inclination to record their knowledge of the Nuer but a study of files in District offices should provide fragments of information of value to the scientific worker.

Para 3. It is doubtful even were there no untoward conditions, such as a military control of the country,[7] to disturb the observer, whether much can be obtained from the Nuer without long and patient residence in their midst.

3. See above, doc. 4.1 n. 17.

4. See above, doc. 1.2.

5. For Fergusson, see above, Introduction, n. 4; for Guek, see above, Section 3.

6. At this time the work by Jackson (1923) was the only attempt at a comprehensive account of the Nuer. Other administrators wrote shorter pieces; see Stigand 1918a, 1918b, 1919, and 1923; Fergusson 1921, 1924.

7. The aftermath of the Nuer Settlement, 1929–30.

They are shy and suspicious of the stranger.

Para 4. It is of interest that the Nuer and Dinka themselves admit a common origin. The story is similar to that of Jacob and Esau in the Bible.[8]

As regards their character and mental outlook there is in my opinion contrast between the Nuer and any single Dinka tribe including the Atwot that I have come across in 9 years dealing with representatives of all sections of Dinka and Nuer except the Dinka of the far west of the Bahr el Ghazal Province.

Para 5.—[9]

Para 6. It is incorrect to state that the tribe is the largest political unit within the nation.

Their history can show many instances where two or more tribes have combined in common offence or defence. As for example Lau and Jekaing [Jikany] against the Annuak [Anuak], Gaweir and Lau against the Dinka. In fact the tribes combined in their first conquests of the Dinka.[10]

Since the disruption of the clans following the advent of the slave raider the political unit has tended to diminish. So great has been the disruption that often the clan or family group became the political unit. The efforts of the present administration in recent years have been to reunite the groups in a Tribal organisation. As the power of hereditary leaders decreased the machinery for settlement of disputes became practically non-existent.

In the past acts of homicide as between members of different Nuer tribes were dealt with by leopard-skin chiefs [*kuar muon*] in the same way as with members of tribal groups.[11]

Tribal and clan segmentation is not only mutually dependent but is also coincident. If the Gajok [Gaajok] and Gajak [Gaajak] are different tribes but one clan, so also are the Leik and Kilwal [Karlual] and Lau and Rangyan [Rengyan].[12] It is not always possible to trace this relationship by name.

8. For the story of the cow and the calf see Evans-Pritchard 1940: 125.

9. Evans-Pritchard here stated that the Nuer were a 'homogenous nation', a point that Coriat felt needed no comment.

10. What Coriat means by 'alliances' is unclear. Very often, individuals from different sections would join raiding parties organized by other sections (as some Lou joined Dual Diu in raiding the Nyareweng and Ghol Dinka in 1928). In the nineteenth century some Lou did combine with the Jikany in raiding the Anuak, but there was no concerted coalition between the whole of the Lou and Jikany. Similarly the Lou and Gaawar did not combine in raids against the Dinka in the nineteenth century, but each fought independently of the other, usually also fighting different groups of Dinka. Evans-Pritchard replied, 'I was aware of these combinations, but preferred to regard them as alliances between two political units' (1933: 12). He later referred to temporary coalitions of different Nuer tribes, using the examples of the Lou and Gaawar and the Lou and Jikany as well as examples of his own (1940: 121), but he tended to treat them as more recent phenomena than Coriat, and as fostered by prophets.

11. Evans-Pritchard (1933: 10–11) acknowledged that this may have been so, but that he was only reporting the principle, as stated to him by Nuer, and not the practice.

12. The Gaajak (Thiang) and Gaajok are two of the three main divisions of both the western

Division of the tribe amounts to division of the clan.

The Gajok will admit that he is a member of the same clan as the Gajak but both claim membership of the Jekaing clan.[13]

To ask the Nuer what his tribe is, is to ask what his clan is. It is merely a matter of how far back one refers. What is your shieng?—TENG [Teny]. What is TENG's BAB (Root)—KERFAIL.[14] Of whom is KERFAIL?—Of Gaweir. What are the Gaweir?—Nath (the people)—Nuer.

Until the clans became disintegrated the tribe was the clan.

In every tribe the sections or groups admit a common ancestry and will trace their descent back to a common ancestor.

The name alone of the Gaweir implies this. GATWEIR—the sons of Weir.[15]

Para 7. It is not necessarily only those which are nuclei of a tribe who form a kind of aristocracy, if such can be said to exist among the Nuer.

In the assessment of blood money for homicide it is the 'DIEL', or pure bred, who receives a special assessment. A diel may long ago have ceased to live with or acknowledge his original clan but pure Nuer ancestry on the paternal side ensures recognition as diel.[16]

Para 8. The subject of totemism is inextricably bound up with tribal spiritual worship.

Whether or not Nuer clans are totemic, I have found invariably that members of the same clan possess a common totem or form of spiritual ritual, though they may also have a distinct and particular family totem or ritual.

Absorption of strangers, intermingling of sections and dispersal has made this a difficult subject for enquiry. The attitude of the Kir of Jekaing to the gourd also the Gaweir and the inderab tree [*Cordia rothii*] does not mean that members of these tribes have no other totems.[17]

In Gaweir, the Kerfail section, one of the oldest and purest of Gaweir

---

and Eastern Jikany. Karlual is one of the three main divisions of the Leek Nuer, and at this time there had been extensive hostility between it and the other primary sections (Evans-Pritchard 1940: 146). Both the Lou and Rengyan were founded by the Jinaca clan, as Evans-Pritchard subsequently pointed out in many of his publications.

13. Both claim membership or association with the Gaatgankir clan. The Jikany are not a clan, in Evans-Pritchard's usage, but the name of a tribe centred around the Gaatgankir clan.

14. Teny, an earth-master lineage of the Kerpeil section, which is the dominant section of the Radh primary section of the Gaawar. See above, doc. 1.2.

15. Gaawar is the name of both a clan and a tribe. The clan around which the tribe was formed are supposed to be descendants of War; thus Gaa (*gaat*, children) of War. See above, doc. 1.2.

16. Evans-Pritchard (1940: 212–20) presents an analysis of the *diel* within the lineage system, but emphasises that it is a relative term (p. 235). The *diel* are not so much 'aristocrats' as 'original settlers' around which 'strangers' subsequently settle.

17. Kir, the ancestor of the Gaatgankir, was supposed to have been found in a gourd (*kir*). War, the ancestor of the Gaawar, is sometimes said to have fallen from the sky with the branch of an inderab tree in his hand. Members of the Gaawar clan sometimes perform ceremonies praying for rain with inderab branches on the strength of this association (Evans-Pritchard 1956: 82).

sections, has a lion totem as a wife of an ancestor of theirs [who] was said to turn herself into a lion at night.[18]

One must assume that apart from clan or tribal totems or spirits, a new totem or spirit is liable to crop up at any time in a family through some supernatural birth or death or other incident.[19]

Except with the Kir of Jekaing,[20] sacred spears do not in my opinion have any great totemic significance. They do not influence the life of the community to the extent that worship of other totems or spirits do and their origin is obscure. Possibly they are connected with war and conquest. Particularly as the sacred spear is common to Dinka tribes.

It is of the utmost importance to note that the Nuer word for a totem—Kwoth—is also the word for the sky, God or spirit. To ask a man what is his totem is to ask what is his Kwoth.

Any object of worship, natural or spiritual and anyone or thing possessed by spirits or of supernatural power is Kwoth. Thus one is, has or is of Kwoth.

Reference has been made to the Gul Weech [*col wic*]. Families with a Gul Weech tradition, the Gul Weech may be an ancestor or near relative, perform certain recognised rituals at birth, marriage and death ceremonies. These are in the nature of propitiatory acts and have nothing whatever to do with the family Kwoth (Totem or God).

It is a common belief that the Gul Weech of a family was spirited away to Heaven in a whirlwind or cloud of fire. He is respected as an entity capable of causing good or evil to the living and his behests which are transmitted by dreams are scrupulously carried out.[21]

Para 9. It is conceivable that at one time the age classes were regulated for the entire nation by one functionary. At any rate two of the oldest age classes within living memory have a common name throughout the tribes.[22]

---

18. While Coriat is probably correct in this statement, the fact that an ancestress was able to change herself into a lion could have other implications. Nuer call such persons *let*, and the *let* often figure in historical traditions as dangerous and unknown foreigners, much in the same way as lions in Dinka lion stories do. According to Gaawar traditions I recorded in 1975–6, most of their current country was originally inhabited by *let*.

19. Evans-Pritchard (1956) discusses at length the accretion of totems in chs. 3 and 4. His evidence basically substantiates Coriat's comment.

20. Kir was supposed to have been found with an iron spear in his gourd. This spear has been retained by the Eastern Jikany and is currently kept in a special shrine in Ethiopia. It was described by Stigand (1919), Jackson (1923), and MacDermot (1972). Coriat's comparison of the spear of Kir with Dinka sacred spears is highly appropriate. He probably had in mind the spear of Lirpiou among the Gualla clan of the Bor Dinka (see Bullen 1982). In fact the Jikany claim that Kir was originally found among the Ngok Dinka, and the Ngok of the Sobat are said to retain part of the spear of Kir and keep it in a shrine of their own.

21. See Evans-Pritchard 1956: 52–5, 60–2, and Crazzolara 1953: 88, 98, for other descriptions of the *col wic*, the departed spirits of persons killed by lightning or lost in the bush.

22. He is referring here to the Tharpi and Thut age-sets (see above, doc. 1.2). There were still

The classes are not regulated by a cattle expert; the Wud 'Ok [*wut ghok*] or man of cattle is responsible only for the initiation ceremony itself. Age classes are now regulated and named by certain 'Kwar Mon' [*kuar muon*] land chiefs with traditional powers.[23]

Whatever their special or general social significance and origin is, the classes have a definite military value as fighting organisations.

In war a man accompanies his village and district and takes part according or not to his age and fitness but he also groups himself with his age class and each particular class singles out those of its own in the enemy to do battle with. In effect they become tactical organisations and are under control of the Niel [*ngul*] or War Leader.

Para 10. The hereditary Kwar Mon was at one time the sole authority for settlement of disputes connected with land or water rights. His powers were autocratic and semi-divine and the practice of hearing disputes in collaboration with older men is born of the present administration.[24]

Both the land and cattle men possessed semi-divine or magical powers. That is, they had 'Kwoth' in them.[25]

The magician who is not also a tribal authority is a growth of the last 50 years [and] probably originated from the Dinka. This class increased as it was found to become lucrative and fundamentally is anti-tribal. The magician contrary to the dictates of Tribal custom was always prepared, in return for suitable emolument, to absolve a Tribesman from the performance of some ritual duty.

The magician and what Mr. Evans-Pritchard terms the Shaman or prophet are one and the same type which has now become either hereditary or acquired.[26]

The Kwoth or magician is said to have 'Kwoth' in him and every wizard possesses his own particular Kwoth spirit each of whom goes by a particular

---

a few old men of the Thut age-set alive in the 1930s.

23. Earth-masters and prophets have in the past been involved in sacrifices made during the initiation of young men, but men of cattle are still the experts most closely connected with the opening and closing of age-sets, conducting the initiation ceremonies, and chosing the age-set names.

24. Evans-Pritchard doubted this and commented, 'I find it hard to believe that the *kuaar muon* even in the heyday of his power ever exercised such judicial or executive authority outside the sphere in which he functioned traditionally as a ritual agent' (Evans-Pritchard 1934: 45).

25. This point is an important one, and one that Evans-Pritchard seems to have underestimated. The *kuoth* of the earth- and cattle-masters is *kuoth rieng*, the divinity of Flesh, and it functions in much the same way that the clan-divinity Flesh (*ring*) functions among the Dinka spear-masters.

26. Coriat was not alone among administrators in confusing the different roles of the prophet (*guk kuoth*), diviner (*tiet*) and magician (*guan wal*). As a rule prophets were opposed to magicians. It was because of this persistent confusion among administrators, and perhaps in reply to this criticism of Coriat's, that Evans-Pritchard wrote in the revised version of his paper (1935: 54–5) that the use of the term 'witchdoctor' to describe 'all the people who seemed to do "odd" things is disastrous to ethnological description and to good administration alike'.

name. The Kwoth of Gwek of Lau was Dengkur[27] that of Dwal Diu of Gaweir was Diu. In Dwal's case the family assumed the spirit name.[28]

The Kwoth should not be confused with the Guk or lesser spirits. These generally 'possess' Healers a class of minor Witchdoctor who confine their work to the cure and relief of ills.[29] It is incorrect to say that Wundeng contented himself with performance of ritual while Gwek exercised Government functions. *Both* father and son were notorious for their secular activities.[30]

Para 11. There is one point in this extremely interesting chapter where Mr. Evans-Pritchard is at fault.[31] A widow may and does marry again if she has no issue by her first husband or other relatives. In rare cases such as this she is paid a small dowry on her second marriage which she retains herself. Her issue become sons of her second husband but with the dowry cattle the woman will eventually marry a girl in her original husband's name. That is she will pay dowry for a girl and obtain the services of a male friend for purposes of procreation. The issue are named after her first husband. It sometimes occurs that a Nuer family or clan will trace its descent back to a woman e.g. Shieng Nyadkwon of Gaweir.

When a widow has married sons, any one of whom has male issue, she is at liberty to contract a woman marriage similar to the practice described in the preceding paragraph.

In this case the issue take her own name. Thus she finds her own line and in due course becomes founder of the family. I do not think it is accurate to say that a man stresses his descent through his mother in proportion to the length of her stay in the matrilocal residence.

On marriage a woman will always live in a hut set aside for her in her family village and will remain apart from her husband for at least a year and sometimes until after the first child has been weaned. This becomes the matrilocal residence and the husband will spend his time equally between his own home and that of his wife.

27. The divinity possessing Ngundeng and Guek was Deng, not Dengkur. Dengkur was Ngundeng's ox-name.

28. Diu is used only sometimes as a family name by the children of Deng Laka. His younger children also took the names of the divinities to whom their mothers were married and in whose name they were conceived and born (see Gau Bang, above, doc. 1.3 n. 15).

29. Coriat appears to be confusing the name of the type of person who is seized by a divinity with the divinity itself. The *guk* is the 'sack' or container of a seizing divinity.

30. Evans-Pritchard cited this criticism (1935: 56) but stood by his original conclusion. If by secular activities one includes hearing complaints about theft, adultery and killing (the sorts of activities the administration asserted were its responsibility), then Coriat is confirmed by modern Lou testimony, and Evans-Pritchard underestimated Ngundeng's influence and authority.

31. Section 11 in Evans-Pritchard's paper read: 'A widow is already married and therefore cannot enter upon a second marriage. She can only cohabit with one of her husband's heirs or with a lover.' Howell (1954: 78–81) essentially substantiates Evans-Pritchard's statement and presents very clearly a complex situation which evidently confused Coriat here.

LIST OF WORKS CITED
IN THE INTRODUCTIONS AND NOTES

ALBAN, A. H. 1940. 'Gwek's Pipe and Pyramid', *SNR*, Vol. XXIII, no. 1, pp. 200–1.
BAKER, S. W. 1867. *The Albert N'Yanza*, London: MacMillan (2 vols.).
[BELL, G., and B. D. DEE] [n.d.] *Sudan Political Service 1899–1956*, Oxford: Oxonian Press.
BEN ASSHER [C. BORRADAILE] 1928. *A Nomad in the South Sudan*, London: H. F. and G. Witherby.
BROUN, A. F., and R. E. MASSEY 1929. *Flora of the Sudan*, London: Sudan Government Office.
BULLEN ALIER BUTTIC 1982. 'The Cult of Lirpiou Spear', *Heritage: A Journal of Southern Sudanese Cultures*, Vol. I, no. 1, pp. 47–60.
CASATI, G. 1891. *Ten Years in Equatoria and the Return of Emin Pasha*, London: Frederick Warne (2 vols.).
COLLINS, R. O. 1972. 'The Sudan Political Service: A Portrait of the Imperialists', *African Affairs*, Vol. LXXI, no. 284, pp. 293–303.
... 1983. *Shadows in the Grass: Britain in the Southern Sudan, 1918–1956*, New Haven and London: Yale University Press.
COLLINS, R. O., and F. M. DENG (eds.) 1984. *The British in the Sudan, 1898–1956: The Sweetness and the Sorrow*, London: Macmillan (in association with St Antony's College, Oxford).
CORIAT, P. 1939. 'Gwek the Witch-doctor and the Pyramid of Dengkur', *SNR*, Vol. XXII, no. 2, pp. 221–37.
... [n.d., c.1961]. *Soldier in Oman*, London: Amalgamated Authors.
COX, J. L. 1985. 'A Splendid Training Ground: The Importance to the Royal Air Force of its Role in Iraq, 1919–32', *Journal of Imperial and Commonwealth History*, Vol. XIII, no. 2, pp. 157–84.
CRAZZOLARA, J. P. 1953. *Zur Gesellschaft und Religion der Nueer*, Vienna: Missionsdrückerei St. Gabriel [Studia Instituti Anthropos Vol. V].
DALY, M. 1980. *British Administration and the Northern Sudan, 1917–1924*, Leiden: Nederlands Historisch-Archaeologisch Instituut Te 'Istanbul.
... 1984. 'Principal Office-Holders in the Sudan Government, 1895–1955', *International Journal of African Historical Studies*, Vol. XVII, no. 2, pp. 309–16.
... 1986. *Empire on the Nile: The Anglo-Egyptian Sudan, 1898–1934*, Cambridge: Cambridge University Press.
DENG, F. 1973. *The Dinka and Their Songs*, Oxford: Clarendon Press.
... 1980. *Dinka Cosmology*, London: Ithaca Press.

DENG, F. M., and M. W. DALY 1989. *Bonds of Silk: The Human Factor in the British Administration of the Sudan*, East Lansing: Michigan State University Press.

DUAL DIU 1930. 'Statement of Dwal Diu Taken on February 3rd. 1930', SRO UNP 5.A.3/43; to appear as text 4.7 in Johnson, in preparation.

EMIN PASHA 1922. *Die Tagebücher von Dr. Emin Pasha*, Vol. II (ed. Franz Stuhlmann), Hamburg: Westermann.

EVANS-PRITCHARD, E. E. 1933–5. 'The Nuer: Tribe and Clan', *SNR*, Vol. XVI, no. 1, pp. 1–53; Vol. XVII, no. 1, pp. 1–57; Vol. XVIII, no. 1, pp. 37–87.

... 1936. 'The Nuer: Age-sets', *SNR*, Vol. XIX, no. 2, pp. 233–69.

... 1940. *The Nuer: A Description of the Modes of Livelihood and Political Institutions of a Nilotic People*, Oxford: Clarendon Press.

... 1946. 'Nuer Bridewealth', *Africa*, Vol. XVI, no. 4, pp. 247–57.

... 1949. 'Burial and Mortuary Rites of the Nuer', *African Affairs*, Vol. XLVIII, no. 190, pp. 56–63.

... 1950. 'Kinship and the Local Community among the Nuer', in A. R. Radcliffe-Brown and D. Forde (eds.), *African Systems of Kinship and Marriage*, London: Oxford University Press for the International African Institute, pp. 360–91.

... 1951. *Kinship and Marriage among the Nuer*, Oxford: Clarendon Press.

... 1956. *Nuer Religion*, Oxford: Clarendon Press.

... 1971. 'Sources with Particular Reference to the Southern Sudan', *Cahiers d'Etudes Africaines*, Vol. XI, no. 4, pp. 129–79.

FERGUSSON, V. H. 1921a. 'Summary of Information on the Nuong Nuer in the Northern Bahr-el-Ghazal extracted from a Report by Capt. V. H. Fergusson, O.B.E. (The Cameronians) on a Tour in the Nuer Country, February and March 1921', Appendix A in *SMIR* 323 (June), pp. 11–12; to appear as document 3.4 in Johnson, in preparation.

... 1921b. 'The Nuong Nuer', *SNR*, Vol. IV, no. 3, pp. 105–12.

... 1923. 'Nuer: Bar el Ghazal', Appendix in *SMIR* 350 (Sept.), p. 5; to appear as document 3.5 in Johnson, in preparation.

... 1924. 'Nuer Beast Tales', *SNR*, Vol. VII, no. 1, pp. 146–55.

... 1930. *The Story of Fergie Bey (Awaraquay) Told by Himself and Some of His Friends*, London: MacMillan.

GESSI, R. 1892. *Seven Years in the Soudan*, London: Sampson Low, Marston.

HASSAN AHMAD IBRAHIM 1979. 'Mahdist Risings against the Condominium Government in the Sudan, 1900–1927', *The International Journal of African Historical Studies*, Vol. XII, no. 3, pp. 440–71.

HENDERSON, K. D. D. 1987. *Set Under Authority*, Somerset: Castle Cary Press.

HILL, R. L. 1970. 'A Register of Named Power-driven River and Marine Harbour Craft Commissioned in the Sudan 1854–1964—I', *SNR*, Vol. LI, pp. 131–46.

... 1972. 'A Register of Named Power-driven River and Marine Harbour Craft Commissioned in the Sudan 1854–1964—II', *SNR*, Vol. LIII, pp. 204–14.

HOWELL, P. P. 1941. 'The Shilluk Settlement', *SNR*, Vol. XXIV, pp. 47–67.
... 1945. 'A Note on Elephants and Elephant Hunting among the Nuer', *SNR*, Vol. XXVI, no. 1, pp. 95–103.
... 1948. ' "Pyramids" in the Upper Nile Region', *Man*, Vol. XLVIII, no. 56, pp. 52–3.
... 1953*a*. 'Some Observations on Divorce among the Nuer', *Journal of the Royal Anthropological Institute*, Vol. LXXXIII, no. 2, pp. 136–46.
... 1953*b*. 'Some Observations on "Earthly Spirits" among the Nuer', *Man*, Vol. LIII, no. 126, pp. 85–8.
... 1954. *A Manual of Nuer Law*, London: Oxford University Press for the International African Institute.
... 1961. 'Appendix to Chapter II', in R. G. Lienhardt, *Divinity and Experience: The Religion of the Dinka*, Oxford: Clarendon Press, pp. 97–103.
JACKSON, H. C. 1923. 'The Nuer of the Upper Nile Province', *SNR*, Vol. VI, no. 1, pp. 59–107; and no. 2, pp. 123–89.
... 1927. 'H.C.J. to Butts, 15.11.1927', NRO Civsec 5/2/10; to appear as document 4.1 in Johnson, in preparation.
... 1954. *Sudan Days and Ways*, London: MacMillan.
JONGLEI INVESTIGATION TEAM 1954. *The Equatorial Nile Project and its Effects in the Anglo-Egyptian Sudan*. Vol. I: *Survey of the Area Affected*, Khartoum.
JOHNSON, D. H. 1979. 'Colonial Policy and Prophets: The "Nuer Settlement", 1929–1930', *JASO*, Vol. X, no. 1, pp. 1–20.
... 1981*a*. 'The Fighting Nuer: Primary Sources and the Origins of a Stereotype', *Africa*, Vol. LI, no. 1, pp. 508–27.
... 1981*b*. 'Percy Coriat on the Nuer', *JASO*, Vol. XII, no. 3, pp. 199–206.
... 1982*a*. 'Tribal Boundaries and Border Wars: Nuer–Dinka Relations in the Sobat and Zaraf Valleys, *c*.1860–1976', *JAH*, Vol. XXIII, no. 2, pp. 183–203.
... 1982*b*. 'Ngundeng and the "Turuk": Two Narratives Compared', *History in Africa*, Vol. IX, pp. 19–39.
... 1982*c*. 'Evans-Pritchard, the Nuer and the Sudan Political Service', *African Affairs*, Vol. LXXXI, no. 323, pp. 231–46.
... 1985*a*. 'C. A. Willis and the "Cult of Deng": A Falsification of the Ethnographic Record', *History in Africa*, Vol. XII, pp. 131–50.
... 1985*b*. 'Foretelling Peace and War: Modern Interpretations of Ngundeng's Prophecies in the Southern Sudan', in M. W. Daly (ed.), *Modernization in the Sudan: Essays in Honor of Richard Hill*, New York: Lilian Barber Press, pp. 121–34.
... 1986*a*. 'Judicial Regulation and Administrative Control: Customary Law and the Nuer, 1898–1954', *JAH*, Vol. XXVII, no. 1, pp. 59–78.
... 1986*b*. 'On the Nilotic Frontier: Imperial Ethiopia in the Southern Sudan, 1898–1936', in D. Donham and W. James (eds.), *The Southern Marches of Imperial Ethiopia: Essays in History and Social Anthropology*, Cambridge: Cambridge University Press, pp. 219–45.

JOHNSON, D. H. 1988. 'Adaptation to Floods in the Jonglei Area: An Historical Analysis', in D. H. Johnson and D. M. Anderson (eds.), *The Ecology of Survival: Case Studies from Northeast African History*, London/Boulder CO: Lester Crook Academic Publishing/Westview Press, pp. 173–92.

... Forthcoming. *Nuer Prophets: A History of Prophecy from the Upper Nile*, Oxford: Clarendon Press.

... In Preparation. *Conquering the Nuer: Documents and Texts in the Pacification of the Southern Sudan, 1898–1930*.

JUNKER, W. 1892. *Travels in Africa during the Years 1882–1886*, London: Chapman and Hall.

KENRICK, R. 1987. *Sudan Tales: Recollections of Some Sudan Political Service Wives, 1926–56*, Cambridge: Oleander Press.

KILLINGRAY, D. 1984. '"A Swift Agent of Government": Air Power in British Colonial Africa, 1916–1939', *JAH*, Vol. XXV, no. 4, pp. 429–44.

KIRK-GREENE, A. H. M. 1982. *The Sudan Political Service: A Preliminary Profile*, Oxford [privately printed].

LEJEAN, G. 1865. *Voyage aux deux Nils*, Paris: Hachette.

LEWIS, B. A. 1951. 'Nuer Spokesmen: A Note on the Institution of the *Ruic*', *SNR*, Vol. XXXII, no. 1, pp. 77–84.

MACDERMOT, B. H. 1972. *Cult of the Sacred Spear*, London: Robert Hale.

MACMEEKAN, G. R. 1929. 'The Demolition of a Pyramid', *The Royal Engineers Journal*, Vol. XLIII, June, pp. 285–9.

MANGAN, J. A. 1982. 'The Education of an Elite Imperial Administration: The Sudan Political Service and the British Public School System', *International Journal of African Historical Studies*, Vol. XV, no. 4, pp. 671–700.

MARNO, E. 1873. 'Der Bahr Seraf', *Petermann's Geographische Mittheilungen*, Vol. XIX, pp. 130–6.

... 1874. *Reisen in Gebiet des Blauen und Weissen Nil, im Egyptischen Sudan 1869–1873*, Vienna: Carl Gerold Sohn.

... 1881. 'Aufnahme des Mittleren Bahr el Abiad und des Bahr el Seraf Sept. 1879 bis März 1880', *Petermann's Geographische Mittheilungen*, Vol. XXVI, Tafel 20.

MATTHEWS, G. E. 1907. 'Report on Journey up the Zeraf Valley to Visit Nuer Chief Diu, and thence across to the Khor Filus and Sobat River', Appendix A in *SIR* 152 (March), pp. 4–7; to appear as document 1.5 in Johnson, in preparation.

O'SULLIVAN, H. D. E. 1910. 'Annual Report: Upper Nile Province 1910', GGR 1910, pp. 407–8; to appear as document 2.3 in Johnson, in preparation.

OWEN, R. C. R. 1910. 'Annual Report: Mongalla Province 1910', GGR 1910, pp. 339–40; to appear as document 2.3 in Johnson, in preparation.

PEDEMONTE, E. 1974. 'A Report on the Voyage of 1849–1850', in E. Toniolo and R. L. Hill (eds.), *The Opening of the Nile Basin*, London: C. Hurst, pp. 55–73.

PETHERICK, Mr and Mrs J. 1869. *Travels in Central Africa*, London: Tinsley

Brothers (2 vols.).
PONCET, J. and A. 1937. *Le Fleuve blanc: Notes géographiques et ethnologiques, et les chasses à l'éléphant dans le pays des Dinka et des Djour*, Alexandria: L'Ecole Professionnelle des Frères.
ROBERTSON, J. [n.d., c.1961]. Foreword to Coriat n.d., pp. 3–4.
SANDERSON, L. M. P., and N. SANDERSON 1981. *Education, Religion & Politics in Southern Sudan 1899–1964*, London/Khartoum: Ithaca Press/Khartoum University Press.
SCHWEINFURTH, G. 1874. *The Heart of Africa*, New York: Harper and Brothers (2 vols.).
SCHWEINFURTH, G., F. RATZEL, R. W. FELKIN and G. HARTLAUB (eds.) 1888. *Emin Pasha in Central Africa*, London: George Philip and Son.
SCHWEITZER, G. 1898. *Emin Pasha, His Life and Work*, Westminster: Archibald Constable (2 vols.).
SELIGMAN, C. G. and B. Z. 1932. *Pagan Tribes of the Nilotic Sudan*, London: Routledge and Kegan Paul.
STIGAND, C. H. 1918a. 'Warrior Classes of the Nuer', *SNR*, Vol. I, no. 2, pp. 116–18.
... 1918b. 'The Dengkur Pyramid', *SNR*, Vol. II, no. 3, p. 210.
... 1919. 'The Story of Kir and the White Spear', *SNR*, Vol. II, no. 3, pp. 224–6.
... 1923. *A Nuer–English Vocabulary*, Cambridge: Cambridge University Press.
STRUVÉ, K. C. P. 1909. 'Report on Administrative Boundaries between the Twi Dinkas and Nuers (Mongalla and Upper Nile Province)', Appendix C in *SIR* 177 (April), pp. 16–17; to appear as document 2.1 in Johnson, in preparation.
SVOBODA, T. 1985. *Cleaned the Crocodile's Teeth: Nuer Song*, Greenfield Center, N.Y.: Greenfield Review Press.
THESIGER, W. 1987. *The Life of My Choice*, London: Collins.
WARBURG, G. 1971. *The Sudan under Wingate*, London: Frank Cass.
WAUHOPE [WAHAB], G. B. 1910. 'G. B. Wahab to governor, UNP, 26.06.1910', SRO UN GOV. CRR. 34 1910; to appear as document 2.2 in Johnson, in preparation.
... 1913. 'G. B. Wauhope to governor, UNP, 22.04.1913', NRO UNP 1/12/101; to appear as document 2.4 in Johnson, in preparation.
WEDDERBURN-MAXWELL, H. G. 1928. 'Note by Mr. Wedderburn-Maxwell on the Duk Faiyuil Affair: August 1928', 16.09.28, NRO Civsec 5/3/12; to appear as document 4.5 in Johnson, in preparation.
WILLIS, C. A. 1928. 'The Cult of Deng', *SNR*, Vol. XI, pp. 195–208.
WILSON, H. H. 1905. 'Report by El Kaimakam H. H. Wilson Bey on a March from the Sobat (Mouth of Filus) to Bor', Appendix A in *SIR* 128 (March), pp. 5–9; to appear as document 1.3 in Johnson, in preparation.
WYLD, J. W. G. 1928. 'Report on the Duk Raid', 10.12.1928, NRO Civsec 5/3/12; to appear as document 4.6 in Johnson, in preparation.

SUBJECT INDEX

administration:
    among the Nuer xxv f., xxxvi f., xlii, xlvii, 136 f., 185 ff., 195
    and Evans-Pritchard xxi, lv f.
    native administration xxi, 75 ff., 186
age-sets xxviii f., liii f., 33 f., 59–65, 197 f.
    initiation 33
agriculture xlix, 24
    cotton cultivation xlii, 156, 174 f., 184, 186
anthropology:
    and administration 191 f.
    Evans-Pritchard xix, xlv, lv f., 191 ff.
    Frazer xxi
    see also ethnography
aristocrats (*diel*) 196
army xxxix ff., 103, 106, 118 ff., 130 ff., 138 ff.
bloodwealth (blood-money) l, 7, 10 f., 19 n. 25, 20, 31 f., 47, 53 ff., 196
boundaries:
    Dinka–Shilluk 57 f.
    district 57, 158 ff.
    Nuer–Dinka xxxiii, 19, 38 f., 50, 57 ff., 85–95
bridewealth xxviii, 27 n. 35, 28 n. 36
    see also marriage
cattle, man of (*wut ghok*) 166 f., 170 n. 39, 172, 198
    and *kuoth rieng* 198 n. 25
chiefs xxix, xxxi f., l ff., 31, 75 ff., 198
    Dinka 69–73, 87 ff., 115, 138, 171
    Gaawar 8 f., 20 ff., 29, 40, 44–9, 87 ff.
    Lou 59–65, 111 ff., 124 ff., 129 ff., 138 ff.
    Western Nuer xliv, 164 ff., 171 f., 184, 187 f.
chiefs' courts *see* law
chiefs' police xxviii, xxxvii f., li, 68 f., 76 f., 116 f., 127, 129 ff., 139 ff., 172
clans *see* political terminology; sections
death and burial 32 f.
    col wic 197
earth-master (*kuaar muon*) l, 8 n. 7, 15 ff., 31 f., 59 n. 17, 61, 65 f., 165, 168 f., 172, 195, 198
    and *kuoth rieng* 198 n. 25
economic development xlix, 174 f., 186 ff.
education 73 f., 177, 185
elephant hunting xxix, 25
ethnography liii
    by administrators xx, 194
    of the Nuer xlvii f.
feuds l, lii, 6 f., 9 ff., 16 f., 19 f., 32, 53 ff., 86 ff.
    inter-sectional fights xliv, 39 f., 47 f.
firearms 23, 43 f., 151, 179
    trade in, with Ethiopia 26
history liii, lvi, 13–20, 92 f., 162 ff.
    Nuer expansion lii, lv, 157
interpreters xx n. 3, xxvii, xxviii, xxxi f., xxxviii, 7 ff., 12, 19, 74, 134, 177 f.
kinship:
    adoption of Dinka 16 n. 12, 17 n. 13, 23
    agnatic kin xxix
    maternal kin xxxii
    maternal uncle xxix
kuaar muon: *see* earth-master
kujur xxix, xxxiii, xxxix, xli, 12, 16–20, 26, 30 ff., 34 f., 59 f., 66 f., 72, 111 f., 117
    as spirit 34, 125
    as witchdoctor xxxiii, xl, 180
    see also prophets
law 12, 27–32
    cases xxxii, 31
    compensation 30 f., 112 n. 16

law (*contd.*)
  chiefs' courts xxxvii *f.*, xlii, xliv, 77, 117, 172, 198
  customary law l
  inheritance 29
  justice xlii
  manslaughter 31 *f.*
  see also bloodwealth
leopard-skin chief *see* earth-master
lineages lii
  see also sections
magic:
  charms 26, 35
  magicians 59 n. 17, 134 n. 27, 165 n. 27, 166, 171, 198
  see also kujur
marriage 27 *ff.*, 199
  adultery 28
  divorce 28
  widow concubinage 29, 199
  see also bridewealth
material culture 24 *ff.*
  houses 24
  iron working 25
  personal adornment 26
medical work 74, 178, 181
missions and missionaries xlv, 177
myth 13 *f.*, 162, 195
1924 Mutiny xxx *f.*
Nuer Settlement xxxvi, 56, 58, 68, 77, 91, 93 *f.*, 99, 123 *f.*, 128 *ff.*
ox-names xxvii, xl n. 43
police xxviii *ff.*, xxxi, 6 *ff.*, 46, 52, 76, 90
  mounted police xxxi, xxiv, xxxix, 107, 121, 130 *ff.*, 138 *ff.*, 179
political prisoners 78 *ff.*, 149 *ff.*
political terminology li *f.*, lvi, 195 *f.*
prophets xxxix, l, 198 *f.*
  Gaawar xxvi *f.*, xxxii *f.*, xxxix, xl *ff.*, l, lvi, 16–20, 33 *f.*, 37 *ff.*, 85 *ff.*, 91, 123,
  127, 139, 144 *ff.*, 150 *ff.*
  guk kuoth 199
  Lou xxxi *ff.*, xxxviii *ff.*, li, liv *ff.*, 56 *f.*, 66, 99 *ff.*, 109 *ff.*, 125 *ff.*, 139 *ff.*, 151
  prophecies 114 *f.*, 133 *f.*
  Western Nuer xliv, li, 165 *ff.*
RAF xxxviii, xl, 101, 103 *ff.*, 108, 118 *ff.*, 142, 164
religion 12, 34 *f.*
  blessing xlvi
  curse xxix
  diviner 198 *f.*
  divinities xxxii, 18, 34, 66
  kuoth (kot, kwoth) 12, 34, 151, 197 *ff.*
  oaths 31
  sacrifice 32, 134, 141
roads xxxvii, 68, 115, 173 *f.*
  road work xxxviii, 58 *f.*, 111 *ff.*
sections (*cieng*) li *f.*, 21 *ff.*, 40 *ff.*, 44–9, 59–66, 161 *f.*
shen see sections
shrines:
  Luak Kuoth 42
  Ngundeng's Mound ('pyramid') xxxii, xl, liv, 109 *f.*, 115, 132, 139 *ff.*
Sudan Political Service vi, xxiii *ff.*, xxx *f.*
taxation (tribute) xlii, xlviii *f.*, 37, 42–9, 51 *f.*, 156, 172 *f.*, 182 *f.*, 187 *f.*
totems 35, 196 *f.*
tribe *see* political terminology; sections
warfare:
  in the 19th century lv
  Nuer–Dinka raids xxxii *f.*, xli, 15, 18, 37 *f.*, 127, 150, 155, 163 *f.*
  punitive patrols 18, 57, 101, 110, 112, 117 *ff.*, 124, 126, 128 *f.*, 133, 150, 164 *f.*, 179 *f.*
  slave raiding 15 *ff.*, 19, 110, 150, 163, 194

www.ingramcontent.com/pod-product-compliance
Lightning Source LLC
Chambersburg PA
CBHW060458010526
44118CB00018B/2456